The Great Illyrian Revolt

The Great Illyrian Revolt

Rome's Forgotten War in the Balkans, AD 6–9

Jason R. Abdale

PEN & SWORD
HISTORY

AN IMPRINT OF PEN & SWORD BOOKS LTD.
YORKSHIRE - PHILADELPHIA

First published in Great Britain in 2019 by
Pen & Sword Military
An imprint of
Pen & Sword Books Ltd
Yorkshire – Philadelphia

ISBN 978 1 52671 817 4

A CIP catalogue record for this book is
available from the British Library.

Printed and bound in the UK by TJ International Ltd, Padstow, Cornwall

Pen & Sword Books Limited incorporates the imprints of Atlas, Archaeology,
Aviation, Discovery, Family History, Fiction, History, Maritime, Military,
Military Classics, Politics, Select, Transport, True Crime, Air World,
Frontline Publishing, Leo Cooper, Remember When, Seaforth Publishing,
The Praetorian Press, Wharncliffe Local History, Wharncliffe Transport,
Wharncliffe True Crime and White Owl.

For a complete list of Pen & Sword titles please contact

PEN & SWORD BOOKS LIMITED
47 Church Street, Barnsley, South Yorkshire, S70 2AS, England
E-mail: enquiries@pen-and-sword.co.uk
Website: www.pen-and-sword.co.uk

Or
PEN AND SWORD BOOKS
1950 Lawrence Rd, Havertown, PA 19083, USA
E-mail: Uspen-and-sword@casematepublishers.com
Website: www.penandswordbooks.com

Contents

Chronology of Events

Approx. 6,000 BC: The earliest recognizable culture within the western Balkans appears.

Approx. 4,500 BC: People living in the western Balkans begin mining, smelting and making objects from copper.

Approx. 1,000 BC: Iron use spreads to the western Balkans. At the same time, the first culture that can be described as 'proto-Illyrian' appears within the region, possibly due to an immigration of Indo-European speakers from Anatolia.

1,000–500 BC?: A group of three Illyrian tribes collectively known as the Iapygians crosses the Adriatic Sea and settles within south-eastern Italy in what is now the region of Apulia.

734 BC: The Greeks expel the Liburnian tribe from the island of Corfu (known then as Corcyra). This is the first recorded conflict between the Illyrians and the ancient Greeks.

691 BC: The first war between the Illyrians and the kingdom of Macedon. These two peoples would continue to fight each other for the next 300 years.

400–300 BC?: The Iapygians of south-eastern Italy are either conquered or driven out by the expanding Roman Republic.

393 BC: The Dardanian tribe conquers Macedon, and holds it for only one year before being expelled.

229–228 BC: The First Roman-Illyrian War. The first time in the historic record when we know that Romans and Illyrians fought each other.

220–219 BC: The Second Roman-Illyrian War.

169 BC: The Third Roman-Illyrian War.

167 BC: Southern Illyria becomes a Roman protectorate. Although nominally independent, it is under the domination of the Roman Republic.

156 BC: The Fourth Roman-Illyrian War.

135–35 BC: A hundred years of sporadic hostilities between the Illyrians and the Romans.

59 BC: The region of southern Illyria called 'Dalmatia' is changed from being a protectorate to being a Roman province, re-named 'Illyricum'. Northern Illyria, known as 'Pannonia', is still independent, but under increasing Roman influence.

35–12 BC: Gaius Octavianus, later to become Caesar Augustus, launches a series of military campaigns against the Illyrians to bring them under complete subjection, with only partial success.

12–9 BC: The region of northern Illyria called 'Pannonia' is conquered by Caesar Augustus' stepson Tiberius Claudius Nero, and is incorporated into the Roman province of Illyricum. Peace in the region is maintained until 6 AD.

6–9 AD: The Great Illyrian Revolt, a massive uprising against Roman rule throughout the province of Illyricum. Romans suffer heavy losses, and are forced to commit tens of thousands of troops to the region to suppress the rebellion. Tiberius Claudius Nero and Aulus Caecina Severus lead Roman forces in this war.

Late September, 9 AD: The Battle of Teutoburg. An estimated 10,000 Romans from the 17th, 18th and 19th Legions are killed by the Germanic barbarians, led by Arminius, during a four-day battle in what is now north-western Germany. Soon afterwards, the Germans drive all surviving Romans out of Germania.

10 AD: Rome launches its revenge campaign against Arminius and his rebel forces in Germania. The war lasts for six years; Tiberius leads the legions in the first two years of the war, and then Tiberius' nephew Germanicus commands the legions during the remaining four years.

14 AD: Caesar Augustus, Rome's first emperor, dies. Tiberius Claudius Nero becomes Rome's second emperor and is crowned Emperor Tiberius Julius Caesar. The Roman legions in both Germania and Pannonia mutiny upon Augustus' death, and both uprisings are bloodily suppressed.

15 AD: Rebellion breaks out in northern Africa, led by the Numidian warlord Tacfarinas, threatening Rome's grain supply.

Late 16 AD: Emperor Tiberius is forced to divert more and more troops to suppress Tacfarinas' rebel army in Africa, and so he halts military operations against Arminius and his Germanic rebels.

17 AD: Tiberius and Germanicus hold their triumphal celebrations for their wars against the Illyrian and Germanic rebels. Tiberius' son Drusus Castor is appointed governor of Illyricum, and he holds this post for three years.

19 AD: Germanicus suddenly dies, possibly assassinated.

19 or 20 AD: Sometime during Emperor Tiberius' reign, the province of Illyricum is split in half into the provinces of Pannonia and Dalmatia.

21 AD: Tacfarinas' rebellion in northern Africa is crushed.

37 AD: Emperor Tiberius dies. Gaius Caligula becomes Rome's third emperor.

Introduction

When people hear the words 'ancient history', they usually think of Egypt, Mesopotamia, Greece or Rome. This is what I like to call 'Ancient History's Big Four', because practically everything that is spoken about in the broad field of ancient history is usually done in relation to one of these four major sub-fields. An incalculable number of books, journals, magazine articles and television documentaries have been produced in relation to these four civilizations. The sheer volume of all of that information will probably destroy your brain.

Once you get beyond the Big Four, then you come across cultures that appear to be of secondary importance. These mostly consist of the civilizations with which one or more members of the Big Four were in contact. Examples would probably be the Nubians, Persians or Celts. There are scholars who devote their entire lives to studying these people and you can find plenty of books about them published in a variety of languages, but it's important to know that each one of these civilizations is inextricably linked with one of the major civilizations that form the Big Four. You can't talk about Nubia without talking about Egypt. You can't talk about the Persians without talking about Greece. You can't talk about the Celts without talking about Rome. You see?

Finally, you get to the absolute bottom of the ancient historical hierarchy: the civilizations, cultures and people of ancient history that hardly anyone knows about, even the so-called 'experts'. These are people that are only mentioned in passing within a few sentences or in the occasional footnote. I guarantee you, most or possibly all of these peripheral ancient cultures are never spoken of in school textbooks and not even the most advanced and specified university courses concerning ancient history are likely to cover these people. Part of the reason why is that available information about these long-forgotten cultures is extremely limited: you might know their name and when and where they existed, but aside from that, their society, their history and how they interacted with the world around them is either a total enigma or is never seriously researched. Another reason why these people are never discussed in detail is because they are simply considered not important enough to be worth studying. Really, what high school freshman studying general world history or even a graduate student writing a thesis for his or her PhD has heard of the Adyrmachidae? Or the Rhaetians? Yet even so, each one of these people is important in their own way. The Adyrmachidae might have been small in number, but they were one of the most powerful of the ancient Libyan tribes and were likely Egypt's major enemy on their western border, and it's possible that they were the ones that prevented the Egyptian civilization from expanding westwards into northern Africa. The Rhaetians were a small minor-ranking collection of tribes dwelling in northern Italy and Austria, but the Romans had to conquer them because their lands blocked off eastern overland access to the Italian Peninsula, and apparently they made the best wine that Caesar Augustus ever had. That might have been the *real* reason why the Romans wanted to conquer them!

What boggles my mind is that there were people in ancient history who *were* important, but are now largely forgotten. For example, hardly anybody talks about the Alans now, but they were one of the major threats to Rome and the Persian Empire from the second to fifth centuries AD. Their legacy has largely been shoved aside by other ancient horse-riding barbarians that are more familiar to us, such as the Scythians and especially the Huns. The Gepids held control over central Europe with a bloody iron fist for three hundred years: other barbarians and the Romans were absolutely terrified of them! However, if you ask somebody with only a general knowledge of ancient Roman or early Byzantine history about the Gepids and the important role that they played in Late Antiquity, that person will likely look at you with a blank stare.

Then there are the people that I wish to discuss in this book: the people who, for centuries, made the Greeks and Romans shake. These were people whose fleets of snake-headed warships terrorized the seas, whose warriors slaughtered the best troops that 'civilization' could offer, whose fortified cities would have made the builders of medieval castles green with envy. They were rich, they were powerful, they were dynamic, they were on the rise, and it's no exaggeration to say that they could have become the *fifth* member of ancient history's hall of greats. They were the Illyrians.

Most people today have never heard of the Illyrians, and those who *do* know about their existence likely learned of them through reading the biographies of Alexander the Great who fought against them or reading the histories of the ancient Romans who conquered them. The Illyrians occupied the land that many people today would still generically call 'Yugoslavia', even though this name has not been used since the early 1990s. The Illyrians controlled this large swath of territory for almost five centuries, and were a major economic and military force in the ancient world. Yet now, they are almost entirely unknown.

The ancient history of the western Balkans is an unfortunately neglected subject of study, largely due to the appeal of other more famous ancient empires and civilizations. The part that this region played in the saga of ancient history has, for the most part, been confined to sideshow references regarding episodes in the histories of other more established and more popularly-appealing cultures. Very little has been done in terms of direct scholarship in which the native inhabitants of the western Balkans are the primary focus, and not something that is sometimes alluded to when speaking of the history of the Greeks, Macedonians or Romans. It is a real shame that the ancient history of this land and the people who once lived there has become academic *terra incognita*. Only a handful of books have been written on that subject in any detail, as opposed to the tens of thousands of texts that have been written concerning the classical civilizations of Europe and Asia. Considering how much physical territory the western Balkans encompasses, and considering how many various cultures must have lived there, the history of this region must surely be on a par with the studies of other European tribal cultures such as the Celts or the ancient Germans.

In all honesty, I must confess that I too am guilty of neglecting the study of the region known in ancient times as 'Illyria'. I was aware to some extent of the people that lived there but again, this was due to studying other cultures, and once in a while the inhabitants of this region would be mentioned in passing. I knew that the ancient Illyrians existed, but absolutely nothing else besides that fact; a name and nothing more.

My interest in the study of ancient Yugoslavia and its enigmatic inhabitants started when I was researching my first book *Four Days in September*, which concerned the Battle of Teutoburg (more commonly but in my opinion incorrectly known as the Battle of the Teutoburg Forest), fought between the Romans and the Germans in the year 9 AD. While doing research on that subject, I learned that three years earlier in 6 AD, a major rebellion against Rome erupted within Illyria. This Illyrian war lasted for three gruelling and tiresome years; you'll find out why I use those adjectives as you read this book. This Balkan rebellion resulted in the deaths of perhaps hundreds of thousands of people, making it one of the first major wars fought in the years after the birth of Jesus Christ. This was unquestionably a major event during the reign of Caesar Augustus, and yet I had never heard of it before. Considering that I was researching another great tribal uprising at the time, in this case that of the Germans, the story of a similar mass uprising taking place only a few years earlier understandably captured my interest and imagination. I decided to write about this important and yet largely unknown event.

Once *Four Days in September* was finished, work began in earnest. I needed to learn as much as I could about the culture of the Illyrians, their convoluted history with other European cultures and especially their relationship with Rome, and of course the story of the rebellion itself – the 'Great Illyrian Revolt', as it has become known to modern scholars, although the Romans themselves never called this war by that name. As I read more, I became more interested, and now I regard the ancient inhabitants of the western Balkans, the Illyrians, as one of the great cultures of classical-age Europe, one that is far richer than I and probably most people had ever thought before.

Information concerning the Great Illyrian Revolt is maddeningly sparse. In contrast to the relative ease of writing a book about the Battle of Teutoburg, which is a well-known event and has already been heavily researched by others, researching the Illyrian uprising was more demanding. Ancient sources written on this subject and on the Illyrians in general were few in number and difficult to track down. As usual, Gaius Paterculus and Cassius Dio provided the bulk of the information. I found a handful of general survey books on the Illyrians, but I found no secondary source material written exclusively about the history of this rebellion. Therefore I could not compare and contrast various viewpoints and hypotheses proposed by modern authors, as I like to do when discussing matters of ancient history. Also, while many Roman artefacts have been found in the western Balkans that can be broadly dated to the first half of the first century AD, I am not aware of any archaeological finds that are directly related to the story of this rebellion, which means that I cannot examine and analyse artefacts to see how they fit in with the historic record. All in all, I knew that researching and writing this book was going to be challenging since I had little material to work with, but I hope that the effort was worth it, and I also hope that the end product is worthy of some praise.

As I am writing this, I am conscious that many of the archaeological sites that I describe in this book are under threat. There are numerous reports that the Muslim terrorist organization known as ISIS has been gaining ground within Bosnia, a predominantly Muslim country within Europe. ISIS already has a reputation for destroying ancient and medieval artefacts and even entire archaeological sites because these things and places do not fit in with their particular ideology about world history. It is possible that Islamic fanaticism might very well lead to the destruction of ancient sites within the western Balkans in the near future, so it's important to have as much scholarship done with regard to the ancient history of this region while we can still do so.

This book relies upon ancient documents, archaeological evidence, analysis by modern historians and my own hypotheses. I have tried to the best of my limited abilities to create an accurate portrayal of locations, persons and events. All quotations are clearly cited as being the words of their authors. My personal interpretations or opinions are clearly stated as such. If there are any errors in facts or translations, I truly apologize.

Chapter One

The Illyrians

'What country, friends, is this?'

The play was called *Twelfth Night*. Its title was based upon a festival undertaken in some Christian countries during the Medieval and Renaissance periods to mark the end of the fabled Twelve Days of Christmas, beginning on Christmas Day itself and ending on the fifth day of January. On the closing day of this festive holiday season, an impressive party would be held, known simply as Twelfth Night. It was a welcome break from the everyday routines of life in the fifteenth, sixteenth and early seventeenth centuries, a day devoted entirely to the Bacchanalian pursuits of drunkenness, rowdiness and general tomfoolery. Status quo social conventions were temporarily cast aside, peasants became lords, masters became the servants, and the whole world in general was turned upside-down.[1]

The play, written by William Shakespeare, was scheduled to be performed as entertainment for the Twelfth Night celebrations. Its first recorded performance was in 1602, during the sunset of Queen Elizabeth's reign; in fact, she only had one more year left to live. Fitting with the festival where everything goes topsy-turvy, the leading character, Viola, disguises herself as a man in order to further ingratiate herself in the company of Duke Orsino, with whom she is rapidly becoming smitten. The plot was not an original one; other authors had thought of similar stories in the past. Indeed, several of Shakespeare's other works dealt with people assuming other identities.[2]

Literary scholars can say a lot about *Twelfth Night*, but what makes Shakespeare's play important for discussion in this book is not the characters or the plot or its possible connections with the history of the Tudor Dynasty, but the setting where much of the story takes place. In Act 1, Scene 2, Viola and her twin brother Sebastian are travelling on the sea when their ship is caught in a violent storm. Viola, the ship's captain and a handful of others manage to make it ashore, but her beloved brother Sebastian is unfortunately nowhere to be found.

'What country, friends, is this?' Viola asks. The captain responds 'This is Illyria, lady.'

The name *Illyria* is an ancient one. The territory known to the ancient Greeks and Romans as 'Illyria' was composed of all lands between Italy and Greece, and between the Adriatic Sea and the Danube River – the land that people of the twentieth century would call 'Yugoslavia'. Many people, especially Americans, equate the term 'Balkan' with Yugoslavia, the large region of land on the eastern side of the Adriatic Sea that is now split apart into the countries of Slovenia, Croatia, Bosnia and Herzegovina, Serbia, Montenegro and Albania. This is due largely to the massive media exposure of the wars in south-eastern Europe that dominated much of the news in the early to middle 1990s, when war reporters used the words 'Yugoslavia' and 'Balkans' interchangeably and also incorrectly. If one uses the term 'the Balkans' in a broad geographic sense, then it refers to *all* of south-eastern Europe. This includes not only the ex-Yugoslav countries but also Greece, Macedonia, Bulgaria and the European part of Turkey. If one uses the term 'Balkan' to refer to a European mountain range, then this refers to the mountains of Bulgaria; the Balkan Mountains or simply 'the Balkans' (known in ancient times as the Haemus Mountains) are located *there*, not in Yugoslavia.

The word 'Balkan' is of Turkish origin, meaning 'forested mountain'. This short description of the landscape is quite accurate. During the late Middle Ages, throughout the Renaissance and into what scholars today call the 'Early Modern' period of European history, south-eastern Europe was referred to as 'Turkish Europe', differentiating it from 'Turkish Asia', since the Ottoman Empire straddled both continents. The name 'Balkan' doesn't appear until the 1400s, when an Italian geographer named Philippus Calimachus used the name to refer to a range of mountains located within what is now Bulgaria. Later during the early years of the nineteenth century, when the Napoleonic Wars were ravaging Europe and nationalism was taking hold, a German scholar named Johann August Zeune incorrectly believed that the Balkan Mountains were not located solely within Bulgaria but stretched the entire width of south-eastern Europe in a crescent, from the Black Sea and curling upwards along the Adriatic coast to the very borders of Italy. It is because of this mistake made two centuries ago that so many people even today use the term 'Balkan' as a blanket statement for all of south-east Europe.[3]

The mountain range that occupies most of what used to be Yugoslavia is called the Dinaric Mountains, also known as the Dinarics or the

Dinarides if one prefers to use a very ancient-sounding Hellenic-type name to make themselves seem more sophisticated. The Dinaric Mountains are named after one particular peak within the centre of its range, Mount Dinara, located on the southern border separating Croatia from Bosnia and measuring almost 2,400ft from its base to its summit. In ancient times, this mountain was known as *Adrian Oros*. The name 'Dinara' is of unknown or at least obscure origin. One idea is that it is based on the name of a now-forgotten tribe that once lived in the region, while another possibility is that the mountain is named after a settlement that was located nearby.[4]

Of course, a great deal changed between the time of Alexander the Great and the time of Queen Elizabeth I. When William Shakespeare was writing *Twelfth Night*, much of the Adriatic coast of the Balkans was controlled by the Republic of Venice, one of the more powerful Italian principalities. Before this, during the Middle Ages, the landscape was carved up among several kingdoms and the territory frequently changed hands. In ancient times, the region was occupied by the Romans from the late 200s BC until the fall of the Roman Empire. Before the Romans came in, the landscape was a patchwork quilt of various independent tribes and tribal confederations, some more powerful than others.

South-east Europe itself is an interesting transition zone, where it seems things are not quite wholly European nor are they quite wholly Asian. Perhaps this had something to do with the fact that this region had once been part of the Roman Empire, which stretched from Spain to Syria. However, during the fourth century AD, the empire was split into western and eastern halves. The capital of the Western Roman Empire changed frequently due to the pressure of barbarian invasions and civil wars, but the capital of the Eastern Roman Empire was always the city of Konstantinopolis, 'Constantine's City', a name that was later Anglicized to Constantinople. From then on, Eastern Europe was somehow different, a buffer zone between the classical Roman homeland in the west and the exotic Persian east. During the late fifth century AD when the Western Roman Empire finally collapsed after decades of being eaten away from both inside and out, that distinction between east and west became ever more apparent. The Western Roman Empire was carved up into numerous small barbarian kingdoms, most of them having Germanic origins, while the Eastern Roman Empire persisted. South-eastern Europe, under the control of what modern scholars call the Byzantine Empire, found itself both literally and figuratively 'in between', between

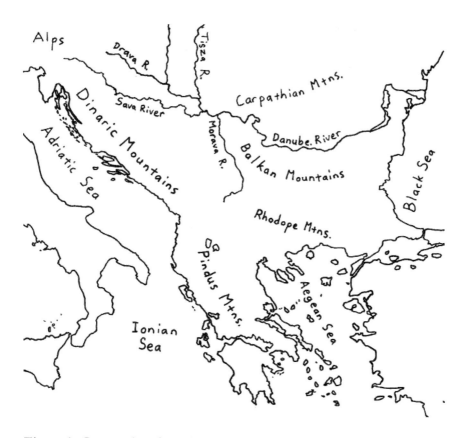

Figure 1: Geography of south-eastern Europe. While the term 'Balkans' refers generically to this whole region, when used specifically in the context of a mountain range, it only applies to the north-eastern part in what is now Bulgaria. The mountains of ancient Illyria were the Dinaric Mountains. (*Illustration by the author*)

Figure 2: A panoramic view of Mount Dinara, the namesake of the Dinaric Mountains, the major mountain range of ancient Illyria. (*Photograph by Zoran Knez, 23 April 2006. Public domain image, Wikimedia Commons*)

the various primitive warlord states run by Germanic tribes to the west and between the Persian Empire to the east. Even today, this 'not quite European and not quite Asian' atmosphere persists.[5]

The Adriatic coast of the Balkans is very rocky and mountainous, and studded throughout with islands of various sizes. In some places, the Dinaric Mountains rise to over 8,000ft tall, forming a wall that splits the western Balkans into two distinct climate regions. On the south-western side that faces towards the Adriatic Sea, the climate is described as 'Mediterranean', whereas on the north-eastern side the climate is described as 'continental'. The British historian John Joseph Wilkes compared the terrain of the Adriatic coast to a limestone sponge, riddled throughout with a complex network of caves and tunnels. Water disappears immediately into the porous rock, making agriculture along the coast difficult. Even in the valleys located between the hills, life is hard. Many of the mountains within the Dinaric range are composed of limestone or some other marine-based rock in their lower parts and harder denser marble towards their tops. The climate is mild for most of the year along the coastline. In the interior in what is now Bosnia, the summer brings oppressive heat and the winter brings freezing cold and fierce winds. In contrast to much of Europe which has been ploughed into farms or developed for human habitation, there are still large portions of the western Balkans that remain covered in thick forests. The land also possesses rich supplies of salt, iron, copper, silver and gold, which no doubt made that land an attractive prize for the Greeks and Romans.[6]

Our oldest information about the landscape and the people who lived in this region comes from the Greek poet Alcaeus of Mitylene, writing in the sixth century BC. Around the year 500 BC, Hecataeus of Miletus described the Balkan coastline of the Adriatic Sea. Unfortunately, his work only survives in fragments, but he names several tribes that lived in the area, such as the Liburnians and the Istrians. In *Periplus*, or *Coastal Passage*, dating from the very end of the sixth century BC, the author Pseudo-Scylax of Caryanda wrote a detailed description of the Balkan Adriatic coastline, but his knowledge of the Balkan interior was sorely lacking. Within this work, he names a few of the Illyrian tribes, including those who inhabited southern Italy at the time, and even wrote a few tantalizing tidbits about their societies. He also asserted that the name 'Illyrian' should apply to a number of different tribes who had a similar culture and not just to one tribe specifically. It appears that the name 'Illyrian' originally referred to just one tribe – the Illyrioi or Illyrii, using the Greek and Roman spellings respectively – but after a while, this name began to be used to refer to all people who inhabited the Balkans and had a similar culture.[7]

Strabo remarks that the coastline of Illyria is dotted everywhere with very good harbours, unlike Italy which has few natural harbours.[8] No wonder, then, that the Illyrians became a dominant naval power in the ancient Mediterranean. Pseudo-Scylax also stated that the Adriatic coastline, especially within Liburnian territory, was dotted everywhere with islands, some of which didn't have names.[9]

The Origin of the Illyrians

Today, it seems that there is a faction within every western Balkan country, from Slovenia to Albania, which claims that their ancestry descends directly from the ancient Illyrians, that they are the true and uncontested heirs to a glorious ancient legacy. Of all of these people, the Albanians voice their claims the loudest, and they have acquired a substantial following who believe their fervent statements. However, contrary to these ethnic-based nationalistic claims, most historians, archaeologists and linguists are convinced that none of the modern-day ethnic groups living within the western Balkans are directly related to the ancient Illyrians. The Slovenians, Bosnians and Montenegrans are of Slavic heritage. The Croatians and Serbians were originally Alanic tribes from the Caucasus Mountains that were granted lands in Illyria by the Byzantines during the sixth century AD for helping them fight the Avars, and afterwards gradually adopted a Slavic culture. As for the Albanians, they are the wildcard because their language bears no similarity to any language currently spoken in the area. It is because of cultural and even physical differences that the Albanians claim that they have no connection, either ethnic or cultural, to any other people presently inhabiting south-eastern Europe, and instead claim to be descended from this region's ancient inhabitants, the Illyrians. The Albanians claim descent from one Illyrian tribe in particular, the Albani, who inhabited what is now central Albania.

Before I dig too deeply into this argument, I think it is important to gain a fundamental understanding of the Illyrian people. Only then can we judge the claims by the Albanians and others to have any merit. The Illyrians were a curious lot. On one hand, both the Greeks and Romans recognized them as distinct from the cultures surrounding them, and yet on the other hand, the Illyrians were something of a melting pot, freely adopting the ways of their neighbours. Even so, ancient scholars regarded the Illyrians as unique enough to be identified with a single ethnic name.

For a long time, modern historians believed that the Illyrians were the original native inhabitants of this region. However, there is a growing body of strong evidence which suggests that they were not. Instead, historians and archaeologists now state that the Illyrians originated from elsewhere, migrated into the western Balkans, displaced the native inhabitants who had been living there since the Stone Age and took over the region, and there they would remain until the Romans conquered them. This leads to two important questions. First, if the Illyrians were not the region's native inhabitants, then who were? Second, if the Illyrians came to this land from elsewhere, then where did they originally come from?

In order to answer these questions, we must look at archaeological finds, the historical records and the use of language. Some anthropologists are convinced that the origin of the Illyrian people lies not in the western Balkans, but in modern-day Turkey. In ancient times, the large rectangular-shaped peninsula that forms the Turkish heartland was called Anatolia. Here lived many different people who spoke a variety of now-extinct languages. The Turks who currently live there are not of Anatolian stock, but instead originated in central Asia and migrated to Anatolia during the early Middle Ages. They speak a language from an entirely different language group, the Turkic languages, which are more closely related to Mongolian than to the languages spoken in ancient Anatolia.

Modern linguistic analysis has determined that the native Anatolian languages are the most primitive of the Indo-European languages, which are spoken natively throughout much of Europe, the Middle East and India. Not much of the Illyrian language has survived. The few pieces that we do have are mostly in the form of personal names, place names and a few isolated vocabulary words, but enough of it exists for scholars to analyse and compare with other ancient languages, and it has been conclusively proven that Illyrian is indeed an Indo-European language. Most of what we know about the Illyrian language comes from the names of people, places and gods. A few basic words survive here and there: *rhinos* for 'fog'; *sabaia* for 'beer'; *sybina* for 'hunting spear'.[10] Here's where things get interesting: linguists have determined that the Illyrian language is only *slightly* more advanced than the Anatolian languages. In other words, Anatolian and Illyrian are very closely related to each other, which suggests that they inhabited the same homeland or were next-door neighbours.

Evidence for just how primitive the Illyrian language is comes from the way that certain words are spelled or pronounced compared to similar words in other Indo-European languages. Such languages generally tend to fall into two categories, based upon the pronunciation of certain words: the 'centrum' and 'satem' branches. The Illyrian language has features of *both* branches, which implies that Illyrian existed before the Indo-European language group split in two, which would place the Illyrian language's existence at a very low point on the family tree, at or near the tree's base.[11]

This seems quite odd if you look at languages from a geographic viewpoint rather than an evolutionary viewpoint. We naturally expect languages to spread geographically in a linear or radiating form, starting off at a central point and radiating outwards like ripples in water, becoming more advanced and more evolved the further they travel. So, keeping this in mind, it would be logical that if the Anatolian languages are the most primitive of the Indo-European languages, then the region closest to Anatolia, Thrace (occupying much of the south-eastern corner of Europe, including most of Bulgaria, eastern Greece and the European part of Turkey), would have a language that would be only slightly more evolved than Anatolian, then Greek would be slightly more advanced than Thracian, and finally Illyrian would be slightly more advanced than Greek. However, this isn't the case. The geographic spread of Indo-European languages starts in Anatolia, completely skips over Thrace and Greece, and suddenly and unexpectedly continues in the western Balkans, and it isn't until later on that the Thracian and Greek languages develop. How does one account for this roundabout geographic spread of language? There are presently two theories that try to explain how the Illyrian and Anatolian languages could be so similar. The first theory is that the Illyrians originally lived in Anatolia and then migrated to the western Balkans. The second theory is that the Illyrians were the western Balkans' original inhabitants who moved to Anatolia for some unknown reason and then moved back into Europe.

Let's look at the first theory. If the theory concerning the Illyrians' Anatolian origins is correct, then how did they end up in the western Balkans? Obviously, they didn't walk there, since miles of ocean separate Anatolia from Illyria. They must have utilized some sort of maritime travel. This can only mean that even at this early stage in their history, the Illyrians or at least people who would become the Illyrians possessed boats or ships. These early water craft were likely of very primitive construction, possibly similar to skin boats called 'currachs' or 'coracles' used by the ancient Celts, consisting of a leather skin stretched over a wooden or wicker frame. Regardless of the actual appearance or construction of these boats or ships, the important thing to realize is that if the Illyrians started off in Anatolia and crossed the seas to the western Balkans, it must mean that the archaic Illyrians of Anatolia were a *coastal* people, not people who dwelt in the mountainous interior.

The second theory concerning the Illyrians and Anatolians states that the Illyrians came from Europe, migrated to Anatolia, and then migrated back to Europe. Part of the evidence for this theory comes from an unlikely source which strongly intermingles history and mythology: the Trojan War. For some modern-day readers, Homer's epic poem *The Iliad* provides the remnants of a historical memory of strange people who came from across the sea and settled in Anatolia, people who would later be called Trojans. The reason why Homer called his epic poem about the Trojan War *The Iliad* and not *The Troad* is because the city of Troy had two names. The first and more well-known is Troy, and the second name was Ilios, and it is this name upon which the poem's title is based. The name *Ilios* looks vaguely similar to *Illyrius*, the name of the heroic progenitor of the Illyrian people, according to Greco-Roman mythology. Furthermore, Homer speaks of Illyrians or people closely related to them (Paeonians and Dardanians, specifically) fighting in the Trojan War.[12] The Dardanians, who fought with the Trojans, had a city called Dardanus that was located very near to Troy. The Dardanelles Strait, which separates Anatolia from the Gallipoli Peninsula, is supposedly named after this tribe. All of this leads to a very exciting question: could the Illyrians and the Trojans be the same people? According to Homer, yes they were.

In *The Iliad*, Homer provides some mythical genealogical information linking the Trojans to the Illyrians. In Book 20 of Homer's mighty epic, Prince Aeneas is boasting of his esteemed parentage, saying that he is a descendant of Zeus himself. In his account, Dardanus, the legendary founder of the Dardanian tribe, was a son of Zeus, and it was Dardanus who founded the city of Dardania. Dardanus' son was named Erichthonius, and he in turn begat a son named Tros, after whom the Trojan people were named, and Tros begat a son named Ilus, who named the capital city of the Trojan people after himself.[13] Other authors like Virgil, Apollodorus, Diodorus Siculus and Dionysius of Halicarnassus provide extra details. In their collective accounts, Dardanus was the child of Zeus and Electra, the daughter of Atlas. Virgil says that he originated from Italy, while Apollodorus says that he came from the Greek island of Samothrace, and Dionysius says that he came from Arcadia. Regardless of Dardanus' exact origins, it is stated in the ancient documents that he came from somewhere in the west and landed in the north-east Anatolian kingdom of Teucria. This kingdom was named after King Teucer, who was the son of the Anatolian river god Scamander. When Dardanus arrived, he was initially welcomed in friendship by King Teucer, who permitted Dardanus to marry his daughter Princess Batia and establish a settlement on Mount Ida, located near the Teucrian capital. This settlement was named Dardanus, after himself. After ruling over his small town for only a short while, Dardanus and his following quickly took control of all of the kingdom of Teucria and renamed it Dardania. Dardanus waged war against his other neighbours and conquered their lands. He had many children, among them a son named Erichthonius. Erichthonius' son was named Tros, who took over the kingdom of Dardania and named it Troad after himself, also renaming the former Teucrian capital city after himself, calling it 'Troy'. Tros' son was named Ilus, whose name inspired Troy's alternate name, Ilios. So, according to Homer, the ancestors of the Illyrians originally came from Greece, migrated to Anatolia, transformed themselves into the Trojans, and then migrated back to Europe after the fall of Troy.[14]

Other stories told by the ancient Greek and Roman authors relate how many of the peoples of Anatolia had originally come from Europe. For example, the Greek historian Herodotus, writing in the fifth century BC, states that the Phrygians and the Bithynians of northern Anatolia were actually Thracians who had migrated across the sea and settled in a new home.[15] The historian Strabo, writing almost five centuries later, reasserts this claim, and there is some evidence to support this. Inscriptions found in the city of Gordium show that the Phrygian language was not one of the native Anatolian languages or even closely related to them.[16]

Considering that the Romans traced their origins back to the Trojans, it is certainly possible that the ancient Illyrians traced their ancestry back to the Trojans as well. What do the Illyrians themselves say about their origins? Stories telling how a group of people or a nation was created are known as 'etiological tales', more commonly called 'origin myths' or 'foundation myths'. Unfortunately, no stories about where the Illyrians came from written by the Illyrians themselves have survived to the present day. Our only historical records about the origins of the Illyrians come from other cultures. Aside from Homer's rather suspect account linking the Illyrians to the Trojans, we currently know of only two existing stories explaining where the Illyrians came from, and both of them are entrenched with mythological references. The first story comes from the Greek historian Pseudo-Apollodorus, who states in his *Library*, which is a collection of various Greek myths and legends, that the creation of Illyria as a formal country was due to the great mythic hero Cadmus, a Phoenician prince who lived around the year 2,000 BC. In Pseudo-Apollodorus' story, the supreme god Zeus kidnapped Cadmus' sister Europa and Cadmus went in search of her, taking his wife Harmonia. The Greeks state that it was Cadmus who introduced the alphabet to the Greeks (the Greek alphabet is somewhat based upon the Phoenician alphabet), and he also founded the city of Thebes. Cadmus and his wife left Thebes, continuing their search for Cadmus' sister, and entered the land of a people known as the Encheleans. During this time, the Encheleans were being attacked by the Illyrians (note that in this story the Illyrians already exist), and the war was not progressing well. Then, one of the gods declared via an oracle that the Encheleans would defeat the Illyrians if they made Cadmus and Harmonia their leaders. The Encheleans obeyed the oracle and, sure enough, the Illyrians were defeated. Cadmus was made king over both the Encheleans and the Illyrians, and when Cadmus had a son, he named him Illyrius, presumably to commemorate his victory (the Romans would do the same thing from time to time). However, the tale ends in tragedy, because Zeus turned Harmonia and Illyrius into snakes, and both of them were taken into the Elysian Fields.[17]

The second origin story concerning the Illyrians is reported by the Roman historian Appianus of Alexandria, commonly referred to in English simply as Appian, who lived in Roman-controlled Egypt from 95 to 165 AD. Unlike the earlier story by Pseudo-Apollodorus, this one does not have the Illyrians already in existence, but has them created from a single founder. According to Appianus, the region was named after Illyrius, who was the son of Polyphemus, the cyclops from *The Odyssey*. Moreover, he states that Polyphemus and his wife had three sons named Celtus, Galus and Illyrius, and that the Britonic Celts, Gallic Celts and Illyrians are descended from these three sons. Appianus further states that Illyrius had many children, and from these children are descended the various Illyrian tribes. As unbelievable as this story sounds, Appianus comments that among the many stories that he has heard concerning the origin of the Illyrians, this one appears the most plausible.[18] This statement indicates that in the past there were many stories pertaining to how the Illyrians appeared, and with the exception of Pseudo-Apollodorus' and Appianus' legendary tales, all of them are unfortunately lost to us. Considering Appianus' comment, one can only speculate as to how wild and outlandish these other tales were!

As stated earlier in Pseudo-Apollodorus' legend, Zeus turned Illyrius into a snake. Taking this as some kind of cue, modern linguists have tried to connect the word 'Illyria' to snakes, and surprisingly, they have come up with some pretty interesting findings. Snakes were rather prominent in the Illyrian religion, and we are fairly certain that the ancient Illyrians' language was part of the vast Indo-European language family. One German scholar named Otto Gruppe stated that 'Illyrius' looks similar to the Greek word *illo*, which means 'to turn or wind' like the slithering movements of a snake. The Slovenian linguist Karel Oštir discovered that the ancient Hittites of Turkey, who spoke a very archaic Indo-European language, called a large mythical snake *Ilurjanka*. According to the history of the Battle of Kadesh, fought between the Egyptians and the Hittites in 1286 BC, an Illyrian tribe called the Dardanians fought on the Hittites' side, which adds further weight to the idea that the Illyrians and Hittites of ancient Anatolia might somehow be related. However, not all scholars have convinced themselves that the name 'Illyrian' somehow involves snakes. Julius Porkorny stated that the name 'Illyrian' comes from the Iller River, which is a tributary of the Danube; the Illyrians were, therefore 'the people of the Iller'. Another hypothesis comes from the study of the Albanian language, because the Albanians are believed by some to be the Illyrians' modern descendants. Ćiro Truhelka stated that the name might be connected with the Albanian word *ilir*, which means 'freeman'; thus *Illyria* would mean 'land of the free men'. There are others who believe that the word 'Illyrian' has absolutely no connection to any Indo-European language and is a 'language isolate', meaning that it is completely unrelated to any other language and any attempts to dissect the word are futile.[19]

Earlier, I made a comment that there is a large community which believes that the Albanians are the descendants of the Illyrians, or who have at least retained numerous aspects of ancient Illyrian culture. This claim originated during the mid-nineteenth century and it has been furiously defended by a sizeable number of Albanians. Some might regard this as archaeology/history-based nationalism, where a modern culture tries to tie itself to a culture from the past to which it might not actually be related in order to give itself greater social clout. However, as outlandish as this may appear at first glance, there is actually quite a bit of evidence to support this claim.[20]

The most important piece of evidence is language. Only a few names and isolated vocabulary words from the ancient Illyrian language have survived to the present day. Some wonder if any trace of this old language can still be found in modern languages, such as Albanian. However, the link between the Illyrian and Albanian languages is sketchy. The Albanian language, as we know it, only appeared in the fifteenth century, and by that time it had already undergone massive changes.[21] Albanian is by no means a pure language. There are obviously loan-words from other languages, the most prominent example of which that springs to my mind is the Slavic word *slava*, 'glory' and the Albanian word *lavdi*, also 'glory'. Some Albanian personal names *might* reflect an Illyrian origin. For example, the name Bardyllis, one of the more famous of the Illyrian rulers, has been preserved in the modern Albanian name Bardhyl, which means 'white star' in Albanian. Yet is this evidence that Albanian is the true ancestor of Illyrian, or does it mean that the Albanians simply adopted a foreign name into their list of names?[22]

Another point of conflict is genetics. Critics of the claim that Albanians are modern-day Illyrians state that Albanians are not genetically related to those from whom they claim to be descended. According to the Human Genome Project, an analysis of Y-chromosomes showed that Albanians are *not* related to the Illyrians. If you were to analyse Albanian DNA, chances are you would not find much in the way of Illyrian genes. After all, the Illyrians lived two thousand years ago, and during the intervening time between then and now, numerous other cultures have moved back and forth into the area: Greeks, Romans, Goths, Huns, Slavs, Turks, Germans and Russians, to name but a few. No doubt, the purity of a potential 100 per cent Illyrian genepool has been substantially polluted by the presence of so many other people who migrated into the area, settled, and had families within the course of twenty centuries. I am quite sure that if you were to take a DNA sample of your average Albanian, that person would show a mixture of Italian, Greek, Slavic, Turkish and possibly a little Scandinavian thrown in just for some added zest.[23]

As for myself, I will not even dare to voice an opinion on a subject that is so controversial, although this controversy exists due more to political reasons than any problems with the actual history and archaeology, *per se*. Genetic evidence has proven impossible, and linguistic evidence is sketchy at best. In short, we just don't know, and I don't think that we ever will. So claims by modern cultures about an Illyrian connection are unreliable, and literary evidence in the form of legendary stories provides only tantalizing glimpses of information. Regardless, all available evidence suggests that the Illyrians came from Anatolia and migrated into southern Europe sometime during the early Bronze Age. Our primary evidence for this is both language and archaeology. Words and archaeological finds that are indicative of an Indo-European culture do not appear in the western Balkans until the early Bronze Age, meaning that a pre-Indo-European culture must have existed in the region beforehand.[24] Who were these people who had been living in what would become Illyria or Yugoslavia since time immemorial? Unfortunately, we don't know what they called themselves or the land that they lived in since they left no written records. Our only evidence for a distinct culture that already existed in the western Balkans before the Illyrians' arrival comes from archaeology.

The Prehistoric Western Balkans

The paleontological and archaeological record of the western Balkans is surprisingly detailed, even though there are of course massive gaps in the record. However, archaeologists have uncovered just enough evidence in terms of human remains and artefacts to construct a probable chronology of what the prehistoric western Balkans were like. The story begins during the Stone Age, when vast glaciers covered much of northern Europe and when beasts like mammoths, mastadons and giant lions and bears roamed the land. The Stone Age is divided into three periods: the Paleolithic ('Old Stone Age'), Mesolithic ('Middle Stone Age') and Neolithic ('New Stone Age'). South-eastern Europe, including the lands of Illyria, was far enough south that temperatures were warmer, and as such was largely free of ice. Because of this, south-eastern Europe had significantly more food than other areas, and the mountainous landscape possessed a vast warren of protective caves. It was an ideal place for the first people to establish themselves.

It is unclear when hominids (humans and their ancestors) first arrived in the western Balkans, but artefacts and skeletal remains dated to the Paleolithic period have been found in this region. At Sićevo Gorge, Serbia, a piece of a jaw was found, possibly being 250,000 years old and believed to have come from *Homo erectus*, a primitive human ancestor.[25] Stone hand axes, believed to be approximately 100,000 to 200,000 years old, have been found in this region. In Montenegro, one cave yielded a massive cache of more than 23,000 stone objects that showed evidence of being manually worked. Based upon the shape of some of the flakes, they were clearly of Neanderthal manufacture.[26] At Bacho Kiro cave in Bulgaria, pieces of two human jawbones were found inside, which were dated to around 43,000 BC. However, it is not clear if these fragmentary jaws belonged to *Homo neanderthalensis* or *Homo sapiens*. The first true humans, though in a very archaic form, entered Europe around 45,000 BC, and Neanderthals became extinct in Europe sometime between 40,000 BC to 37,000 BC. In 2002, a skull that was positively identified as belonging to *Homo sapiens sapiens*, modern humans, was uncovered in Romania, dated to about 40,000 BC. To date, this is the oldest-known modern human skull that has been found in Europe.[27]

In the centuries following the end of the Ice Age, the geography and climate of the western Balkans began to take on their present form. The Mesolithic, the Middle Stone Age, was a period of renewed prosperity. The warmer temperatures led to a lush landscape full of food. Forests of deciduous trees began to spread, while fields of wild grain sprang up along the Danube River Valley. With warmer temperatures and more available food, populations grew. As the landscape presumably returned to its pre-Ice Age state, the primitive people who inhabited this region maintained their hunter-gatherer lifestyle. In some places within Mesolithic Europe, food was so abundant that the people significantly delayed the adoption of agriculture.[28]

The most well-known Mesolithic site within the western Balkans is Lepenski Vir, Serbia, located on the western bank of the Danube River. Examinations at the site show that it was inhabited for more than a thousand years, beginning in the Mesolithic and ending well into the Neolithic at about 3,000 BC, when habitation abruptly ended. The buildings that are evident at Lepenski Vir and the other nearby villages show that these were not permanent buildings, at least not at first. In its early stages, Lepenski Vir might have been a seasonal campsite that was inhabited year after year. The site itself is rather confining, occupying a small area squeezed between the Danube and steep rising cliffs. The small huts, which were of various sizes (the smallest ones were just barely large enough to accommodate one person, and the largest ones were not that much bigger), were laid out in the shape of bell-shaped trapezoids.

The huts themselves were not arranged in any sort of pattern, but all of them had their wide flaring end facing towards the river. Amazingly, each of these huts was built according to extremely precise geometric measurements, long before geometry was thought to have been invented. The architectural proportions of the huts remain the same throughout all of the habitation phases at the site. The differences in size might be due to social status, since the larger huts appear to be concentrated in the centre of the camp.[29]

Human burials at Lepenski Vir are of several types. In the site's earliest stage, dubbed 'Lepenski Vir I', the dead are buried underneath the hut, usually at the far end away from the entrance; these consist almost entirely of newborns to 5-month-olds. In some cases, the bones are of a much wider age bracket, but they seldom consist of whole skeletons. Usually they consist of isolated bones here and there, such as a skull, or a jawbone, or some ribs, or a femur. This shows that the body was not buried whole underneath the hut. Instead, the body was likely left out in the open to decompose or to be picked clean by carrion birds, similar to the custom of many native North American tribes of the Great Plains, and then afterwards some of the physical remains were brought back and buried underneath the house, presumably to strengthen the house through the spiritual power of the ancestors.[30] The dead were also buried outside the village in collective cemeteries located either to the north or west of the settlement. These burials date mostly to the occupation phase called 'Lepenski Vir II'. Almost all of them are buried lying on their backs and orientated parallel to the river, being laid out in a north-south direction.[31]

Larger populations meant more advanced cultures and societies, and this leads to a phenomenon peculiar to humans: art. The site of Lepenski Vir contains some of the oldest artwork found in the western Balkans. The most notable of these are stone sculptures carved from the rocks found in and around the Danube River, some dated as far back as 6,500 BC. Some of these figurines were placed by the hut's central stone hearth, while others were placed in association with the graves. Both of these locations indicate that these figures represent protective gods or spirits, either protecting the house or protecting the body and/ or soul of the dead. Some of these figures are quite large. For example, one of them is two feet long and weighs almost two hundred pounds, and would have been virtually impossible to carry around as part of a nomadic society. Therefore the presence of stone sculptures indicates that the people at Lepenski Vir had transitioned from a nomadic to a non-nomadic society.[32]

However, becoming sedentary has its risks. Unless your habitation site is especially lush and overflowing with bounty, your local food supply *will* run out eventually. If you cannot easily obtain food from the landscape through a hunter-gatherer lifestyle, then you have to obtain food through other means; you must provide your own food by growing it yourself.

Agriculture appeared in the western Balkans rather early on. The oldest digging tools found in this region, made from bones and deer antlers, are dated to about 6,000 BC. It is interesting to note that even well into the Roman period when iron was readily available, tools made from bone were still being used. Archaeologists have grouped these Neolithic artefacts into what is called the Starčevo Culture, named after an archeological site on the Danube River close to the city of Belgrade where some of these artefacts were discovered. The Starčevo Culture lasted from about 6,000 to 4,500 BC. Farming seems to have occurred in the north first, in the area of the central Danube and its various tributaries, in the areas of northern Serbia, Bulgaria and southern Romania, and it was not until later that farming spread southwards into the rocky hills and mountains of the southern Balkans and northwards into what is now Hungary. It is not surprising that farming would develop in the river valleys first. As said earlier, the fertile soils around the Danube River were favourable for the growth of various types of wild grain such as wheat, barley, oats and rye. In time, people would learn to harvest them and raise them as crops. They would also begin cultivating millet and beans. Furthermore, when growing crops, it helps to have a good water supply.[33]

With the adoption of agriculture, semi-nomadic camps were replaced by permanent farming communities. Based upon what archaeological discoveries can illustrate, some of these settlements were continuously occupied for thousands of years. Not long after farming took hold, the people in the western Balkans began domesticating animals as well. Cattle, pigs, sheep and goats were raised and butchered for their meat and skins and possibly for their milk. The bones also provided a great source for sculpting utilitarian items such as needles, eating utensils and tools. Ceramic loom weights and spindle whorls indicate that the people were using clay, and were also raising sheep for their wool to make clothing instead of relying upon leather skins.[34]

During the Neolithic, artwork became more sophisticated. Cylindrical human and animal figurines with crudely-fashioned heads have been discovered dating from Neolithic times. These finds are similar to artefacts found in Greece and Turkey, indicating a common eastern Mediterranean culture, or possibly even early trade. All of this corresponds to what is called the Balkan-Anatolian Complex, an archaeological term for several related cultures that existed at the same time within south-eastern Europe and Anatolia.[35] Some of the best-known pottery from the prehistoric western Balkans comes from the Butmir Culture, which was exclusive to the region of Bosnia's capital of Sarajevo, although it was part of the larger Mediterranean Neolithic Culture that spanned the entire Italian Peninsula, the western Balkans, southern and central Gaul and the eastern coast of Spain. The artefacts were first discovered in 1893, and it was determined that they came from a single recognizable culture unique to this region dating from 5,500 to 4,500 BC. Butmir has been declared both the oldest and most well-known Neolithic settlement in all of Bosnia. In addition to the pottery, Butmir is also known for the presence of a substantial number of female figurines, likely representing a fertility cult. The Butmir Culture is divided into three phases, all of them dated to the Late Neolithic. Of these, Butmir II is especially noteworthy for its remarkable artwork. The region around Butmir, which is a neighbourhood in the town of Ilidža, which is itself a suburb of the city of Sarajevo, is rich in flint, and this is what likely drew large numbers of human settlers here since there was a vast abundance of tool-making stone. At Butmir, there were found large flint knives, arrowheads and axes. Ilidža is also the home of Bosna Spring, the source of fresh water from which the Bosna River emerges. On the whole, it was an ideal place for settlement.[36]

With a readily-available food source also came a substantial increase in the region's population. At Okolište, Bosnia, the remains of a massive Neolithic settlement were discovered, dated to 5,200–4,500 BC. At its height, it covered an area of just over 18.5 acres and is estimated to have contained a population of about 1,000 people, which is unheard-of for this time period. This village was also fortified, surrounded by a ditch and a wooden palisade wall with only one entrance. At Obre, located in the fertile valley of the Trstionica River, not far from the town of Kakanj, Bosnia, excavations were conducted showing that its history stretched back to the Neolithic. During Obre's earliest phase, the people's homes were 'pit houses', common among the Slavic, Baltic and other eastern and northern European peoples from ancient to modern times. As time progressed, both the houses and the settlement as a whole became more sophisticated. At Butmir, in the layers identified as Butmir II and Butmir III, the houses were rectangular longhouses made of wattle-and-daub, which would have been very similar to those constructed by the Celts of the Hallstat Culture or the ancient Germanic tribes, and were arranged in rows on a grid pattern like modern streets. One of the houses that was excavated actually had a floor made of wooden boards, and at one end was a dome-shaped oven with an ash pit, along with a separate area for grinding grains. The oven, commonly called a 'calotte', is similar to modern-day bread ovens used by the Serbians and other people living today in the western Balkans called a *furuna*, also spelled as *vuruna* or *vurnja*, possibly a derivative of the word 'furnace'. Food, especially grain, was stored inside the house in large ceramic containers. Outside the house were buildings that archaeologists suspect might have been workshops to craft the pottery and other artwork that we see in this region dated to this time.[37]

In addition to sculptures and decorated household goods, artwork can also take the form of personal ornamentation. We have many examples of jewellery made from the shells of *Spondylus gaederopus*, commonly called the European Thorny Oyster.[38] The shells of this marine animal have been found in archaeological sites throughout Europe dating as far back as the Paleolithic. The fact that we have people from an *inland* culture wearing jewellery made from the shells of *oceanic* invertebrates indicates that there must have been some sort of early trade network in the western Balkans at this time, in which inland settlements could obtain goods from the sea coast. The trade in *Spondylus* shells was almost pan-European, with specimens being found as far away as central Germania, the Carpathian Basin and even in the foothills of the Swiss Alps, which is about as far from the European coast as you can get.[39]

In addition to art, another important addition to culture occurred during this time: writing. It is possible that one of the world's oldest writing systems appeared in the Danube River Valley at around 5,500 BC. The 'Vinča symbols' are a series of symbols that have been found on pieces of pottery and other clay objects. Some of them are geometric in shape, while others can be described as hieroglyphic in appearance. I was always taught that the oldest-known writing that appeared in the world had occurred in Egypt and Mesopotamia, and scholars of these two regions state with pride that these areas were the birthplace of writing. However, the symbols uncovered in Romania and Serbia pre-date the oldest-known writing by more than a thousand years. Many scholars, especially those of Egypt and Mesopotamia, express high doubts that these symbols represent a language and might refer to something else.[40]

Illyria Modernizes through Metal

The Stone Age ended when people began using metal to make tools instead of relying on stones and bones, and the first metal to be exploited by early Man was copper. In 2008, the oldest-known copper axe from Europe was found in Prokuplje, Serbia, dated to around 5,500 BC.[41] While some might have claimed that this showed copper being imported into the western Balkans from elsewhere, possibly Mesopotamia where it was long-believed that copper production began, this view dramatically changed in 2010 when it was discovered that Belovode, Serbia, located on Mount Rudnik, contained the oldest-known site for copper smelting, also dated to about 5,500 BC.[42] The adoption of copper in the region possibly marks the beginning of the Butmir Culture.

Around the year 4,500 BC, the Butmir Culture, which had dominated much of what is now Bosnia for a thousand years, fell away and other cultures took its place. One of them was the 'Vinča Culture', named after a settlement on the Danube River near the city of Belgrade. It was during this time that agriculture finally broke out of the well-watered river valleys and began encroaching into the hills. Vinča-style pottery can be distinguished by a much wider variety of forms and decoration than that seen in previous archaeological cultures. The Vinča Culture of central Illyria directly replaced the Butmir Culture, and it lasted for five hundred years.[43] During the same time in southern Illyria along the Adriatic coast, the 'Danilo Culture' was taking shape. At the hilltop settlement of Danilo Gorje, the remains of twenty-four houses were found, and some of their floors were paved with stone. There also appears to have been some cultural contact across the Adriatic Sea between the Neolithic inhabitants of the western Balkans and the people of eastern Italy, since some of the pottery found at Danilo Gorje reflects Italian style. This could mean that there was active trade between the eastern Italians and the people along the Balkan coast. After all, only a few miles separate Italy's heel from the Balkans, and even small primitive boats could easily make the trip back and forth. Therefore trade is not an unreasonable idea. It could also mean that the native inhabitants of the western Balkans had seen Italian-style pottery and decided to copy it. Either way, the people of the Danilo Culture liked what the eastern Italians were doing and decided to have Italian-style goods.[44]

Illyria during the Bronze Age

Unlike agriculture, the adoption of metal tools by the people of the Balkans appears to have been a slow process.[45] As said earlier, even after metal tools were in use, some were still using farming tools made out of bone instead of metal. When they finally did decide to switch over to using bronze tools in large quantities, iron had emerged onto the scene.[46]

By the Bronze Age, the people of the western Balkans were definitely in contact with the outside world, and there appears to have been an especially strong trade connection with the people of modern-day Greece and Turkey. Bronze weapons start turning up in sizeable numbers, including daggers, swords and Minoan-style double-bladed axes. They even had contact either directly or indirectly with the Baltic tribes, because amber from the Baltic region has been found within Illyria, possibly traded down the Vistula River, across the Carpathians, and ending at the northern end of the Adriatic Sea on the border between Italian and Illyrian territory. Amber jewellery was rather popular with the Illyrians, because it is found in some quantity in graves in the form of necklaces, pendants and set within metal brooches. A laboratory analysis conducted in 1976 of amber recovered at Illyrian archaeological sites shows that almost all of it came from the Baltic region. Amazingly, the Illyrians recognized that amber was solidified tree resin, in contrast to Greeks and Romans who thought that it was simply a rock, and they tried to make their own home-made imitation amber from pine resin in their own land, but it didn't work.[47]

The ties between Greece and the people of the western Balkans during the Bronze Age are confirmed by the presence of numerous Greek artefacts found within Albania. Most of the artefacts that were found were weapons of Mycenaean design, indicating an impressive arms trade between the early Greeks and the early Illyrians.[48] One wonders what the Illyrians traded in exchange for all of these weapons. John J. Wilkes states that manufactured goods were exported to Illyria from Italy and Greece, and in exchange, the Illyrians traded natural products such as grain and animal skins, and possibly slaves.[49] However, 'natural products' is a bit vague; what does the Illyrian landscape have to offer? From our earlier survey of Illyrian geography, we know that this region is rich in forests, grain and livestock. The Illyrians could have traded timber, grain, live animals, meat and leather. Such products, especially food, would have been in high demand within Greece because the Greek landscape does not have much farmland. Even today, nearly 70 per cent of Greek territory is not suitable for growing crops. The vast grain fields and livestock pastures of Illyria, separated from each other by thickly-forested mountains, must have been viewed by the ancient Greeks as a great centre of natural resource wealth. Grain may have been sent to feed the people and animals, wood was sent for construction and ship-building, and leather was used for making clothing and body armour.

Illyria during the Iron Age

Iron became available in the Balkans beginning at around 1,000 BC. It is also around this time that we begin to see the emergence of cultures that can be described as 'proto-Illyrian'. By the eighth century BC, iron usage had spread entirely through the western Balkans, probably due to increasing contact with Greece and the Celtic tribes.[50] The ancient world was getting smaller and less isolated. Expanding populations, improved technologies and the creation of vast trade networks made people more interconnected than ever before. The tribes of the Dinaric Mountains were now in contact all around the 'civilized' world. Primary influences upon the lives of these people were the Celts, Greece and northern Italy, notably the Venetics and Etruscans.[51]

A typical Illyrian settlement during this time consisted of a fortified hilltop settlement, or 'hill fort' as it is commonly called. Burial practices took a noticeable shift. During the early Bronze Age, tumulus burials were common, but as the Bronze Age progressed, they were increasingly replaced by cremation burials. By the end of the Bronze Age, cremation graves were common throughout all of south-eastern Europe. In a cremation burial, the dead would be burned and the ashes laid to rest in the ground, sometimes in a ceramic container. With the beginning of the Iron Age, burial rituals abruptly swung back towards laying the dead to rest within circular burial mounds, in many cases defined by stone circles about thirty to forty feet in diameter, often containing two to four graves.[52] Since there are numerous archaeological sites of earthen mound burial tombs that have been uncovered in Western Europe and have been attributed to the Celts, the presence of these types of tombs possibly shows the influence of Celtic culture upon the Illyrians, or at least this particular region of Illyria. Some ornamentation was laid with the dead, but not much.[53]

Until the sixth century BC, tumuli occurred in groups of ten, but afterwards there were more. Major tombs consisted of a central burial chamber lined with roughly-cut stones, with secondary burials around the main central tomb, outside the stone enclosure, and orientated in an east-west direction. Cremation graves became more popular from the end of the sixth century BC onwards. In the sixth and fifth centuries BC, burials became increasingly richer with a lavish profusion of grave goods, including jewellery, weapons, armour and imported Greek and Italian pottery and glassware. Other grave goods appear to be the work of Illyrian craftsmen who were either trained in classical artistic styles or trying to imitate them.[54] In the late fifth century and into the early fourth century BC, the dominant burial practices in central and eastern Europe changed from burial mounds to individuals being buried in flat graves in vast cemeteries. At the same time, many of the hilltop settlements that prevailed in that region were abandoned and people moved down into the fertile lowlands.[55]

Metal-working of all sorts became a major industry in Illyria from about the fourth century BC onwards. Archaeologists have uncovered numerous metal-working tools, smelting furnaces, casting moulds and even the graves of the craftsmen themselves. Understandably, local mineral deposits determined what sort of materials would be worked. If a silver mine was found in a certain area, then that location and the area immediately surrounding it would become a centre for silver production. One of the most famous, located in eastern Bosnia, was aptly named 'Argentaria' ('silver place') by the Romans. Domavia (modern-day Gradina) was also an important centre of silver production, whose job it was to supply silver for the imperial mints to be produced into coins. In Salona, there was a government bureau tasked with overseeing gold-mining.[56] Some Illyrian tribes made their own coinage. At first, they were simply copies of existing Greek coins, manufactured in the fifth century BC. The Greek colonies located along the Adriatic coast minted their own coins for their own personal use, not for trade with the Illyrians. Later, Illyrian tribes that had gained power and notoriety minted their own coins, but they were not widely circulated.[57]

The Illyrians had a tendency to adopt aspects of the cultures with which they were in contact. Southern Illyrians were very Hellenized, northern Illyrians were Celtic in appearance, and the Illyrians in the far west were similar to the Etruscans and northern Italians. Among the eastern Illyrians where Greek culture was the dominant force, there were even small aspects of Thracian and Scythian influence.[58]

When the Celts entered the western Balkans during the third century BC, it profoundly changed the culture of the people who lived in those areas. The Celts introduced the pottery wheel into the western Balkans, as well as new weapons and tools. They also introduced their La Tène culture to Illyria, which gave the Illyrians new art and new styles.[59]

As I've stated before, there is no such thing as 'Illyrian culture'; that is to say that there was no single unifying dominant culture that existed throughout this whole area. Different regions of Illyria could have radically different practices and customs. I have stated previously that in Roman times there were two main Illyrian culture groups: the Dalmatians and the Pannonians. Within these two main spheres, there were several smaller localized culture areas. Archaeologists and anthropologists have determined that there are several regions within Illyria that show signs of having been culturally distinct. In the south in what is now Bulgaria and southern Albania, there was the 'Trebenište Culture', which lasted from the twelfth to the mid-fourth centuries BC, with its high point during the sixth century BC. Based upon the dates of its existence, we can attribute the collapse of the Trebenište Culture with the rise of Alexander the Great and his conquest of the Illyrians that bordered his realm. This society was long extinct by the time that the Great Illyrian Revolt took place during the reign of Caesar Augustus. The people who lived here were heavily Hellenized, especially from the sixth or fifth century BC onwards.[60] In northern Albania and stretching to the Morava and Drina Rivers deep into Serbia and eastern Bosnia, there was the 'Glasinac Culture'. Of all the Illyrian or proto-Illyrian cultures that existed, this one appears to have lasted the longest, while other people changed their cultural practices depending on circumstances.[61] The Alpine areas of western Illyria tend to have more cultural zones, smaller in area and tightly packed together. In mountainous landscapes where travel and cultural interaction is difficult, societies which may only be a few miles apart can be radically different from one another. At least three cultural regions have been identified: the Sveta Lucija, Notranjska and Dolenjska Cultures. Many of these are similar to the Etruscans and other northern Italic groups.[62] To the north in what the Romans would have considered southern Pannonia was the 'Dalj Culture'. It is named after Dalj, located at the confluence of the Sava and Danube Rivers, where a large ancient cemetery was discovered. It appears to have been a further development of the 'ash urn culture' that was located here during the Bronze Age.[63]

The Illyrian Tribes

The Illyrians may seem sophisticated to us, but to the ancient Greeks and Romans they were nothing more than barbarians. The word comes from the ancient Greek word *barbaros*, which means 'foreigner' or 'outsider'. As such, 'barbarian' is merely a generalized term for anyone who wasn't Greek, regardless of how advanced or primitive they were. This is different from the word *xenos*, meaning 'stranger' or 'unknown person', from which we get our word xenophobia. Reputation has it that the word 'barbarian' comes from the Greeks' perception of the various languages that foreign peoples spoke; it sounded like 'ba-ba-ba'.

The Romans had a more exact definition of what the word 'barbarian' meant, and this is the definition that has permeated the English language to this day. To the Romans, 'barbarians' were people that were primitive, dirty, hairy, animal-like, bloodthirsty, uncultured and uncivilized. They only lived in small villages. They could neither read nor write. They had no laws or morals. They had no logic or reason and acted without restraint. They had no high culture or art, music or philosophy. They were either naked, semi-naked or clothed themselves in animal skins. They were inferior in every way to the advanced Mediterranean civilizations of Egypt, Greece, and Rome, fit only to be conquered.

By these Roman perceptions, the Illyrians were *not* barbarians. The historical records from both Greece and Rome state that the Illyrians lived in cities; not villages or towns but full-fledged *cities*, usually built atop mountains and heavily fortified with stone walls and towers, turning their cities into nearly impregnable fortresses. They had fleets of modern warships that were the equals and possible superiors to any ships used at that time by the Greeks or Romans. Their warriors, although not professional full-time soldiers like the Roman legionnaires, were nevertheless disciplined and professionally-equipped with metal body armour, shields and weapons, and they fought in tactical cohesive formations rather than simply charging in one massive horde. Illyrian armies frequently gave the Greeks and Macedonians a run for their money, and many times the professional hoplite phalanxes were butchered by these warriors. They also traded goods throughout large portions of the

Mediterranean and became wealthy. The Illyrians were no push-overs: they were a serious power in the region, an entity to be reckoned with.

However, as impressive as they were, there was a great flaw in their culture, a flaw unfortunately common to many 'barbarians' like the Celts, Germans and others: the Illyrians never united to become a single nation. The Greeks, Macedonians and Romans must have been very grateful for that. The individual Illyrian tribes – and the ancient sources collectively name almost sixty of them – were powerful enough as they were. Had they joined together to form a single country ruled by a single king, then they might have become one of the great civilizations of ancient times, and the histories of Greece, Macedon, and Rome might have been drastically altered. The kingdom of Macedon might have been destroyed long before Alexander the Great was born, Greece might have been reduced to a second-rate power, possibly even becoming vassals to the Illyrians and forced to pay regular tributes, and Rome might never have expanded into central and eastern Europe. One is led to wonder about what possible cultural contributions such a nation could have made to the western world. It is more than probable that if a single Illyrian kingdom existed, modern-day historians and scholars might speak of their grand artwork, architecture and writings. We might speak of great kings, courageous generals, wise philosophers and gifted artists and poets. Yet it was not to be. One can only imagine 'What if?'

Although the Illyrians were not united into a single nation, it appeared that they were coming close to doing so. The Romans recognized fairly early on that the Illyrians were divided into two main culture groups; northern Illyrians were culturally different from southern Illyrians. Outsiders like the Romans gave these culture groups names, usually based upon the dominant tribe within that group. Northern Illyrians were generically called 'Pannonians'. The name actually referred to just one tribe, the most powerful one, but since the other tribes shared the same culture as the powerful Pannonian tribe, all of the tribes were called by that name, the Pannonian culture group. Southern Illyrians were referred to as Dalmatians because that was the name of the dominant tribe in that area.

Since we are unaware of any surviving Illyrian texts aside from a few fragmentary inscriptions, all that we know about the Illyrians comes from what the Greeks and Romans wrote about them. Since both the Greeks and Romans tended to look down upon anyone who was considered to be non-Greek or non-Roman, and since the Illyrians were often at war with the Greeks and Romans, one can surmise that the written accounts are not exactly unbiased, but there are a few notable exceptions. An unknown Greek writer who was ascribed the name 'Scymnus' or 'Pseudo-Scymnus' by modern scholars wrote about the Illyrians in a work entitled *Periodos to Nicomedes* written in the late second century BC. This work is known as a *periegesis*, meaning 'being shown around' in ancient Greek; essentially, it's a geography and travel guide. He portrays the Illyrians as the stereotypical 'noble savages', rather comparable to Tacitus' analysis of the ancient Germanic tribes in his landmark ethnographic work *Germania*. However, such Romanticized views are just as invalid as the prejudiced accounts written by other ancient historians.[64]

At Most Na Soči, the remains of 2,730 skeletons were found. Of these, 770 were those of children, indicating that between one-quarter and one-third of Illyrian children never made it to adulthood. In Roman-era Illyricum, life expectancies varied from region to region. In the south, the average life expectancy for a man was 39 and for a woman it was 36, while in the northern territories, men had an average life expectancy of 43 and women 44.[65]

The first record of the various tribes that lived along the Adriatic coast of the Balkans comes from Hecataeus of Miletus, written sometime in the sixth century BC. Unfortunately, only fragments of his work survive. Among the tribes listed are the Kaulikoi, Liburnoi (Liburnians), Mentores, Sypioi, Hythmitai and the Iapygians who would establish settlements in southern Italy. However, Hecataeus merely mentions their names and goes little into cultural studies. *Periplus*, written by Pseudo-Scylax of Caryanda around 330 BC, mentions the names of various tribes including the Liburnoi, Hierastamnai, Boulinoi, Hylloi, Nestoi, Manioi, Autariatai, Enchelleis, Taulantioi and, most importantly, the Illyrioi. This shows that the name 'Illyrian' was originally the name of one particular tribe, but this name eventually became ascribed to the whole ethnic group. *Periodos to Nicomedes*, written by Pseudo-Scymnus around 110 BC, lists the Ismenoi, Mentores, Pelagoni, Liburnoi, Boulinoi and Illyrioi.[66] This last piece of information shows that even in the late second century BC, when the name 'Illyria' was already commonly used by both Greeks and Romans to refer to an entire geographic region, the name 'Illyrian' was still being used to refer to just one specific tribe that existed within that region.

If you were to look at an ethnic map of Illyria in the third century BC, you'd soon see that it was not populated exclusively by Illyrians. There were Venetics in the west, Illyrians throughout, Celtic tribes scattered in isolated pockets here and there, and Thracians pushing in from the east. Even back then, the western Balkans possessed a mixed multi-ethnic population.

In Italy's north-east were the Venetic-speaking peoples, coastal-orientated tribes whose life depended upon the sea. The most prominent of these were the Veneti, who occupied the northern tip of the Adriatic Sea and who would become the founders of the city of Venice. However, there were more of these 'Venetic people', such as the Catali and Secusses. Slightly further to the east were the Istrians or Histrians, located in eastern Italy, Slovenia and western Croatia. They gave their name to Croatia's Istrian Peninsula, where many of them lived.[67] Strabo states that the Istrians were the first people to inhabit the Balkan coast, that they were of Italian ethnicity and it is due to their heritage that Rome's rulers had redrawn the boundaries of the imperial province of Italia to include the Istrian Peninsula.[68]

The Istrians' immediate eastern neighbours living along the coast of the Balkan Adriatic were the Liburnians. Their lands stretched from the Istrian Peninsula eastwards to the Krka River, called the Titus River in Roman times. The Liburnians' ethnic identity is questionable. Some historians and anthropologists classify them as Illyrian, but others consider them to be Venetic. Even the ancients were unsure of how to classify them.[69] Regardless of their exact ethnicity, the Liburnians were *the* naval power in the Adriatic. They commanded vast fleets of ships of all sorts, including warships. Their claim to fame was one specific kind of ship, a small light craft named after them called the 'liburnus' or 'liburna', which the Romans enthusiastically copied for their own navy. Many Greeks and Romans equated the Illyrians in general with pirates, but the Liburnians in particular seem to have been associated with this label. Their maritime superiority over the Adriatic led to them exerting intense control over travel and trade, and this made them very rich. Pseudo-Scylax comments that they were a strong powerful people who possessed many cities along the coast. Liburnian domination of the Adriatic eventually led to them spreading beyond their traditional tribal borders, including taking possession of the entire island of Corfu (in ancient times, both this island and its main city were called Corcyra), and even setting up small outposts within Italian territory.[70] Although the Liburnians are commonly associated with the sea and probably got a great deal of their food from fishing, the ancient writers tell us that they were also pastoralists raising flocks of sheep.[71] Both Greek and Roman writers recorded the sensational aspects of Liburnian culture with the goal to shock their audiences with their supposed cruelty and immorality. Pseudo-Scylax states that the Liburnians were ruled over by powerful sexually promiscuous queens who used their power to take any man that they fancied into their beds, even slaves – a far cry from the ideal image of the dutiful stay-at-home Roman matron.[72] The Roman historian Marcus Terrentius Varro states that both women and children were held in common, and that once a boy reached 8 years old, he would be *allotted* to a man who bore the closest physical resemblance to him, who would then act as the boy's father.[73]

North of the Istrians and Liburnians were the Japodes, the first people that we can definitely identify as Illyrian. They were either a single large tribe or a collection of small culturally-similar tribes. The Japodes inhabited the eastern Alps in areas that now cover Slovenia, western Croatia, north-eastern Italy and possibly southern Austria. Strabo states that the Japodes were a perfect fusion between Celtic and Illyrian cultures; as examples of this, he comments that they wore Celtic-style armour and covered their bodies with tattoos 'like the rest of the Illyrians and the Thracians'.[74] Their main settlement was Metulum (modern-day Josipodol, Croatia),[75] and Strabo lists other Japode settlements such as Arupini (Auersberg), Monetium (Mottnig) and Vendo (Crkvinje Kampolje). In the mountain valleys, they grew spelt and millet, but making a living was hard. In many places where abundance cannot be obtained, people are reduced to raiding to get what they need, and the Japodes appear to have fallen into this category. Strabo calls the Japodes 'a war-mad people'[76] and Appianus describes them as 'a strong and savage tribe'.[77] Their domain lay upon or near important trade routes. Strabo states that on the perimeter of Japode territory was the town of Segestica (which was originally a settlement of the Illyrian Segestani tribe), and that both waggons on main roads and cargo ships travelling on the rivers leading to this town brought in goods from all locations.[78] These economic hubs became targets for Japode attacks. Appianus states that they had defeated the Romans twice within the span of twenty years, and had even taken and sacked the Roman towns of Aquileia and Tergestus.[79] The Roman military historian Sextus Frontinus describes how on one occasion a group of Japode warriors joined forces with the Romans, only to use the opportunity to massacre a large number of legionnaires:

> Under pretence of surrender, the Iapydes [the Japodes] handed over some of their to [*sic*] best men to Publius Licinius, the Roman proconsul. These were received and placed in the last line, whereupon they cut to pieces the Romans who were bringing up the rear.[80]

Directly east of the Japodes in what is now western Hungary, northern Croatia and northern Serbia were a large number of tribes that the Romans referred to collectively as 'Pannonians'. Cassius Dio comments that the name 'Pannonia' comes from the clothing that they wore: sleeved tunics made by sewing together strips of cloth called *panni* which were cut from old clothes.[81] It isn't too much of a stretch of the imagination to envision the Pannonians wearing striped clothes of various colours, similar to the 'coat of many colours' worn by Joseph in the Bible. Strabo lists the Pannonian tribes as being the Andizetes, Breuci, Daesitiatae,[82] Ditiones, Mazaei, Peirustae 'and also other small tribes of less significance' which he does not name.[83]

Appianus describes the Pannonian Illyrians (referred to incorrectly as Paeones, who actually lived just east of Macedonia) as a vast nation living south of the Danube River, with their lands stretching from the Japodes in the west to the Dardani in the east. Their country was thickly forested, and the Pannonians themselves did not live in towns or cities but in isolated villages scattered throughout the land. They were divided up into many tribes totalling 100,000 warriors, but they had no single ruler. The Pannonians occupied high mountainous terrain, difficult to access, with only narrow paths that were hard to climb, and had managed to preserve their independence purely due to the remoteness and ruggedness of their homeland, and anyone who wanted to pass through had to pay a toll.[84] The Roman author Publius Florus, writing during the reign of Emperor Tiberius, said 'The Pannonians are protected by two swiftly-flowing rivers, the Drave and the Save; after ravaging the territory of their neighbours, they used to withdraw behind the banks of these streams.'[85]

Appianus' claims are corroborated to a slight extent by the Greco-Roman writer Cassius Dio, who describes the Pannonians as being very poor and unfortunate people 'and lead the most miserable existence of all mankind'.[86] In his words, the climate of their territory was dreary, their soil was unproductive for growing crops, they had no olives (something which was absolutely unheard-of for a Greek!), and they had hardly any grape vineyards and the little wine that they did produce was wretched. Their winters were harsh and brutal, and cold weather occupied a majority of the year, so their growing season was short. Their diet consisted mostly of barley and millet, which they ate as bread and drank as beer. However, as is the case with many societies in world history, a hard life breeds hard people, and Cassius Dio lauded the Pannonians as being the bravest men that the Romans had faced up to that point, bloodthirsty and full of high spirits. Cassius Dio knew all about the Pannonians because he had once been the Roman governor posted there. In fact, just to assuage any criticisms that could have appeared concerning his description of Pannonia and its people, Cassius Dio wrote 'After my command in Africa and in Dalmatia (the latter position my father also held for a time) I was appointed to what is known as Upper Pannonia, and hence it is with exact knowledge of all conditions among them that I write.'[87]

One thing that Appianus definitely got wrong was his claim that the Pannonians didn't live in towns or cities, because they assuredly did. The most prominent of their settlements was called Segestica, the centre of power for the Segestani tribe, which was a member of the Pannonian culture.[88] Sometime after the Great Illyrian Revolt, possibly during the reign of Emperor Tiberius, the Romans changed the name of the city from Segestica to Siscia (the name 'Siscia' does not appear in the ancient sources until the reign of Tiberius), which serves as the basis for the town's modern name, Sissek.[89] Archaeology has shown that Segestica was surrounded by a wooden wall before and during the Great Illyrian Revolt of 6–9 AD. Either during the rebellion or just after it, the wooden walls were destroyed by fire. Replacing them would be a brick wall with a stone base.[90] Were the wooden walls destroyed in an act of war, or were they deliberately set fire to as a way to clear the space for the construction of the brick walls that would replace them? Segestica was ideally suited for trade and military operations, as described by Strabo:

> The city Segestica, belonging to the Pannonians, is at the confluence of several rivers, all of them navigable, and is naturally fitted to be a base of operations for making war against the Dacians; for it lies beneath that part of the Alps which extends as far as the country of the Iapodes, a tribe which is at the same time both Celtic and Illyrian. And thence, too, flow rivers which bring down into Segestica much merchandise both from other countries and from Italy.[91]

The historian Paterculus states that even though they were barbarians by birth, the Pannonians had become very heavily Romanized by the beginning of the first century AD and actually showed a degree of intelligence! He says: 'Now all the Pannonians possessed not only a knowledge of Roman [military] discipline but also of the Roman tongue, many also had some measure of literary culture, and the exercise of the intellect was not uncommon among them.'⁹²

Such statements are in line with other statements made by Roman authors, who in the same breath compliment and insult the tribes of which they speak. I'm especially reminded of Tacitus' description of the Germanic rebel leader Arminius, in which he states that he was unusually smart for a barbarian. If Arminius actually heard people say that about himself, I'm not sure as to whether he would take such a statement as a compliment or not. However, not all authors were willing to grant haughty concessions to their ethnocentric arrogance. Herodianus of Antioch flatly accused the Pannonians of having all brawn and no brains: 'Although the men of those regions [Pannonia] have huge and powerful bodies and are skillful and murderous in battle, they are dull of wit and slow to realize that they are being deceived.'⁹³

Central and southern Illyria were inhabited by Illyrian tribes that were collectively referred to as the Dalmatians, the second of the two main Illyrian culture groups. This group's name is based upon one particular tribe known as the Dalmatians, Dalmatae or Delmatae, depending upon which source you read. The Dalmatian Illyrians were more heavily influenced by Greek culture than their northern Pannonian brothers, who were more Celtic-influenced. The Dalmatian tribe specifically was one of the more powerful and well-known of the Illyrian tribes. They were originally small and weak, and were named in reference to their founding city called Dalmium (modern-day Tomislavgrad, Bosnia); the name was later changed to Delminium by the Romans. Dalmium was a fortified walled town built atop a mountain, like almost every Illyrian settlement. Strabo describes it as a large city. As the people of this city gained power, they spread out, conquering adjacent territories. This is similar to the rise of Rome during its very early stages. As the Dalmatian tribe expanded, it added more territory and settlements to its domains until the region that they ruled over was called Dalmatia, and the ancient city of Dalmium served as the epicentre of their realm.⁹⁴

The Greek geographer Strabo gives us the most information about this particular tribe:

Then comes the seaboard of the Dalmatians, and also their seaport, Salo [Salona]. This tribe is one of those which carried on war against the Romans for a long time; it had as many as fifty noteworthy settlements; and some of these were cities — Salo, Priamo, Ninia, and Sinotium (both the Old and the New), all of which were set on fire by Augustus. And there is Andretium, a fortified place; and also Dalmium (whence the name of the tribe), which was once a large city, but because of the greed of the people Nasica[95] reduced it to a small city and made the plain a mere sheep-pasture. The Dalmatians have the peculiar custom of making a redistribution of land every seven years; and that they make no use of coined money is peculiar to them as compared with the other peoples in that part of the world, although as compared with many other barbarian peoples it is common.[96]

The Daesidiates (also called Daesitiatae, Desiadates and Desidiatians) and Breucians deserve special attention, since these were the two main tribes that were involved in the Great Illyrian Revolt. The Daesidiates were Pannonians who lived in central Bosnia near modern-day Sarajevo. We know this due to an ancient inscription that was found near the Bosnian capital at Breža: VALENS VIRRON F PRINCEPS DESITIATI (*Valens Virronis, filius princeps Desitiati*; 'Valens Virronis, the son of the chief of Daesidiates'). The reason why Cassius Dio called the Daesidiates 'Dalmatians' is because they dwelt within Dalmatian territory. Strabo calls them Pannonians.[97] Not a lot of info is known about the Breucians. They might have been named after a mythical founder, since Breucas was an Illyrian name (also sometimes spelled Breukoi, Breigos or Brykos, indicating that the 'c' in Breucus and Breuci was a hard c, not a soft c). Pliny the Elder states that the Sava River flowed through their territory.[98]

Illyrian Warfare

During the Iron Age, Illyria became very prosperous. Trade brought in wealth from foreign lands and farms were growing more food than ever. A testament as to how well the people were doing was their sheer number. Between the eighth and sixth centuries BC, it is estimated that the overall population of this land increased by 700 per cent. Because of this staggering rise in population, Illyria became very crowded. No wonder that the tribes began to develop very sharp elbows. Tribes that had previously lived in relative peace with their neighbours now began to ferociously compete for land and resources.[99]

Another visible way to assess the growing power of Illyria was the status of their rulers. Fuelled by wealth in the form of trade and prestige goods, the tribal chiefs began to amass more and more power to themselves and their followers. Now they began to be elevated to the status of petty kings. Eager to gain even more power, the Illyrian chiefs and kings began expanding their realms through military conquest and political sovereignty.[100]

This combination of an overcrowded landscape, intense competition over farmland and other resources, growing industrialization and the desire of the tribal chiefs to expand their power created the ideal circumstances for a sudden upsurge in warfare within this region. Equipped with armour and weapons traded to them by foreign states and fueled by large trade-based treasuries, armies of hundreds or perhaps thousands of warriors began marching into adjacent tribal lands. Some were annexed, some were subdued, others were outright destroyed. It is of little doubt that the growing militarization of the Illyrians caught the attention of their neighbours across the border, like Macedon and Greece. Border defences began to be strengthened in anticipation of attack.

Archaeologists have discovered large numbers of weapons in Illyrian graves dated to both the Bronze Age and the Iron Age. The unusually high number of military artefacts may demonstrate that Illyrian culture placed a very strong focus on warriors and that fighting men had a dominant role within their society.[101] Many of these weapons were of foreign manufacture and were either traded or sold to the Illyrians in exchange for unknown commodities.

One wonders why any nation would willingly sell weapons to a group of people who might become future enemies. I think that there are a few reasons. First, natural resources in some areas might have been so scarce that one nation might have been willing to do anything to get their hands on them, even if it amounted to the equivalent of trading millions of dollars worth of military hardware in exchange for it. The United States is a prime modern example of this sort of operation.

Another reason is using a foreign culture to one's own advantage. If Illyrians placed a high value on martial prowess, as almost all tribal societies do, then owning weapons would have been very important to them. Knowing this, sly foreign merchants would have sold weapons to the Illyrians at absolutely extortionate rates, demanding an excessive amount of lumber, grain or precious stones in exchange for only one sword. The naïve Illyrians, believing that this was a fair exchange, submitted to it willingly. To me, this sounds very similar to stories that I have heard of dishonest American and Canadian fur traders operating in North America who would sell a single rifle to an Indian or Eskimo in exchange for a waggon-load of fur pelts. Sometimes, the number of furs stacked one atop the other was equivalent to the length of the rifle standing upwards. Often, guns with ridiculously long barrels were traded to the Indians knowing that they would have to give up a correspondingly large number of pelts.

So far, I've talked about economic reasons for trading weapons to the Illyrians, but what about political reasons? Foreign states could have traded weapons to the Illyrians with the understanding that they would use them on the state's enemies. According to the old adage 'the enemy of my enemy is my friend', the Greeks or Macedonians might have been willing to trade weapons to the Illyrians in exchange for these tribesmen fighting a sort of proxy war against that state's foes. Even today, countries that want to beat their rivals but don't necessarily want to get their own hands dirty doing it will often employ some weaker power to do their fighting for them.

Then again, the Greeks and Macedonians could also have traded the weapons to the Illyrians, fully knowing that they were current or future enemies, with the understanding that they would eventually turn these weapons on *each other*. The rising power of Illyria was a definite threat to those on the other side of the border, and so one would think that giving large numbers of weapons and armour to them would be the stupidest decision that you could possibly make. However, the Greeks, Macedonians and others must have been watching the situation in Illyria very closely. Tribes were attacking each other over controlling farmland and other resources. These foreign powers might have seen an opportunity to reduce both the population and power of the Illyrians by aggressively fuelling the inter-tribal warfare that was going on. I wouldn't be a bit surprised if they traded weapons to both sides. Why send in the hoplites to kill the Illyrians when they seemed to be doing just fine killing each other? Once the Illyrians had exhausted themselves from constant fighting, they could be deemed safe and the borders would not suffer the threat of an invasion anytime soon. Furthermore, if their populations were reduced to a significant extent, then land would become available, and with the warriors too weak to stop them, the armies of the foreign states could then sweep in and claim the land for themselves.

Well, this might have been the original idea of the foreign states and for a while it seemed to work. Illyrian tribal chiefs now envisioned themselves as kings and wanted to preside over large domains, but in order to gain their kingdoms, there had to be war. For a time, armies of Illyrian warriors fought and slaughtered other armies of Illyrian warriors, but then something changed. Illyria didn't implode: it _ex_ploded. Seemingly overnight, hordes of Illyrian warriors were seen on the horizon, preparing to invade and conquer the foreign lands. Fleets of Illyrian warships rampaged over the seas, sinking foreign ships and pillaging shoreline settlements. Something had obviously gone horribly wrong for those on the outside who wanted to benefit from Illyria's troubles. Maybe the chiefs and war-leaders finally realized that others were trying to benefit at the expense of their lives.

The Illyrians didn't just import weapons, they also made their own once they acquired the skills to do so. Near the town of Sanski Most, Bosnia, located near the lower length of the Sana River, there were and still are rich iron-ore deposits. Here were found the remains of an Iron Age village with an accompanying cemetery, dated to the fifth and fourth centuries BC. That in itself is impressive, but what makes this site really stand out is that it is one of the earliest-known sites in this area for native ironworking. Forges were discovered near the houses, along with tools used for both smelting iron ore and forging iron objects made from the processed ore. Weapons found in the graves nearby include not only imported ones, like a Greek double-edged _xyphos_ sword, but also natively-manufactured weapons, such as spears and single-edged curved short swords, the latter seeming to be a rather common telltale feature of Illyrian warrior graves dated to Classical times.[102]

What did Illyrian warriors look like? How did they arm themselves? How did they fight? Thankfully, we have numerous portrayals of Illyrian fighting men from the Greeks and Romans, so we have a lot of information regarding their appearance, although most of it comes from centuries before the Great Illyrian Revolt took place. The Illyrians experienced a lot of cultural interchange, and so they tended to adopt aspects of other cultures that were located nearby; ditto with regard to military matters. The tribes that were in contact with the Celts of northern and western Europe were somewhat Celtic in terms of their armour and weaponry. By the same token, the Illyrian tribes that were proximate to Macedon and the various Greek states were heavily Hellenized. As such, their warriors and their battle strategy differed very little from the Greeks. They wore similar armour and carried similar weapons, and likely fought using similar tactics. If someone took an Illyrian warrior and a Greek hoplite, both of them wearing full armour and carrying their shield and weapons, put them side by side and then asked you to identify which one was Illyrian and which one was Greek, you would be very hard pressed to tell the difference between them.

With regard to how the Illyrians equipped themselves for battle, it came down to what they could afford, just like every early ancient society. Obviously the rich would be the most kitted out, since they could afford to purchase weapons, a shield and a full set of armour. Those who had less money would have to be content with just a weapon, shield and perhaps a helmet. The poorest of the poor would wear no body armour at all, and possibly act as light skirmishers armed with slingshots or javelins. Since horses were and still are expensive, only the aristocrats would act as cavalrymen, taking their horses into battle with them. As an example of what rich Illyrians could afford, one burial in Glasinac dated to the seventh century BC holds the grave of a prominent chief or warrior. In addition to jewellery and pottery, the grave contains a bronze-handled sword and two spearheads which have a central rib running down the middle to give them increased strength and rigidity. The skeleton also has a pair of highly-decorated bronze greaves (lower leg armour) and what appears to be the remains of a shirt affixed with rows of round metal studs. The garment itself has long rotted away, but it might have been made of leather or some other tough material.[103]

The most ready form of protection for a warrior was neither a helmet nor body armour but a shield; every warrior, regardless of status, carried a shield into battle. Shields, even small ones, were essential in pre-gunpowder warfare. Illyrian shields came in various sizes and shapes, depending largely on cultural contact rather than on specific shields used by specific types of soldiers. Some Illyrians in the south and along the Adriatic coastline carried large round shields that were very similar to the Greek *aspis*, the large round shield carried by hoplites. Round Illyrian shields are commonly shown with designs of rings, dots and sometimes a 'sun wheel' in the centre. Depictions of shields used by the Macedonians under Philip II and his son Alexander the Great show similar designs. However, it is not clear if the Illyrians copied Macedonian artistic styles or vice versa. As for central and northern Illyrians who were in contact with the Celts, their shields were oval or rectangular in shape, and were held using just a single central hand grip as opposed to the double grip commonly seen on other shields in which the arm passes through one loop and the hand holds onto the other loop. Many of these Celtic-style shields had a large central rib running up the middle which either took up half the length of the shield or sometimes even ran up its entire length. A large metal boss made of bronze or iron was fitted in the middle to protect the hand and act as a 'puncher' when the shield was used offensively. This type of shield was also commonly used by Roman soldiers before the adoption of the famous half-cylindrical *scutum* shield that is identified with post-Marius Roman legionnaires.

The head was always a vulnerable target, so those who had a bit more money would be able to afford a helmet for added protection. The Illyrians wore different types of helmets. Conical helmets made of bronze or iron were common, and these were sometimes decorated with plumes of feathers or horsehair. The Japodes, who lived in what is now the eastern Alps and Slovenia, wore a conical helmet made of wicker reeds and chain mail, and occasionally having large round metal plates fixed onto the surface; this is called the Šmarjeta Helmet, named after the locality where the first example was found. Some Illyrians who were in contact with both the Celts of the Hallstat Culture of central Europe as well as the peoples of northern Italy wore the 'pot helmet', common in the sixth century BC and almost always made of bronze, consisting of a dome with a fairly wide brim around the edge and often fitted with a front-to-back horsehair crest. Another helmet was the so-called Negau or Negova Helmet, named after the first specimen found in Negau, Slovenia and dating from the fifth to fourth centuries BC. It was more conical than the previous pot helmet and the decorative crest had been done away with, opting instead for a sharp ridge running across the top, all of which were designed to deflect blows more easily. One example found at Novo Mesto even has large dents which, in all likelihood, were made by a battle-axe.[104] However, the helmet most associated with the Illyrians is called, not surprisingly, the Illyrian Helmet. It looks similar to the Corinthian helmet worn by Greek hoplites except that the Illyrian Helmet has an open squared face as opposed to the nose guard, leaf-shaped eye-holes and large cheek plates of the Greek helmets. These helmets first appeared during the seventh century BC and were used until the second century BC. They were always made of bronze, and a pair of small ridges running down the middle of the helmet indicated

Figure 3: A reconstruction of the Glasinac Warrior, seventh century BC. Although a shield was not found in the grave, one is portrayed here based upon other shield examples from that time. (*Illustration by the author*)

where a detachable crest could have been affixed. This helmet design was used throughout the ancient region of Dalmatia. It is unclear if the Illyrians imported these helmets or if they were natively manufactured, but I'm leaning towards the idea that they did both.[105]

As to which kinds of helmets the Illyrians wore *after* the second century BC, they almost certainly wore various copies of Roman helmets. There are two reasons for this. First, by this time, the Roman Republic had conquered all of northern Italy (previously under the control of the Gallic Celts) and Greece, both of whom were the Illyrians' neighbouring territories. The Illyrians were thus sandwiched in between these two Roman provinces. While the Illyrians had previously been under the influence of the Celtic tribes to the north-west and the Greeks to the south-east, cultural influence upon the Illyrians was now almost wholly Roman. Secondly and more importantly, beginning a century earlier, the Romans had become militarily involved in Illyria. By the year 200 BC, the Romans had already fought two wars in the region and controlled a sizeable portion of the Illyrian coast. So the Illyrians had direct first-hand contact with Roman military technology, weaponry, armour, equipment and battlefield tactics. With the success that the Romans had in the previous two wars, the Illyrians must have put the Romans' success down to their superior military, and therefore wanted to emulate it in order to preserve their existing territory against further Roman aggression or even to regain hegemony over the region. Being the enterprising people that they were, they would surely have remodelled their warrior bands along the lines of Roman military units and would have begun copying the Roman way of war in every detail: their armour, their weapons, their shields, their equipment, their training and how they fought. By the time of Gaius Octavianus' campaigns against the Illyrians during the 30s BC, it is highly likely that the Roman legionnaires and the native Illyrian warriors would have been almost indistinguishable from one another.

For even more protection, Illyrians wore body armour consisting of a cuirass and greaves; armour was rarely worn on the arms, despite what is depicted in movies and TV shows. A metal plaque found in Slovenia shows Illyrian warriors, both infantry and cavalry, wearing what appear to be padded sleeveless jackets reaching down to just above the knee. These vestments, similar to medieval aketons or gambesons, would be able to defend against glancing blows and against some blunt hits, but they would be absolutely useless when it came to a stab. Another warrior from this same plaque is shown wearing a Greek-style cuirass, complete with *pteruges* decorated with a single row of T-shaped designs or possibly T-shaped metal studs, with the bottom edges of each leather strap trimmed with fringe.

In terms of weaponry, there was much to choose from. The Illyrians armed themselves with short swords like the Greek *xyphos* or the Roman *gladius*. Some also carried a curved chopper known as the *falcata*, also called a *machaira* or *kopis*, popular throughout southern Europe from Spain to Greece. However, the weapon that the Romans felt was distinctly Illyrian was a curved bladed weapon known as the *sica*. The word is derived from the Latin verb *secare*, meaning 'to slice'; we have no idea what the Illyrians themselves called this weapon. They were typically short, no more than two feet long, but were most common in 'large knife size' for lack of a better term. They could be either single-edged (knife) or double-edged (dagger). Both the single-edged and double-edged versions have curved blades, but what is interesting is that in the single-bladed specimens, the blade is on the *concave* edge, looking like a backwards sabre or a stretched-out hand sickle.

How were these knives and daggers used, especially the single-edged ones? A tantalizing hypothesis is found in comparing the Illyrian *sica* with the Levantine *khanjar* dagger and the teeth of prehistoric sabre-toothed cats. The late palaeontologist Larry Martin hypothesized that the curved teeth of sabre-toothed cats functioned in the same way as Middle Eastern-style curved daggers like the khanjar. *What are these knives used for?* he asked. They are specially designed for ripping open people's throats.[106] Let us imagine that you intend to kill someone with this weapon. Ideally, you sneak up behind them, reach around in front, clamp their nose and mouth shut with your open left hand to prevent them from screaming and giving your presence away, yank back your victim's head, exposing his throat, and use your *sica* to dispatch him. When that moment comes, you have two ways of handling it. First, you can place the sharp concave edge across the surface of your victim's throat (that is, have the bladed edge pointed *towards* you and your victim) and pull across sharply from left to right. The curved edge of the knife hugs the curvature of your victim's throat, and results in slicing open the jugular vein, the oesophagus and the carotid artery in one swipe. The second technique is somewhat more vicious and requires a bit more muscle to get the job done. This involves physically piercing the right side of your victim's throat with the knife, with the bladed edge pointed *away* from you and your victim, and pushing the blade to the left into your victim's neck. Because the shape of the knife is curved instead of straight, it will follow a curved path as it stabs into your victim's neck. The curved shape of the knife will cut a C-shaped slice out of your victim's throat, first going in, then rounding, and then working its way out in a clean C-shaped swoop. This technique doesn't just slice open your victim's throat, but physically rips it open. You have to get through a lot more muscle and fibrous tissue to do this, but with this technique, you are guaranteed a quicker kill. No wonder that the Illyrian *sica* soon became the preferred weapon of murderers and assassins in the ancient world, and the people who carried these knives became known as the *sicarii*, or sicarians in English. Today, the word *sicario* means 'murderer' or 'hit-man' in Italian and Spanish.

The Illyrians also carried pole-arms, but it seems that they did not conform to a single distinctive style; their spears came in a variety of lengths and shapes. Of all of the pole-arms carried by the Illyrians, the most intriguing is the one called the *sibyna*. This is one of the few words from the Illyrian language that have survived to this day. Various ancient authors provide different spellings for this weapon, but what is important is what the weapon looked like and how it was used. The famous Roman poet Quintus Ennius, writing in the late-third to mid-second centuries BC, mentions the sibyna in his *Annales*, which unfortunately have only survived in isolated fragments. While describing a sea battle, he states '*Illyrici restant sicis sibynisque fodantes*',[107] which translates as 'The Illyrians stood fast and stabbed with sicas and sibynas.' Aulus Gellius simply provides the word 'sibones' in a list of vocabulary terms pertaining to different weapons used at the time and doesn't go into any description of it, but since it is lumped into a section of words devoted to pole-arms, we are fairly confident that the word referred to some kind of spear or spear-like weapon.[108] The word that the Romans used to describe the sibyna was *venabulum*, the Latin word for 'hunting spear',[109] although the word literally translates to 'an instrument used in hunting', which could mean anything. Hunting spears are differentiated from combat spears by being typically fitted with larger-than-average heads that are used to take down large and dangerous prey like lions, bears and especially wild boars. In fact, during the Middle Ages, these kinds of spears were called 'boar spears'. In addition to having larger heads, they are also fitted with a cross-guard at the base of the spearhead to prevent the spear from digging into the animal so far that it penetrates the animal's body up to the shaft. The ancient Roman *venabulum* looked remarkably similar to medieval and modern hunting spears, and they were a common tool used by the *bestiarii*, the 'beast men' who fought against wild animals in the arena. The only difference between the ancient and medieval versions that I can see is that the crossguards on the Roman spears are V-shaped with the two points directed towards the front, while on the medieval ones they are fashioned into a straight horizontal bar.

Javelins were also used: light spears with short thin shafts and small but long metallic heads that could be hurled from a distance; these appear to have been native-made copies of Roman *pilum* javelins. The reason why is because a tenth-century AD Byzantine document called the *Suda* describes the Illyrian spears as being made of metal, as in *mostly* metal. There were no all-metal spears in ancient or medieval times. The only ancient pole-arm that I can think of that is composed of a higher-than-average amount of metal would be the Roman pilum javelin. If this is true, then this would be a concrete example of the Illyrians adopting Roman weapons.

In terms of sheer numbers of weapons that have been found by archaeologists, the axe is the weapon most frequently uncovered. They were made of iron, bronze and even stone; these stone axes probably had some ritualistic significance.[110] Metal arrowheads have been found in sites attributed to the Illyrians.[111] The Roman doctor Paulus Aegineta (Paul of Aegina), who wrote an epic medical textbook entitled *De Re Medica* (*On Medical Matters*), states that the Dalmatian Illyrians put a type of poison on their arrows called 'ninum'. He adds that this poison was deadly when it infected an animal's blood. However, the flesh of the animal was still edible, so there was no risk of the hunter being killed by eating poisoned meat.[112] One scholar named Mirko Dražen Grmek proposes that this type of poison was not made from plants, since no toxic plants grow in the area with poisons matching the qualities that Paulus Aegineta describes. Instead, he suggests that this poison was made from snake venom.[113]

Nicolaus of Damascus states that the Autariate tribe used to kill their own wounded warriors to prevent them from being captured by the enemy.[114] This shows that the Autariates, at least, considered it an act of great shame to be captured by their enemies and they would rather die than be taken prisoner. Aleksandar Stipčević claims that this was done to prevent the enemy from cannibalizing the prisoners. I find Stipčević's statement to be wholly bizarre because no ancient author mentions that the Illyrians practised cannibalism, nor is there any archaeological evidence, at least to my knowledge, that shows proof of cannibalism. The basis for the idea that the Illyrians were cannibals and ritually consumed the bodies of their enemies in order to gain their power comes from a description of the Scordisci tribe, who were not ethnic Illyrians. The Scordisci, known in the ancient Greek sources as 'Skordiskoi', were Celts who had migrated south into the Balkans. They were named after the place where they first settled, Mount Scordus.[115] Florus states that the Scordisci (whom he calls Thracians, not Celts) tortured their prisoners, offered human blood as sacrifices to their gods, and drank out of the hollowed-out skulls of their enemies.[116] Other such tales can be found in the writings of other ancient writers. Whether such stories represent real facts about their behaviour and culture or if they are just sensationalized over-the-top works of fiction, we don't know.[117]

The Illyrian Navy

A discussion of the ancient Illyrians would be incomplete without mentioning their ships. The Illyrians were renowned as being some of the best sailors in the world, and their ships were renowned as being some of the best in the world. Two kinds of ships deserve close attention: the *lembus* and the *liburnus*. The *lembus* (from the ancient Greek *lembos*, 'boat') was the most common type of Illyrian warship, which had only one level of oars and no sails. It was small, fast and manoeuvrable, and capable of carrying fifty men in addition to the rowers.[118] The *liburnus*, also called the *liburna* or *navis liburnica*, 'the Liburnian ship', had both oars and a sail. Early versions had a single level of fifty oars, twenty-five on each side, while later versions had a double level of oars; these ships are called 'biremes'. This later version was a hundred feet or so long, sixteen feet wide and only had a three-foot draft, which meant that despite its large size, it could move in very shallow water. In the double-decker version of the *liburnus*, there were eighteen oars on each side of each level, totalling thirty-six on each side and seventy-two oars overall. The Romans enthusiastically copied this ship for their own use, and Liburnian-style biremes played a crucial role at the Battle of Actium in 31 BC.[119]

There is an engraving of an early Liburnian-style ship on a pair of bronze greaves (lower leg armour) found in Ilijak and dated to the seventh century BC. In this engraving, there is a single large rectangular sail mounted on a central mast. Atop the mast is a crow's nest for a lookout who may have doubled as an archer when the ship was engaged in battle. There are four large ropes that hold the sail in place: two are fixed to the yard-arms and are tied to the hull. These ropes are likely used for 'tacking': changing the angle of the sail so that it can catch the wind from a certain direction. The other two ropes are fixed to the bottom corners of the sail and are likely used for raising and lowering the sail. The ship has a forward-projecting prow like the ram's head on a trireme, but there doesn't appear to be an actual ram's head. This hull design is for cutting through the water, not for ramming other ships. Liburnian ships were built for speed, not brute force. Above the prow is a large horned dragon's head with a long serpentine neck. These Illyrian dragons appear to have two large ears, a pair of Texas-style longhorn horns and a large rectangular head. Note the similarity of this design to that of the giant horned snake seen on the bronze belt plate found in Gradiste, Serbia. The similarity of these two designs indicates that a giant horned serpent must have been part of Illyrian legend, or was perhaps a named character from Illyrian mythology. The Illyrian religion will be discussed later on in this chapter. The ship's hull has a row of diamond-shaped shields mounted along the side. There is an aftcastle (a raised platform commonly used

Figure 4: The *ketos* or *cetus*, a beast from Roman mythology; the word 'cetacean' comes from this. The cetus was a sea dragon with a long serpentine body, crocodile-like jaws and a pair of horns on its head. Could this be an example of the Romans adopting a character from Illyrian mythology? This mosaic is dated to the third century BC and was found at Monasterace in southern Italy. (*Photo by Carole Raddato, 17 December 2014. Ancient History Encyclopedia, www.ancient.eu Creative Commons: Attribution-ShareAlike. Used with permission*)

as a command post or a tower-like defensive position) in the rear of the ship, but no forecastle towards the front. On the back of the ship, there is a large rudder mounted centrally on a pivot, as opposed to other rudders used on other ships that were mounted on the ship's side. This would have made Liburnian ships much easier to steer and manoeuvre than other contemporary ships used by other Mediterranean cultures.[120]

The Illyrian Religion

Hardly anything is known about the Illyrian religion. There are a few names of Illyrian gods that survive, mostly in carved inscriptions rather than in paper texts. It is almost certain that, like many ethnic groups composed of many individual tribes, they had a certain standardized pantheon of important gods, accompanied by a host of lesser local deities that were worshipped only by one specific tribe or another.

Polytheistic peoples tend to be more religiously tolerant than monotheists. In societies that worship multiple gods and divine spirits, the idea that other people worship gods that are different from your own isn't a point of contention. In fact, polytheists will sometimes incorporate foreign gods into their own native pantheon. However, the only times when the Illyrians appeared to actually accept other gods were if those gods were similar to theirs. It essentially means that gods that are from different cultures and have different names but have the same attributes and perform the same functions are regarded as being more or less identical. When it came to gods and religion, the Illyrians rejected foreign gods unless those gods were similar to the deities that they themselves worshipped. As evidence of this, there are inscriptions that mention the names of certain Illyrian gods, and the names of corresponding Roman gods are listed immediately afterwards.[121]

However, perhaps we are looking at these artefacts incorrectly. The Romans seldom took the time or effort to learn the names of the gods that were worshipped by the peoples that they conquered, so they simply called other gods by Roman names. When the Roman historian Tacitus wrote his famous ethnography on the Germanic tribes during the last years of the first century AD, he stated that the Germanic barbarians mostly worshipped the god Mercury.[122] Mercury was a Roman god who was almost exactly identical to the Greek god Hermes. The Germans certainly didn't worship Mercury; they worshipped their own native gods. In this case, Mercury is a synonym for either Odin or Thor. Tacitus used the name of a Roman god because he was writing for a Roman (preferably Italian) audience, one that was certainly knowledgeable about the Roman pantheon but who may have been completely ignorant about the Germanic religion and, quite frankly, were not interested in learning all of those foreign-sounding names. The fact that the names of Roman gods are listed alongside Illyrian ones may not be due to the idea that the Illyrians accepted Roman gods into their polytheistic pantheon. Instead, it might be due more to letting the Romans know which of their gods corresponded with which Illyrian gods, almost like a reference guide or a cheat-sheet.

As stated many times in this chapter, the topic of snakes appears to have been something commonly associated with the Illyrians. Images of snakes and other serpent-like creatures are seen on Illyrian jewellery and body armour, and they recur frequently in legend and lore. Among the Illyrians, snake imagery seems to have been confined largely to the southern region of Dalmatia. The western and northern lands, occupied by the Japodes and Pannonians respectively, have very little in the way of snake imagery.[123] It might be too much of a stretch, though, to think that the Illyrians referred to themselves as 'the Serpent People'. The reason why is that snakes and snake-worship were a common motif in ancient Europe, not just in Illyria. While the Abrahamic religions of Judaism, Christianity and Islam associate snakes with evil due to the story of Adam, Eve and the Garden of Eden, in many ancient European cultures, snakes had the complete opposite image. They were believed to be good luck charms, or the embodiments of friendly spirits that could bestow good fortune, prosperity and protection on someone's house. The Baltic tribes of northern Europe venerated divine snake-like spirits called 'zaltys', which were the guardians of the house and all who dwelt within, and would bring good luck to the family. The ancient Romans believed that the protective spirit or *genius* of a household looked like a snake in its physical form. Famously, Queen Olympias, the mother of Alexander the Great, was a snake-worshipper. Even outside Europe, snakes were seen as protective entities. Famously, the kings of ancient Egypt had cobras adorning their crowns and headdresses, believed to spit venom into the eyes of the king's enemies. There were also numerous serpentine gods and goddesses in the Egyptian pantheon who served as protectors. The span of snake-worship in ancient Europe and elsewhere indicates that there must have been some common feature among either Indo-European or pre-Indo-European faiths in which snakes were seen as protective good luck symbols.

If there were symbols of good luck, then there was also bad luck as well. Pliny states that Illyrians believed in curses and 'the evil eye'.[124] If you suffered from a curse or just plain bad luck, then there were ways to gain the favour of the gods and spirits. The most notable of these was sacrifice. Like many ancient cultures, the Illyrians practised human sacrifice. The Roman historian Arrian states that when Alexander the Great besieged the Illyrian town of Pelion, located in central Albania, the defenders killed three rams, three boys and three girls to gain divine favour.[125] Regrettably, no Illyrian temples have survived, nor do we have any written descriptions of them, so we have no idea what they would have looked like. Following Hellenization, they presumably built their temples according to Greek architectural styles. After the Romans came in, Roman-style temples became the norm.

Interring the dead either as a whole body or a cremated one within a burial mound, often called by the Latin name *tumulus*, appears to have been the most common funerary practice throughout Illyria. A mound of earth, earth mixed with stones, or exclusively of stones would be piled up atop the grave; a mound of stones piled atop a grave is called a 'cairn'. This practice lasted from the Bronze Age until well into the Roman period. The size of the burial mound, its location and the grave goods associated with the person buried within denoted the status of the deceased. Some of these could be quite huge. The impressive burial mound of Jalžabet, located near Varaždin, measured twelve metres high and two hundred metres in diameter. However, the mounds were usually much smaller than this one, which is one of the largest tumulus grave sites in all of Europe. At first, a mound was the site of just one grave, almost certainly that of a chief or another important person. However, as time went on, secondary graves tend to appear arranged in close proximity to the central grave. Apparently, other people of the community had expressed their wishes to be buried near their leader; as they followed him in life, so too do they follow him in death. They are often arranged in a rectangle around the chief's grave, possibly so that their spiritual power can protect their chief from outside harm. One mound excavated at Stična, Slovenia contained 183 graves, but evidence shows that these graves were placed here within a broad 300-year timespan, which shows that mounds such as this were continuously added onto year after year.[126] Illyrians sometimes buried their dead in stone-lined graves, like underground crypts. This practice was widespread throughout Illyria. The rectangular grave would be lined with five large flat stone slabs, one for each side and one to serve as a lid; there was no stone for the bottom. These types of graves are not associated with burial mounds.[127] Cremation graves increase beginning in the late 500s BC and continuing into the early 400s BC. This could indicate a shift in religious beliefs, possibly due to the influence of the Celtic tribes that were expanding into south-eastern Europe, since the Celts practised cremation rather than burying their dead.[128]

Illyrian Architecture

Illyrian-made buildings are very hard to find. After more than two thousand years of occupation and invasions, most of the old buildings that are in the western Balkans are of Roman, Byzantine, Venetian, Slavic, Austro-Hungarian or Ottoman Turkish construction. Very little architecture constructed by the region's pre-Roman inhabitants is left. However, there are a few places where it can still be seen.

Many sources describe the Illyrians as living in heavily-fortified cities with massive stone walls. Modern archaeologists call these fortified settlements by the Serbian name *gradina*, based upon the Slavic words *grad* or *grod*, meaning either a fort or a fortified settlement (as in Leningrad, Stalingrad, etc.). You can still see the crumbling ruins of a few of these Illyrian forts today. Even now, they are impressive, and you can get an idea about what Roman soldiers were thinking when they were ordered to march up a steep hillside and assault the defences, all the while being hammered by rocks, arrows, javelins and ancient Molotov cocktails. These walls could be anywhere from six feet to thirty feet high, depending on how accessible the terrain was: places that could be easily attacked needed large walls, whereas places that were difficult to access could do just as well with smaller walls because the natural landscape itself provided some defence. The ancient authors themselves stated that the Illyrians were very astute in using the terrain to their advantage, and archaeology has proved this. Unlike Roman forts, Illyrian fortified settlements were not built according to a more or less standardized plan. The shape of the forts depended upon the topography of the landscape. Walls and even the locations of buildings within the fort followed the contours of hillsides and canyons. In that way, you can see how the Illyrians managed to incorporate their fortifications into the landscape rather than simply imposing their buildings upon it. In places where there was level ground, the fortifications were almost perfectly circular, while in more jagged terrain the fortifications were built in accordance with the topography. Many times, these fortified towns only had one or two gates. This would make it difficult for an attacking army to get in, but it would also make it equally difficult for the population inside to quickly evacuate if there was an emergency.[129]

Of all of the Illyrians' fortified settlements that are still discernible today, arguably the most impressive is Daorson, now known as Ošanići, located near the town of Stolac, Bosnia. The site was inhabited since the Bronze Age and possibly earlier. It began as a hill fort, constructed between 1,600 and 1,500 BC; very little evidence of this original fortified settlement remains. However, it really came into its own during the time of Alexander when the city was surrounded by massive stone walls and towers. Obviously, Daorson had grown very prosperous, so much so that it minted its own coins, had a thriving manufacturing centre and was a major exporter of pottery and metal products. The oldest sections of the walls have been dated to the fourth century BC, while the rest of the fortifications date up to the middle of the first century BC. The reason for the abrupt end date is because during that exact time, the inhabitants of Daorson were crushed by the Romans led by Publius Vatinius. Since that date, the site has been abandoned.[130]

The stones that form the walls of Daorson are very large. Although they are cut into various-sized blocks that are more or less rectangular, they have a certain organic free-form quality to them. Many of the stones that make up the city walls are not perfectly square or rectangular but are multi-angled, which helps to better lock the stones together and resist the punishing effects of earthquakes, battering-rams and catapults. The construction seen in the walls of Daorson looks eerily similar to the walls of ancient Mycaenae or that of the Hittite capital city of Hattusha, which perhaps hints at an architectural tradition or a historical memory of building brought from further east. Before the arrival of the Romans, the Illyrians built their fortifications using 'dry wall' construction, meaning that they simply stacked the stones on top of one another without using any cement or mortar to hold them in place. After the Romans began coming in, the Illyrians began to use mortar.

Sometimes the Illyrians settled close to rivers, which made very good natural barriers. They could be fished and they served as highways for boat-based trade, rowing up and down the rivers trading goods with other riparian settlements. However, sometimes these rivers flooded and damaged the buildings. The clever Illyrians adapted to this situation by doing something that many people who live in or near flood zones do

Figure 5: Ruins of the city walls of Daorson. (*Photo by Lsimon, 5 September 2009. Public domain image. Wikimedia Commons*)

today: they built elevated houses, mounted on wooden stilts. It should be said that archaeologists have only found a small handful of sites that follow this construction plan. Considering that these buildings were constructed atop wooden piles and that wood rots (especially in a waterlogged setting like that), no wonder that few traces of such dwellings have been uncovered. Actually, the very fact that people have discovered these remains at all is nothing short of miraculous.[131]

If the riverbank was rather steeply sloped, then the buildings would be terraced, like a set of stairs, leading from the river up the slope of the hill. Archaeologists have discovered one such settlement as this located at Donja Dolina, approximately eight miles upstream from the town of Bosanska Gradiška, on the banks of the Sava River. A wooden palisade wall made of vertical logs was placed on the upstream side of the village, arranged perpendicular to the river's flow. It was made of two rows of logs, and the empty space in between was packed with dirt. Buildings were arranged in rows, with narrow streets and alleyways running parallel to the river. The houses were all square-shaped and constructed around a framework of thick wooden beams. The houses' walls were made of wooden rounded beams laid horizontally, one on top of the other. The ends of these beams were narrow, and the points of the beams of one wall fit into the empty gaps between the pointed ends of the beams of another wall, interlocking and interleaving together. Afterwards, the floors and walls were covered with a smooth layer of plaster-like clay. The roofs were made either of flat wooden planks or were thatched with straw; in a riverine setting like this, reeds to make thatched roofs would be readily available. The floor plan of a single house averaged at twenty-five square metres in area, and was usually divided into three sections: the large main room which contained an open hearth, a smaller bedroom, and a small storage room. The central hearth itself was usually made of clay. Archaeologists have hypothesized that this was not simply a fireplace where food was cooked but possibly had a multi-purpose role, acting as both a fireplace to keep warm, a place to cook food and a place to give religious offerings. In one of the storage rooms, archaeologists found several pottery jars filled with carbonized grain. Animal pens were even built in this fashion. We know this because large amounts of preserved animal manure have been uncovered at one of these sites, so we can hypothesize that one of these elevated buildings was actually used as a barn.[132]

Despite the preserved remains found at Donja Dolina, this should not be taken as the standard form of Illyrian architecture. Not all Illyrian villages were built in this way. Indeed, it seems that there was no discernible 'Illyrian' style of architecture. Houses could be constructed of wood or stone. They could be square or circular, large or small. They could be separate or attached to each other. Architecture, therefore, depended upon regional style, geography and the availability of building materials. Most Illyrian houses consisted of one large room rather than several small rooms. The houses themselves were also fairly small by many people's standards. The remains of one stone dwelling, discovered at Monkas near Rovinj, measured only 4 × 6 metres in area. Like the impressive stone walls, pre-Roman stone houses were also constructed using a dry-stacking technique. The roofs could either be made of a thick layer of thatch or overlapping flat tiles made of limestone.[133]

Everyday Life for the Ancient Illyrians

Regrettably, very little information exists concerning how the Illyrians went about their everyday lives or how their societies were laid out. We know the obvious facts: they were ruled by chiefs, they had warriors, etc., but we have very little in the way of specific cultural anthropological information. We do not know if there were such things as 'man's work or woman's work', we don't know the role that religious officials played in society, and we don't know about the exact role played by the tribal chief.

Like every ancient society, the Illyrians had slaves. In fact, the Greek historian Theopompus says that the Ardiaei tribe (pronounced AR-dee-AY-ee) alone had 300,000 slaves as part of its population. This is assuredly an exaggerated number, since the city of Rome had 200,000 slaves during its height, and the population of the entire Ardiaei tribe was certainly smaller than the number of people who dwelt in the Eternal City. A more reasonable figure is given by Agatharchides of Cnidos, who states that some of the wealthy elites of the Dardanian tribe could possess up to 1,000 slaves; in peace they worked the fields and in war they fought under the command of their masters.[134]

Our earliest records of Illyrian clothing come from the sixth century BC, and consist almost entirely of carved stone depictions, especially tombstones, of the Illyrians by Greek artists or perhaps by native Illyrians trained in Greek artistic styles. However, I have to say that most of these date to the last few centuries of the Roman Empire, when the state was already in decline. Since fashion styles change considerably from one decade to the next, let alone from one century to the next, we cannot automatically take it for granted that the clothing seen on these monuments would have been identical to the clothing that the Illyrians wore five or six centuries earlier.

The men mostly wore sleeved long tunics; short tunics are rarely portrayed in art. During Roman times, the sleeves were wider and they could also be removed, fixed into place by clasps on the shoulders. These long tunics are believed to be the precursor of the garment called the *dalmatic* (i.e., the 'Dalmatian tunic') worn by members of the Catholic clergy. Sometimes they wore a cloak over this, presumably during wet or cold weather, which was similar to the Greek *chlamys* or the Roman *sagum*, fastened at one shoulder with a brooch. It is uncertain if Illyrian men wore trousers; Aleksandar Stipčević states that Illyrian men seldom wore trousers, while John Wilkes hypothesizes that their use was common.[135]

We have more evidence of what Illyrian women wore, mostly in the form of grave goods and depictions in stone carvings. A typical woman's outfit consisted of three parts: an undergarment, an outer garment and a cloak. The undergarment was similar to a man's long tunic, except that it was longer, reaching down to the floor. Over this sleeved undergarment, the women wore an outer garment that came in various styles. One was a sleeveless version, which was fastened on the shoulders with *fibula* clasps. A belt would then be tied around the waist so that the upper part would blouse over it, and then a second belt would be tied over that bloused-over part. Another style of outer garment was designed so that the upper part would be tight-fitting, like a bodice or a corset, but from the waist down it would be pleated and bell-shaped. The cloaks that women wore were often hooded. Ancient authors called it the *cucullus Liburnicus*, or 'the Liburnian cloak'. In artwork that does not show women wearing hooded cloaks, the women are portrayed wearing scarves covering their heads. The scarves were not tied around their heads: the ends freely fell down the sides and were draped on the shoulders. At other times, they wore large shawls made of thick heavy material that covered the head and upper body. Therefore it would appear that according to Illyrian social custom, women were banned from appearing bare-headed and must always have their heads covered out of modesty.[136]

Hats or other types of head coverings were mostly worn by Illyrian women and they came in various styles:[137]

1. A small skullcap that was similar in style to the small white fez called the *qeleshe*, worn in Albania. It is suspected that the qeleshe is a modern version of this earlier Illyrian cap.
2. A conical leather or fur cap, similar in shape to a Slavic cap called the *šubura*.
3. A skullcap with a wide wavy brim, worn only by soldiers; essentially an Illyrian 'boonie hat'.

The types of shoes that were commonly worn by men were made of leather with upturned toes. These types of shoes are today called *opanci*, and are still worn today in some areas of the Balkans. It is possible that the Slavs who moved into the region copied this style of shoe from the Illyrians. Although they conformed more or less to a general form, some were more boot-like, others more sandal-like.[138] Japode-style shoes were made from a single piece of leather that had the toe turned backwards and held in that position with a leather strap that was tied around the ankle.[139]

As in all societies from ancient times to modern times, appearance could be augmented with the use of jewellery. If you've got, you flaunt it.

The Illyrians were no exception, and they could be just as glittering and gaudy as anyone around in those days. Belt plates were broad enough for highly-complex decoration; many of them depict warriors and battle scenes. Brooches and necklaces were common, used both by men and women. Pendants suspended from necklaces could be geometric or organic in shape. Pendants in the shape of human heads were common among the Japodes and Liburnians. The triangle was the most common geometric ornament, and who knows what it might have represented? Possibly a representation of the mountainous landscape in which the Illyrians lived? Or maybe an abstract depiction of the rays of the sun radiating downwards from the sky? Or maybe an axe that gave protection, similar to amulets worn by Germans and Scandinavians that represented Thor's hammer? Or maybe it was simply a design or a shape that had no meaning at all. Since there are no ancient written records explaining what these shapes and designs mean, and since we can't ask any Illyrians about their meaning, we'll never know what these things represent, and any ideas that modern historians propose are purely guesswork that will never be conclusively proven. Regional styles were also prevalent in terms of the jewellery that people wore. Northern Illyrians, like the Japodes and Liburnians, wore pendant necklaces with images of the human face. Southern Illyrians were fond of wearing pendants shaped like birds. Necklaces made of Baltic amber beads, or necklaces decorated with an amber pendant, were also common. Illyrian chiefs also sometimes wore large bronze Celtic-style torques around their neck as a symbol of their rank.[140]

One of the few things that we can call thoroughly Illyrian is the spiral-shaped fibula clasp. This consists of a pin and two round discs made out of wire (almost always bronze) coiled around and around in a spiral. Fibulae of this design first appeared in the 700s BC, but appear to have been rather common during the 600s and 500s BC.[141] Another type of fibula clasp that was found throughout much of Illyria was a curved fibula. Sometimes, especially in the western areas like Slovenia, the arch of this clasp was decorated with small beads. The Japodes and Liburnians decorated their arched clasps with amber beads.[142]

Bronze and silver bangles were worn on the wrists and arms. A large number of these were uncovered at a tumulus at Stična, dated to the sixth century BC. C-shaped metal bracelets were also worn, with the terminals shaped like animal heads. Snake heads were a particularly common design; interesting how the subject of snakes

Figure 6: Illyrian noblewoman's clothing, sixth to fourth century BC, based upon graves and artefacts found at Donja Dolina, Ribič, Zaton, Gorica, Stična and Opačići. Items include a veil with a decorated metal band, large hoop earrings, circular fibulae, a cloak, a long-sleeved dress with a pleated skirt, a triangle-shaped amber necklace, a wide belt decorated with metal studs and bronze wrist bangles. (*Illustration by the author*)

keeps popping up in our discussion of the Illyrians, isn't it? Mostly, these C-shaped bracelets are found in southern Illyria, in the lands bordering Greece and Macedonia, which might mean that they were either trade goods imported from that region specifically for the Illyrian tribes, or that they were of native manufacture made by smiths who learned metalworking using the Hellenic methods. The best examples of Illyrian bracelets come from Mramorac, near Belgrade, Serbia, made of gold and dated to either the fifth or fourth century BC. Metal diadems made of bronze or gold and decorated with geometric patterns are notable among the Japodes and Liburnians, and seem to have been worn only by women. Mostly, these objects are dated to the 500s BC.[143]

Personal appearance didn't apply just to clothing and jewellery. The historian Strabo states that the Illyrians decorated their bodies with tattoos. In several places, such as Glasinac and Donja Dolina, archaeologists have found sharp bronze needles affixed to wooden handles, which many have assumed to be used for pricking the skin with ink. As to what the tattoos looked like, it is anyone's guess since no descriptions of Illyrian tattoos exist and no mummified remains of Illyrian skin with preserved tattoo patterns have been discovered. Even though we have no idea what the tattoos themselves looked like, we might yet be able to ascertain their significance. Writing five centuries earlier, Herodotus wrote of the Illyrians' eastern neighbours the Thracians that tattooing was a sign of noble birth while commoners were not allowed to have tattoos; the Illyrians might have had a similar practice. One's appearance also applied to facial hair. Along the coastline, where people were in contact with the obsessively clean Romans, Illyrian men were clean-shaven, while men who lived in the interior wore beards.[144]

The Illyrian diet had a balanced mixture of farmed crops, livestock and seafood. Of course, depending upon where a certain community existed, their diet would be biased towards one aspect or another. In the Illyrian lowlands, especially the famed Pannonian Plain, farming was essential, whereas livestock-raising was the primary source of food in the mountainous highlands. With some Illyrian tribes, as with other tribes in other parts of the world, livestock was regarded as a form of wealth: the more horses or cows that you had, the richer you were. In northern Illyria, pigs were the dominant form of livestock. Of lesser importance were sheep and goats, and to an even lesser extent were cattle. However, along the southern Illyrian coastline, sheep and goats were the dominant form of livestock – more than 50 per cent of the meat consumed, in fact – with pigs and cattle being seldom seen. Surprisingly, hunting appears to have formed a very tiny part of the Illyrian diet. Most of their meat came from farm-raised livestock, not wild animals. At one site, 6,500 animal bones were uncovered and, of these, only 100 belonged to wildlife, mostly deer; that's a rate of just 1.5 per cent. Hunting may have been rare, but fishing was practised to a greater degree. Large numbers of fish bones have been uncovered at excavations of riverside settlements, as well as metal and bone hooks, harpoons and tridents. Pyramid-shaped clay weights might have been used as weights for fishing nets or bird-catching nets. At the site of Nesactium, located in the region of Istria, large numbers of seashells were found, including mussels and cockles.[145]

We know a lot about Illyrian agriculture because we found their farming tools and even the remains of their crops. Wheat was their primary crop, while those of secondary importance were other grains like barley and millet. Grains were used for bread, as well as to make alcohol. Apparently, the Illyrians were fond of beer, ale and mead. Pseudo-Aristotelus says that the Taulanti drank very high-quality mead. In fact, the word 'mead' comes from the Pannonian word *medos*, and the Illyrians called beer *sabaia* or *sabaium*. Archaeologists have also found the remains of grapes. Illyria was renowned for its wine, but this wasn't always so. Our earliest accounts of the Illyrians state that they did not grow grapes or make wine, so vine culture must have been a feature that the Illyrians adopted after contact with the Greeks. However, once the Illyrians got going, they made some of the best wine that the ancient world had to offer. In particular, the north-western region of Illyria known as Istria produced a vintage of especially good quality.[146] Other crops that were raised were vegetables, lentils, peas and beans. By looking at the crops that they grew, the Illyrians as a whole had a very protein-heavy and carb-heavy diet, which would be good for a life of hard work.[147]

The most common farming tool that archaeologists have discovered is the mattock, the earth-chopper. It seems that the Illyrians had originally used mattocks made of bone and deer antlers for doing simple ploughing. As stated before, even when metal tools became available, tools made of bone were still widely in use. When the Celts arrived in the Balkans, they introduced the horse-drawn iron plough, but it doesn't seem to have been popular. After all, ploughing is something best suited to wide expanses of flat land, which are seldom found throughout much of the western Balkans. Archaeologists have discovered scythes and sickles, large pottery jars stuffed with carbonized grains, and tools for flour-grinding and bread-baking. Archaeologists have found hand-grinders and larger grist mills used for grinding grain into flour. At first, the Illyrians used what is called a 'saddle quern' for grinding their grains, in which the grain was spread along the bottom of a flattened U-shaped stone and was then ground into flour by crushing it with another smaller hand-held stone. Following contact with the Romans, many Illyrians began to adopt the rotary quern. While some Roman settlements used large industrial-scale grist mills powered by oxen or donkeys walking round and round in a circle, the Illyrians do not appear to have adopted this, preferring smaller hand-cranked mills.[148]

The region of Illyria may have been famous for alcohol *production*, but the people of Illyria were famous for alcohol *consumption*. It seems that the native Illyrians were constantly drunk, which is yet another common feature of the crude European barbarian archetype that Greeks and Romans like to poke fun at.[149] Polybius states that the Illyrian leader Genthius, who we shall be hearing about in much more detail in the next chapter, was 'constantly drunk night and day',[150] in addition to other vices. When the Celts invaded Illyria, they easily defeated the Ardiaei tribe in battle because the Illyrians were so drunk that they couldn't fight. The fourth-century BC Greek historian Theopompus, whose work *The History of Philip* is now unfortunately lost although a few snippits are quoted within Athanaeus' book *Deipnosophistae*, where it states

> Theopompus, in the second book of his *History of Philip*, says that 'the Illyrians dine and drink seated, and even bring their wives to parties; and it is good form for the women to pledge any of the guests, no matter who they may be. They conduct their husbands home from drinking-bouts. The men all live a hard life, and when they drink they gird their bellies with wide belts. This they do, at first, with tolerable looseness; but as the drinking becomes more intense, they pull their belts more and more tightly together. The people of Ardia (he continues) own 300,000 bondmen who are like helots. They get drunk every day and have parties, and are too uncontrolled in their predilection for eating and drinking. Hence the Celts, when they made war on them, knowing their lack of self-control, ordered all the troops to prepare a dinner in their tents with the utmost possible

splendour, but to put into the food a certain poisonous herb which had the effect of upsetting the bowels and thoroughly purging them. When this had been done some of the Ardiaeans were overcome by the Celts and put to death, while others threw themselves into the rivers, being unable to bear the pain in their stomachs.'[151]

Illyrian ovens were mostly located outside houses to reduce the risk of fire, but a few Illyrian houses had indoor ovens. Often these were nothing more than hearths made of a circle of rocks laid on the bare ground, but there are a few examples of bowl-shaped hearths with vertical sides made of hardened clay, standing about six inches tall. The top of this ridge had a pair of grooves for placing a rotating spit. It also had two tube extensions, almost certainly for affixing a bellows or some other venting mechanism. In hearths constructed in elevated houses, the bottom of the hearth was perforated with holes, like a strainer. These holes probably aided air circulation, and the ashes would fall through the holes into the ground or water below.[152] One cooking implement that archaeologists have found is identical to the Slavic *pekva*, also called a *crepulja*. This was a large round domed lid made from ceramic, and attached to the top would be a handle. To bake bread the Illyrian way, the pekva would first be placed over a fire to heat it up. Then all of the hot embers in the middle of the hearth would be pushed out of the way to make an open space in the middle. The soft bread dough would then be dropped down into the middle of the hot ground where the fireplace embers had been. Then the heavy terracotta pekva, still hot, would be placed on top of the bread dough. The hot coals and embers would then be piled on top. Sometimes, these pekvas would have one or more ridges running around the lid to hold the hot coals in place and prevent them from sliding off. Pekvas are still used in cooking today in the Balkans.[153]

A number of various tools and other objects have been found at Illyrian sites. Ceramic weights, mostly pyramid-shaped, some plain and others decorated, have been found in almost every excavated Illyrian settlement. In some places, hundreds of these weights have been uncovered. They possibly served as weights for fishing nets or for keeping string stretched taut when on a loom. Many of these have been found in graves, which some find curious. Usually, the term 'grave goods' is associated with prestige items such as weapons, jewellery and fine table goods. However, the term applies to any object that is placed in the grave, be it spectacular or mundane. They are things that would be needed in the next world, and weaving would be essential. Remains of spinning wheels, scissors, bone and metal sewing needles, loom shuttles and ceramic thread spindles have also been found in excavated settlements. All of this demonstrates that textile manufacturing was very prominent in Illyrian households. Other objects include metal sheep-shearers, double-bladed axes for wood-chopping, billhooks for cutting tree branches, chisels for shaping wood, pickaxes, shovels, rakes, strainers and whetstones for sharpening metal blades. Most tools were made of iron and date to the Roman period.[154]

Several archaeological sites prove that the Illyrians engaged in active manufacturing. Near Bugojno, Bosnia is an Illyrian fortified settlement named 'Pod', situated atop a plateau sticking out of the side of Mount Koprivnica, overlooking the Porid'ž"nica River. Pod seems to have been a centre for pottery production since large amounts of pottery shards were uncovered. Other objects were for bronze-casting and iron-working, indicating weapons or tools manufacturing. At Ošanići, a massive collection of finds dating between the fourth and second centuries BC was uncovered including pottery, moulds for bronze-casting, an iron anvil, blacksmithing tools, carpentry tools, silver wire and glass. All of this indicates that Ošanići was a very active industrial centre.[155]

It would therefore appear that ancient Illyria was a beehive of activity. It was a land of great wealth and great potential. It is no wonder that it began to attract the attention of its eastern and western neighbours, Greece and Italy.

Chapter Two

Rome and the Balkans

Illyria and Greece

Before Rome discovered the inhabitants of the Balkans, the Illyrians had definitely made their presence known to the Greeks, which isn't surprising considering that their respective territories adjoined one another. Such close proximity was bound to invite both contact and conflict. Strabo states that Chersicrates, the leader of the Greek state of Corinth, forced the Liburnian tribe to withdraw from the island of Corfu, known in ancient times as Corcyra. Although Strabo himself doesn't give any specific date as to when this event took place, it is typically dated to 734 BC by modern scholars. It is also unclear if there was a battle to wrest control of the island of Corfu from the Liburnians, or if the Liburnians left without incident after Chersicrates' sabre-rattling. After the island was completely depopulated, Chersicrates brought in his own people to colonize it.[1] This appears to have been the earliest hostile episode between the Greeks and Illyrians.

When the Greeks began setting up their *apoikia* outposts along the Balkan Adriatic coastline, beginning with the Greek takeover of Corfu, it was an important event with vast repercussions, because it served to further accelerate the process of Hellenization among the Illyrian tribes. The Greeks started in the south and gradually worked their way northwards. In 627 BC, settlers from the island state of Corfu founded the colony of Epidamnus, later renamed by the Romans as Dyrrhachium (modern-day Durrës, Albania). In 588 BC, people from the cities of Corcyra and Corinth founded the settlement of Apollonia, built atop a hill commanding a strategic view of both the Aous River and overland trade routes connecting Greece with the rest of Illyria. In the early 300s BC, Dionysius of Syracuse established the colonies of Issa (Vis Island) and Pharos (Starigrad, Hvar Island). The Greeks fought a significant naval battle against the Illyrians in order to establish their colony at Pharos, resulting in 5,000 Illyrians being killed and another 2,000 being taken prisoner; this shows that the Illyrians didn't simply let the Greeks set up settlements without resistance. All of these settlements would play important roles in the histories of Illyria, Greece and Rome. It should also be stated that while the Illyrians were becoming more 'civilized' due to their contact with the Greeks, the Greek colonists were becoming more 'barbarized' due to their contact with the Illyrians, especially with regard to Greeks having Illyrian names or Illyrianized versions of Greek names. By the 200s BC, the Greek colonies had essentially ceased to be mono-culturally Greek. This is a prime example of typical Illyrian cultural exchange in action.[2]

The ancient Greeks had mixed views about their Illyrian neighbours to the west. In the book *Periegesis*, written in the second century BC by an unknown author (though modern scholars have given the author the name Pseudo-Skymnos), the Illyrians are portrayed as being utterly barbaric but at the same time being pure, free from the corrupting influences of civilization, virtuous, devoted to their gods, and being just and hospitable in the treatment of others.[3] Such a kind view would have raised a lot of eyebrows and outcries among the ancient Greeks. If you read the ancient documents written by the Greeks and Romans, you will very quickly see that the tone is almost always hostile. The Illyrians are frequently described as nothing more than violent thugs, savages and especially pirates.

I'm sure that there were benefits for both sides when these two cultures met, but what the historical sources tell us about mostly concerning the Greeks and Illyrians is war. As the Greeks expanded, they came into conflict with the Illyrians, who were more than a match for them. The western state of Epirus, being located on the border of the territories of some of the strongest Illyrian tribes, endured many attacks from their north-western neighbours. However, the Hellenic state that suffered the most bloodshed at the hands of the Illyrians was Macedon. The antipathy between the Macedonians and the Illyrians has a long history extending back to the early seventh century BC. After diplomatic relations between the Macedonian court and the Illyrians soured, the Illyrians invaded Macedon in 691 BC. For the better part of three hundred years, the Macedonians and Illyrians slogged it out in an on-off feud for power in the region. In 602 BC, King Philip I of Macedon was killed in battle by the Illyrians. In 424 BC, a combined army of Spartans and Macedonians, two of the strongest Greek states of that time, was defeated by the Illyrians at the Battle of Lyncestis and the survivors were forced to flee for their lives.

The Greek historian Thucydides reports that the Spartan commander Brasidas tried to raise the morale of his men by giving an inspiring speech, stating that while the Illyrians' shouting and swinging their weapons around in the air might have an intimidating appearance, when it comes to hand-to-hand fighting, they are no match for professional troops.[4]

The Spartans, Macedonians and others would come to discover that the Illyrians were, in fact, far *more* than a match for the hoplites, especially under the leadership of arguably the most famous name in Illyrian history, King Bardyllis of the Dardanians. In 393 BC, the large and powerful Dardanian tribe actually *conquered* Macedon, forcing King Amyntas III to flee his kingdom, taking as many refugees as he could with him, and seek asylum in the neighbouring Greek state of Thessaly. For a year, the Illyrians controlled Macedon, ruling through a puppet king named Argaeus. However, the deposed Amyntas rallied support in Thessaly, kicked the Illyrian invaders out and regained control of his realm. To cement the peace, he married Eurydice, the sister of the Illyrian general who had conquered his kingdom the previous year, who would bear him four children. Even so, in later years, the Macedonians would be forced to pay a regular tribute to their Illyrian foes to ward off their armies. In 359 BC, the Macedonians lost another battle with the Illyrians, which resulted in 4,000 Macedonians being killed, including King Perdiccas III; it is said that Bardyllis personally slew Perdiccas in single combat on the battlefield. Afterwards, the Illyrians seized control of the western half of Macedon. Diodorus Siculus records that the Macedonians had 'become exceedingly afraid of the Illyrian armies and had lost heart for continuing the war'.[5] However, Perdiccas' younger brother Philip, now King Philip II, Alexander the Great's father, forced the Illyrians to withdraw, killing Bardyllis in battle. In 337 BC, Philip just barely escaped being killed himself by the Illyrians in battle.[6] After three centuries of fighting, the Greeks had made relatively no progress against their traditional western foe. Perhaps a new power rising to dominance on the Italian Peninsula would have better luck.

Rome and Illyria: First Contact

The city of Rome was founded in the year 793 BC by the divine twins Romulus and Remus. For the next 200 or so years, the tiny western Italian city-state was ruled by a series of kings. It slowly expanded its dominion in Italy by conquering and assimilating neighbouring tribes and city-states. In the year

509 BC, Rome expelled the monarchy and proclaimed the creation of the Republic. The civil war between the monarchists and republicans would last for ten years. In the end, the republicans won, the monarchy was abolished, and the Roman Republic was officially created in 499 BC.

It is unknown when Rome first became aware of the Illyrians' existence. The Greek poet Callimachus reports that not long after the Republic was founded, the city of Rome came under attack by an Illyrian tribe called the Peucetians, who had settled in southern Italy, but they were driven off. Callimachus' story is probably a work of fiction, since no other ancient account mentions this event, and the only foreign attack upon the city during this time was by the Etruscans led by Lars Porsenna. Moreover, Callimachus lived two centuries after the events in question supposedly happened. However, it should be stated that the Celtic assault on the city, which occurred in the early 300s BC, was a much more recent event and a fairly famous one, and would have been well-known. Perhaps Callimachus substituted the Peucetians in place of Brennus' Gallic warriors. In Callimachus' story, a Roman man named Gaius attacks and kills the Peucetian commander, but he is wounded in the thigh in the process. He complained about his limp, but was scolded by his mother to stop whining, and he did. Stories such as this are meant to portray *exempla*, models of correct behaviour that other people should emulate. In this case, the lesson is not to complain or whine about personal injuries and not to indulge in self-pity.

Okay, so we can rule out Callimachus' story, so where does that leave us? It's almost certain that the Romans first came into contact with the Illyrians when they were expanding in the Italian Peninsula, conquering and assimilating other tribes into their domain. The questions are when, where and who?

Sometime in the first millenium BC, a group of Illyrians crossed the Adriatic from their homeland in the Balkans and settled in southern Italy. This group of Illyrian tribes collectively called themselves the Iapygians, and may have formed a distinct cultural group separate from other Illyrians. According to the geographer and historian Strabo, they were named after Iapyx, the son of Daedalus.[7] The Iapygians were divided into three tribes: the Daunians, the Peucetians and the Messapians. It's not clear exactly from where these people came, but one idea is that they were from southern Illyria, possibly from what is now Albania. The trip from here to Italy's boot would be short, and considering that Illyrians were known to be good sailors, the journey must have been rather easy.

The date of the arrival of the Iapygians is open to academic speculation. Some claim that they arrived between 1000–900 BC, long before Rome was even established. Others claim that the migration was a bit more recent, say about 500 BC or thereabouts. The exact date doesn't really matter. Furthermore, it was almost assuredly not a single massive event but a gradual migration of people across the Adriatic that occurred in small batches over a prolonged period of time.[8]

When the Iapygian colonists landed on the Italian coast, they quickly realized that they were not alone. The landscape of southern Italy was already inhabited by numerous Italic tribes. Also by this time, the Greeks had established a sizable colony in southern Italy, stretching from Naples southwards. The name Naples is, in fact, of Greek origin: *Neopolis*, the 'new city'. Although I have not found any record of it, I imagine that when the Iapygians landed on Italy's south-eastern coast, there was considerable conflict between themselves and both the Italic natives and the Greek colonists. I have two reasons for proposing this. First, it has been established both in archaeology and in historical records that the area now known as Apulia was originally home to numerous Italic tribes. Strabo comments that while the Greeks of southern Italy referred to this area by the Iapygian territorial names, the Italic natives persistently referred to the landscape using the original native names. Strabo further comments that the native people of southern Apulia were squeezed into a tiny area around the city of Tarentum between the lands of the Peucetians to the north and the Messapians to the south. In order for this to have happened, the native Salentini and Calabri tribes would have to have been driven off their lands and forced to relocate into this small pocket of territory, under the protection of the Tarentine city-state. Second, the Iapygians are not described as being under the overlordship of the Greek and southern Italic city-states but were three independent powers. Consistently, the Greeks seem to regard the Iapygians as the people 'over there', implying that Iapygian territory was considered foreign and therefore not included within the broader region of *Magna Graecia*. The Iapygians were never able to take over all of southern Italy, but restricted themselves to Italy's heel and a thin strip of land immediately north of it along the peninsula's eastern coast. This largely corresponds to the modern-day region of Apulia.[9]

In the northern part of the Iapygians' newly-claimed territory were the Daunians. Since they were the furthest north, and as such were the furthest away from the Greek colonies in the south, the Daunians were not as Hellenized as their neighbours. The Daunians were known for their pottery and for their funerary monuments, many of which are kept within the museum in the town of Siponto. Siponto may, in fact, have been their main settlement.[10]

South of the Daunians were the Peucetians. According to Dionysius of Halicarnassus, they named themselves after a heroic ancestor, Peucetis. In the legend that he reports, Peucetis was one of many sons of Lycaon of Arcadia. Lycaon had already divided up his land among his other sons, so Peucetis was forced to go elsewhere to seek his fortune, and thus he and a troupe of followers came to Italy. According to the Greco-Roman historian Strabo, the Peucetians lived where the city of Bari stands today, and extended as far south as Brundisium (Brentesion in Greek; modern-day Brindisi).[11]

The southernmost of the Iapygian Illyrian tribes was called the Messapians. Strabo says that the border of Messapian territory stretched between the cities of Brundisium and Taras, later known as Tarentum (modern-day Taranto).[12] By 500 BC, the Messapians had become strong, so strong that they were regarded as rivals for power by some of the existing Greek and Italian city-states in the region, especially the Greek city-state of Tarentum. Wars between Tarentum and the Messapian tribe would continue on and off for the better part of a century. In fact, Strabo states that on one occasion, when the Messapians and the Tarentines were fighting over control of Heracleia, the Daunians and Peucetians actually joined Tarentum's side. This shows firstly that the Iapygians were not united, and secondly that there was competition and even hostility between them.[13]

Strabo hints that the Iapygian tribes were long gone by the time that he was writing his *Geography*, and that these regional names of Daunia, Peucetia and Messapia had fallen out of usage. By the late third century BC, the Messapians had disappeared and their territory was taken over by the city-state of Tarentum. The Tarentines became such a powerful force in southern Italy that they were a major enemy of the expanding Roman Republic. However, even into the first century AD, the tip of Italy's heel was referred to as the 'Iapygian Cape'. Moreover, while the Iapygian Illyrians had faded into the past, their successors known as the Apuli spoke the Iapygian language and practised Iapygian culture.[14]

In addition to the dominant Illyrian populations in the south-eastern territory of Apulia, there is also evidence that small pocket populations of Illyrians inhabited lands all along the eastern coast of Italy. The

Liburnians, especially, seemed to be fairly aggressive colonizers. Florus states that they were spread throughout the whole Mediterranean, including establishing settlements in Italy.[15] Theopompus states that the Liburnians established the settlement of Adria in Italy; the name may be related to 'Adriatic'.[16] According to Pliny the Elder, the Liburnians had a few outposts established along Italy's Adriatic coast, until they were eventually expelled. In time, the Umbrians of central Italy drove the Liburnians out of their last Italian stronghold: the port of Truentus.[17] In addition to written historical evidence, we also have archaeological evidence for Illyrian populations in central Italy. The Iguvium Tablets, dated to the fifth to fourth centuries BC, state that the *Japuzkum numen* ('those named the Japodes') were banned from attending religious rites.[18]

Figure 7: Map of the Iapygian Illyrian tribes of south–eastern Italy, circa 500 BC. Note the area claimed by the city-state of Tarentum. (*Illustration by the author*)

The First Roman-Illyrian War: 229–228 BC

The Romans may indeed have come into conflict with the Iapygian Illyrians who lived in south-eastern Italy, and it is possible that they had small conflicts with Liburnian outposts on Italy's coast, but when did the Romans become militarily involved in Illyria proper? Thankfully, that question is easy to answer, unlike a lot of others in ancient studies, because several ancient Greek and Roman historians relate how hostilities between the Illyrians and Romans began. One writer who deserves special attention is Polybius, whose account is lengthy and detailed, and comments that the First Roman-Illyrian War was an important event that should be very carefully studied.[19] Other historians who write about this conflict include Appianus, Publius Annius Florus and Cassius Dio. It is important to take note of the fact that none of the ancient authors who wrote about this war were contemporaries of this conflict, or even shortly removed from it. Polybius likely began writing his monumental work, *Histories*, sometime after 167 BC, when the Romans conquered Greece. By then, the First Roman-Illyrian War was sixty years in the past. Both Florus and Appianus wrote during the time of Emperor Hadrian in the early second century AD. Cassius Dio was the latest one of the whole lot, writing in the early third century AD. As such, each account written by these authors is often dramatically different from the others.

Because the focus of this book centres upon one particular war during the reign of Caesar Augustus and is not meant to be a complete military history of ancient Illyria, I will not go into great and exhausting detail regarding the various wars fought between the Illyrians and Romans – that could be the subject of an entire book in itself – nor will I go into protracted length comparing and contrasting the various ancient sources who write about these conflicts. Instead, I will provide a summarized account with a few side notes here and there concerning the various Roman–Illyrian wars.

The first time that blood between the Illyrians and the Romans was shed upon Illyrian soil was in 229 BC. The ancient sources provide some background information to this conflict as follows. During the mid-third century BC, the kingdom of Macedon was at war with a confederacy of Greek city-states known as the Aetolian League. The Macedonians were losing the war and, in desperation, King Demetrius II of Macedon appealed to his neighbours, some of them being former enemies, for help. One of them was a nearby Illyrian tribe, the Ardiaei, ruled by a rough-and-tumble man named Agron. He saw Demetrius' entreaty as an opportunity to expand his power into Greece and he agreed to fight alongside the Macedonians. Shortly, 5,000 Illyrian warriors in 100 ships landed on the coast, scored a great victory against the Greeks and helped to turn the tide in King Demetrius' favour. However, once the war was over, the Illyrians refused to leave, and they continued attacking other Greek city-states while Illyrian pirates ravaged the Greek coastline.[20]

The Romans largely ignored these events, but the Illyrian pirates were also threatening maritime shipping. Now, not only Greek ships but *Roman* ships were coming under attack. The Roman Senate decided to send some diplomats to the Illyrian court to gather information about what was happening and to bring an end to the pirate attacks. By now, King Agron was dead, and his wife Queen Teuta was in control. The meeting between the two sides went badly. Afterwards, the Roman envoys were assassinated on Queen Teuta's orders. The public outcry in Rome was immense. Rome could never allow such an offence to go unpunished. Almost immediately, they began preparing for war.[21]

Meanwhile, the Illyrians were still attacking and seizing control of various Greek ports. The Greek city-states agreed to ally together to fight a common foe, but things went poorly for them. At the Battle of Paxi Island, the Greek fleet was thoroughly destroyed and the Illyrian fleet was hardly damaged. This crushing naval victory marked the high point of the war from the Illyrian perspective. At this time, the Roman army, numbering about 20,000 men, finally got under way after lengthy preparation and set sail from the port of Brundisium. With the help of an Illyrian traitor named Demetrius of Pharos, the Romans began gaining the upper hand, driving out the Illyrians from some of the Greek territories that they had seized earlier, although the Romans did claim some of the 'liberated' territory for themselves. After this was accomplished, the Romans took the next step and attacked several of the Illyrian tribes on their home turf, who either surrendered or were slaughtered. Knowing that the war was lost, Queen Teuta retreated to the fortified town of Rhizon and in 228 BC, just one year after the war began, she sent word that she was willing to negotiate. Rome's terms were humiliating: an excessively large tribute would be paid to the Roman treasury; several large islands on the Balkan side of the Adriatic, some originally Greek and some originally Illyrian, became Roman territory, and all the people dwelling upon those islands were now Roman subjects; almost all of the southern Illyrian tribes would be placed under Roman control as a massive collection of semi-independent vassal states; Illyrian ships of any sort were restricted to operating only within the Adriatic Sea; Queen Teuta would be forced to abdicate and place her young son on the throne as Rome's puppet ruler. In response to all of this and with no other choice, Queen Teuta agreed to all of the conditions. As a final act of power, Rome had all the enemy commanders who had been taken prisoner executed.[22]

After the treaty was concluded, the Romans sent messengers to the Achaean and Aetolian Leagues, who explained the causes and conduct of the war, and recited the terms of the treaty. Now that the threat of Illyrian piracy had been greatly reduced, the Romans and the Greeks drew closer together. However, Macedon was angered that the Romans muscled in and began to view the Romans as a new threat in the region.[23] As a reward for his treachery in handing over his territories to Roman control, notably the island of Corcyra, Demetrius of Pharos was given some estates and also became the guardian of the young Illyrian prince, thereby ruling much of southern Illyria as a royal regent. Yet the Romans suspected that this man was not to be trusted and their suspicions were well-founded.[24]

The Second Roman-Illyrian War, 220–219 BC

Several years later in 225 BC, the Romans were busy fighting the Gauls in the Po River Valley, and Rome's old enemy Carthage, now under the leadership of a rising star named Hannibal, was once again causing trouble. Meanwhile in Illyria, Demetrius of Pharos had become disillusioned with Rome, believing that the Republic was not as strong as it claimed. Growing increasingly contemptuous of Rome and with ambitions of ruling over southern Illyria as something much more than a regional vassal lord, he decided to make a power-play for dominance in the region, supported by his new ally, the kingdom of Macedon. Although Macedon was far weaker than it had been during the glory days of Philip and Alexander, it was still strong enough to act as a prominent regional power, and Demetrius wanted to have as many cards to play as possible. So he allied himself with Macedon to counteract any designs that Rome would have that could interfere with his future ambitions. Believing that the Romans were distracted with affairs elsewhere, Demetrius began sponsoring widespread piracy throughout the Adriatic Sea. He used fifty ships and his own private army to attack cities in Illyria that were loyal to Rome, causing havoc throughout the Adriatic and even penetrating as far

Figure 8: Roman mosaic floor from the ancient Illyrian city of Rhizon (mod-ern-day Risan, Montenegro). When this city came under Roman control, it was re-named 'Risinium'. At its height during the late first century and early second century AD, Risinium had a population of approximately 10,000 people, far larger than the population of the town today. (*Photo by Julo, 30 July 2006. Public domain image. Wikimedia Commons*)

east as the Cycladic Islands in the middle of the Aegean Sea. He brought the Istrians into his scheme and had the pro-Roman Atintani tribe placed under his rule.[25]

The Romans were too busy with affairs concerning Carthage and the northern barbarians to once again worry about Illyrian pirates. However, once the war with the Gauls was over, Rome immediately turned its attention to settling accounts with the treacherous Demetrius. Believing that war between Rome and Carthage was inevitable by this time, the Senate decided that Rome's position in eastern Europe had to be better secured, or else the Republic would be weakened on two fronts. The Romans sent a small fleet to deal with the pirates in 220 BC, hoping to smash them quickly so they could turn their full attention towards Hannibal. That same year, the Romans declared war on Carthage.[26]

While the Romans and Carthaginians fought in Spain, Demetrius consolidated his power. In every town and city that he controlled, he had the opposition executed and placed his supporters there in positions of power and authority. When he was informed about the approach of Roman warships, he bolstered his defences. The small Roman fleet did not accomplish much. The Senate was informed that Demetrius and his pirates were much stronger than they had supposed, and that a larger force was needed to deal with the pirates effectively.[27]

The following year in 219 BC, the Romans sent an army to attack the pirates, commanded by the Senatorial consuls Lucius Aemilius Paullus and Marcus Livius Salinator. Demetrius was well-prepared for their arrival. Yet in spite of Demetrius' preparations, the Romans captured the heavily-fortified city of Dimale (also spelled Dimallum) after a seven-day siege. After this impressive stronghold fell so quickly, the neighbouring settlements soon submitted with minimal or no resistance.[28]

However, the war wasn't over yet. Demetrius had escaped to his home base on the island of Pharos and he still had many armed men under his command. After Dimale fell, Lucius Paullus sailed to Pharos to deal with Demetrius personally. After learning that Pharos was very well-defended, he decided to attack the city in a pincer movement and it worked. The Romans won the battle and seized control of the city, but Demetrius once again escaped. Believing that he had smashed the Illyrians sufficiently, Paullus and many of his troops returned to Italy. As for the crestfallen Demetrius, the Greek historian Polybius states that he found refuge in the court of the Macedonian king, but was killed in battle some time later during an ill-executed attack upon the Greek city of Messene. By contrast, Appianus claims that Demetrius was captured and executed by the Romans.[29]

In 217 BC, the young King Pinnes, who had nominally reigned over southern Illyria, died at the age of 15. Taking his place as the new leader in the region was one of Demetrius' battle-captains named Scerdilaidas. Unlike the crafty and shifty Demetrius, his subordinate proved to be far more loyal to Roman interests as well as being more interested in 'the big picture' when it came to Illyria's place in the scheme of world affairs. Scerdilaidas made sure that ties to Rome were maintained and, under his guidance, peace in the region was preserved and Illyria fared well under his rule.[30]

However, the kingdom of Macedon was still a player in this drama. It had signed an alliance agreement with Demetrius of Pharos against

Macedon's Greek opponents as well as against the expanding Roman Republic. Macedon had made no such deal with Illyria's new vassal chief Scerdilaidas, and due to Scerdilaidas' pro-Roman stance, Macedon had no intention of ever acknowledging this man as a friend. Therefore King Philip V of Macedon signed a new alliance agreement with Carthage and the Greek city-state of Syracuse in the hope that all three would conduct a jointly-coordinated war against Rome. This never happened, much to Philip's frustration. All this alliance resulted in was Rome becoming more and more wary of Macedon, and had begun seriously contemplating destroying the ancient kingdom to prevent it from continuing as a threat to Roman power.[31]

Well, Macedon certainly couldn't tackle the full might of the Roman Republic all by itself, so instead, Philip decided to launch an attack against a much softer target: Rome's Illyrian ally Scerdilaidas. The campaign was initially successful for the Macedonians, because the Romans were too busy fighting a losing war against Hannibal. However, once the situation in Italy had been stabilized, Rome could once again turn its attention to the troublesome Balkans. A shaky cease-fire between Rome and Macedon was signed in 205 BC, but once Hannibal was defeated for good and the Second Punic War came to an end, the Romans now turned their full military attention upon King Philip. The Second Macedonian War had begun. In 197 BC at Thessalonika, the legions scored their final decisive victory and Macedon was defeated but not conquered.[32]

The Third Roman-Illyrian War, 169 BC

For the next few decades after King Philip V's forces were driven out of Illyria, the western Balkans remained quiet. Rome's Illyrian vassal Scerdilaidas had kept the peace, and so too had his successor Pleuratus. Then in 180 BC Pleuratus died, and under his successor Genthius, hostilities between Rome and Illyria renewed.[33]

This conflict had its roots in the Third Macedonian War, which began in 171 BC. Rome had declared war on Macedon when it appeared that this kingdom was once again becoming a threat to Rome's eastern interests. Although the war went well for Macedon at first, the Romans quickly gained the upper hand. Desperate for help, in 169 BC King Perseus of Macedon appealed to the neighbouring Illyrian tribes under Genthius for help. When the Romans found out about King Perseus' alliance proposal with Genthius, they sent envoys to Genthius to get him to maintain his pro-Roman stance but to their surprise, he had them imprisoned. The Republic responded accordingly.[34]

Unlike previous conflicts with the Illyrians, the Romans were not going to start off with halfway measures this time. The Senate sent Lucius Ancius (also spelled Anicius) Gallus with a huge army of 30,000 men with orders to crush Genthius as soon as possible. In the opening engagement, the Romans smashed the Illyrian fleet. Soon afterwards in the second battle, the Romans defeated the Illyrian forces on land. In a short time, Genthius' forces had almost been entirely destroyed, so he fled to the heavily-fortified mountaintop city of Scodra (modern-day Shkodër, Albania) where the last of his followers had garrisoned themselves. The Romans pursued and demanded that he and his men surrender.[35]

After this, the several historical records concerning this war vary wildly and can get a bit confusing with each other, so I'll take the liberty of combining the accounts to make a cohesive storyline (take note that what I'm stating in the following lines is only my hypothesis and should not be taken as literal fact). Genthius was forced to retreat to Scodra. General Lucius Gallus knew that his legions could never break into such a heavily-fortified place, so he called upon Genthius and his men to give themselves up. Genthius knew what Romans were like, and believed that they would surely have attacked him immediately if they were as powerful as they boasted. If they wished him to surrender, it must mean that they were afraid of attacking him, which meant that the Romans were far weaker than they claimed. In a flush of poor judgement, Genthius believed that he could destroy the Romans in an open battle. Therefore he stupidly ordered his men out from behind the protective fortifications and took up a position in front of the city walls. Now that the Illyrian pirates were no longer protected inside their city, General Gallus sent his legions forward and obliterated Genthius' forces. Genthius himself managed to escape back into the protection of the city and prevented the Romans from breaking in. Once again, General Gallus called upon Genthius to surrender. Genthius replied that he would need three days to consider it. In the end, Genthius agreed to give himself up and he begged for mercy. Genthius, his family and followers were imprisoned and were brought to Rome. Afterwards, they were taken to Gubbium. The Third Roman-Illyrian War had lasted for just twenty days and, in the end, the Romans gained control of that whole area.[36] Lucius Gallus gathered the Illyrian chiefs at Scodra and announced that all of the tribes

Figure 9: Rozafa Castle, located near the town of Shkodër, Albania. In ancient times, this fortified settlement located atop this hill was called Scodra, and the modern town located near this ancient site has taken on a version of that name. It was here that Genthius conducted his last stand against the Romans. Like almost all Illyrian settlements, it was strategically located. The hill was steep and rocky, making it difficult for attackers to storm the town. The hill commanded the valley and, most importantly, it is located on the spot where the Buna and Drin rivers converge. The ancient fortifications were demolished sometime during either ancient or medieval times. The castle that sits upon the hill today, Rozafa Castle, was built by the Venetians. (*Photo by Josef Székely, late August 1863. Public domain image. Wikimedia Commons*)

and settlements that had remained loyal to Rome during the war were exempt from paying any more taxes. Specifically, he was referring to the Taulanti, Pirusti and Daorsi tribes as well as the towns of Rhizon and Olcinum, and possibly Lissos.[37]

For Rome, the Third Roman–Illyrian War (which was actually a small sideshow conflict of the Third Macedonian War) was an easy victory.

Although this campaign was short and presumably the loss of life was rather minimal compared with other bloodier Roman campaigns, the Republic gained a lot out of this conflict. The western Balkan territory, stretching from the northern tip of the Adriatic Sea to the Greek border, was now firmly under Roman control, although not yet directly incorporated into the Republic. Rome was now the undisputed master of the Adriatic Sea. In 167 BC, two years after the war ended, southern Illyria became a Roman protectorate, and it would remain as such until 59 BC when it was incorporated into the Roman Republic as the province of 'Illyricum' with its capital in Salona (modern-day Solin, Croatia).[38] A 'protectorate' is an independent territory that is protected diplomatically and militarily by another country. In exchange for this protection (hence the name), it must agree to certain terms imposed upon it by the protecting country. However, the protected state itself is still considered an independent country and not under any legislative or submissive obligations. This is what makes a protectorate different from a 'vassal state', in which a territory is semi-independent, having its own laws and leaders but having to acknowledge another country or foreign ruler as its overlord. A modern example of a protectorate would be Monaco, a small independent country ruled by its own monarch but also under the military protection of France.

However, this arrangement would not put an end to the hostilities in the western Balkans.

The Fourth Roman-Illyrian War, 156 BC

Following Rome's victory over Macedon's Illyrian allies during the Third Macedonian War, southern Illyria was designated as a Roman protectorate. Although technically an independent country, this did not stop Roman colonists from entering the territory and establishing new settlements there. Understandably, this caused a great deal of animosity. This land was not supposed to be open to foreign settlement, and the continuous influx of Roman immigrants made some Illyrians believe that the Roman Republic would not be satisfied with having southern Illyria merely as a territory under Roman military protection; they wanted to turn it into a fully-fledged province, with the people subject to Roman laws and Roman taxation. Something had to be done about it.

The Dalmatians attacked the former Greek colonies as well as the Daorsi tribe, who had pledged loyalty to Rome. After receiving numerous complaints from the colonists and the Daorsi tribesmen about the Dalmatian raids, the Roman Senate decided to send an emissary named Gaius Fannius. He arrived at the town of Delminium, the Dalmatian tribe's capital, in 158 BC, but the chief refused to grant him an audience. Later, the Roman emissary and his escorts were attacked and a few of them were killed.[39] Amazingly, there does not seem to have been any retaliation by Rome for this action.

Two years later in 156 BC, the Dalmatians attacked Roman settlements in Illyria. When the Romans sent messengers demanding that the Illyrians offer amends for what they had done, they were ignored. Cassius Dio reports that the Dalmatians even imprisoned and killed envoys sent to them from *other* countries. Now the Romans decided to do something, and they sent an army against the Dalmatians. The army was commanded by the Senatorial consul Gaius Marcius Figulus, with his fellow consul Scipio Nasica acting as his second-in-command. The two men would lead two different forces: Figulus would transport his men by ship and land on the Illyrian coast, while Nasica would march his troops overland. Figulus' amphibious force landed at a place called Narona, located near the Neretva River, known in ancient times as the Naro River. The modern town of Vid, which is often stated to be the modern site for this ancient town, is actually located two miles *away* from the Neretva River, and is instead situated on a strategic bend of a small creek that hooks around the eastern side of the village. The expedition went off to a bad start right on the first day. The landing itself was unopposed, but while the disembarked Roman troops were in the process of laying out their camp, the Dalmatians launched an all-out massive attack against the legionnaires stuck on the coastline. The attack was apparently so sudden, so unexpected and so overwhelming that the entire Roman force, or what was left of it, was forced to flee for their lives. Not exactly an auspicious beginning for the war.[40] Meanwhile, Nasica's men fared no better. Setting out from the northern Adriatic port-city of Aquileia, he and his troops pushed eastwards as far as the town of Segestica. However, upon reaching his destination, he and his men were defeated and were forced to turn back. Many Illyrian tribes, notably the Japodes, used this opportunity to attack along the frontier, especially Rome's recently-acquired possessions in Istria, which lay right on the Japodes' front doorstep.[41]

Examination of both history and geography can give us a good idea about the progression of the war's opening stages. The Neretva River, which measures five hundred feet wide, is one of the major rivers in the region. The Roman force likely took ship up this wide river. No word of any battles takes place before the conflict at Narona. So this must mean that either the Roman fleet sailed up the Neretva River, bypassing all settlements until they made landfall near the town of Narona, or that the Roman fleet landed on the coastline at the mouth of the Neretva River and the army advanced inland but didn't encounter any resistance. I believe that the second option is more likely. Why penetrate far inland in the opening stages of the war, bypassing other settlements that could potentially serve as enemy bases?

No information is given about the progress of the war immediately after this event. Therefore, we can only assume that both sides had entered some kind of stalemate. Presumably the Romans had relocated to a more defendable location, but they were unable to launch attacks, unwilling to risk leaving their position. Likewise, the Dalmatians were not strong enough to assault the Romans where they were, but if they should be foolish enough to advance beyond their lines, the Illyrians could have easily slaughtered them. So the two sides stared at each other, waiting for the other to make the first mistake. Meanwhile, I imagine that the Romans were being constantly supplied by ship, preparing for a renewed offensive.

With winter now approaching, the Dalmatians were returning to their homes. Gaius Figulus wanted revenge for the embarrassing defeat that he had suffered on the first day of the war. He could never live down the insult of being defeated by 'barbarians', nor could he stand the almost assured investigation of events that was bound to follow, so he planned to ambush the Dalmatians as they made their way back in the hope of saving his reputation.[42] Unfortunately, things didn't go as planned. The Dalmatians found out about the Romans' approach and chose to stand and fight instead of retreating. Regardless of the fact that the Dalmatians had been tipped off, the Romans managed to defeat them anyway and drove the warriors back to their capital of Delminium.[43]

Gaius Figulus didn't have the power to attack such a strongly-defended position since he would have to advance his men out in the open in plain view of enemy archers and other various missile troops, and he couldn't use his catapults because they couldn't hit such a high target. However, there was something that he *could* do. The Dalmatians had pulled all of their warriors out of the nearby villages to defend Delminium, and this meant that the surrounding villages were undefended. So, rather than attacking the town, the Romans rampaged across the countryside attacking the smaller softer targets. Presumably, he did this with the hope of drawing the Dalmatians out from behind their walls, but it didn't work; the Dalmatians sternly remained within their fortifications. I assume they recognized a trap when they saw one and, despite the damage and destruction that they could plainly see, they would not take the bait. Frustrated, the Romans now were forced to resort to more direct measures. Using their catapults, they shot torches over the walls and into the town (note that this is in *complete* contradiction to Strabo's earlier statement that the catapults couldn't hit the walls, let alone shoot over them!) in the hope of burning the defenders out. It worked and a large portion of the town was burned. Satisfied with the destruction he had caused, Gaius Figulus left, but the Dalmatians were still more or less intact and they would return to raid and pillage again. Gaius Figulus turned over control of the war to his second-in-command, Scipio Nasica, and under his direction the war was prosecuted with full intensity. Nasica completely subjugated the Dalmatians, capturing several of their towns and obtaining a large number of prisoners, which were later sold off as slaves.[44] Strabo says that before the Romans attacked, Delminium was a large city, but 'Nasica reduced it to a small city and made the plain a mere sheep-pasture.'[45] Nasica was awarded a triumph for his victory.[46]

Hostilities Continue

In 135 BC, while the Romans were busy fighting a war in Spain against the Numantines and another war against a slave rebellion in Sicily, two Illyrian tribes called the Ardiaei and the Palarians (also called Pleraei) raided Roman possessions in Illyria. Since the Romans could not afford to spare any troops at that time, they decided to send some messengers to scare the tribes into stopping their attacks. However, the Ardiaei and Palarians were not intimidated by the Romans' threats and continued their attacks on Roman settlements in the area. Realizing now that they had no choice but to send men, the Senate sent two legions and two cavalry detachments (10,000 infantry and 600 cavalry) under the command of the consul Servius Fulvius Flaccus to attack the two aggressive tribes. Raiding local villages and towns was one thing, but now the Illyrians would have to face the professional Roman army, which was a different matter entirely. When the Ardiaeans and Palarians heard about this, they were not prepared to defend themselves against such a large military force and begged for mercy. The Roman Senate ordered the two tribes to make things right with those to whom they had done harm. I assume this means to hand over the perpetrators and to pay tribute. However, when the Illyrians were too slow in obeying the Senate's command, a second army was sent out. The record of events stops here, because Appianus states that he was unable to find any record of what happened afterwards.[47] This goes to show that even in ancient times, records of historical events could be lost. Appianus was writing more than 250 years after the events in question happened.

In 129 BC, the famous orator and writer Gaius Sempronius Tuditanus and Tiberius Pandusa attacked and subjugated the Japodes and the Liburnians. After a rough start, he eventually made some headway and penetrated as far as the Krka River, bringing the Japodes and Liburnians under his control, at least for the time being. Just ten years later in 119 BC, the Romans were forced to yet again suppress the Japodes, this time led by Lucius Cornelius Cotta and Lucius Cecilius Metellus.[48] Cotta and Metellus attacked and subjugated the Segestani tribe, but the Japodes and Segestani launched an offensive soon afterwards. Cotta turned back to Italy while his companion pressed onwards and attacked the Japodes. Not content with this, he marched on the Dalmatians, even though the Dalmatians had done nothing to provoke them. Appianus states that Metellus urged the war because he wanted to be granted a triumph. However, it was all a play; the Romans really weren't going to attack the Dalmatians after all. Appianus states that when the Roman soldiers came to the land of the Dalmatians, they were received with friendship and hospitality, and spent the winter resting in Salona. During the following spring, Lucius Metellus returned to Rome. I imagine that he concocted some great lie about how he had subjugated and slaughtered the entire tribe and laid the entire country to waste. He was granted a triumph and given the agnomen *Dalmaticus*.[49]

The Dalmatians remained placid for forty years until trouble flared up with them yet again. By then, the Romans must have been groaning about having to constantly repeat their conquests. In 78 BC, the Dalmatians rebelled and seized control of the city of Salona. In response, the consul Gaius Consconius was sent against them. The war lasted for two years before the Dalmatians were driven out and Salona was once again in Roman hands.[50]

The Province of Illyricum

According to the *Lex Vatinia*, in 59 BC, Illyricum's status changed from being a protectorate to a *provincia*, and the province's first governor would be Gaius Julius Caesar.[51] Despite its name, Illyricum was not a province in our modern sense of the word but was instead a 'zone of responsibility'. Illyricum did not become a real Roman full-fledged administrative province until 27 BC, when the region was declared a propraetorial province under direct control of Caesar Augustus.

The settlement that became the capital of Roman Illyricum was Salona (modern-day Solin, Croatia), situated on the northern side of the mouth of the Jadro River. This was an ideal location for trade into the interior, but it was also established at this site for practical reasons. The area occupied by the city of Salona is one of the few areas of flat land in the vicinity; to the city's east lies a range of ridges like fingers on a hand, and directly to the city's north is a steep ridge measuring 1,800ft above sea level. In early days, Salona was a small coastal village of the Dalmatian tribe, which soon came under the economic influence of the Greeks. At first, the newcomers from the Greek colony of Issa set up a trading post within the village, but afterwards they essentially took over the place and Salona became a mixed Illyrian-Greek settlement. However, the village remained small and relatively unimportant until the Romans became interested in the area during the third century BC.[52] The road connecting Salona with the Greek colony of Tragurion, the *Via Munita*, is the oldest-known road within the region of Dalmatia. Salona did possess stone walls at the time of its founding, possibly during the third century BC, but they only protected the city centre or *acropolis*, not the entire settlement. They were rather simple structures and did not have any towers. In fact, Julius Caesar writes that when he and his troops occupied Salona during the civil wars of the late Republic, they had to build wooden towers in order to better improve the town's defences.[53] Julius Caesar, who at that time was Governor of Illyricum, upgraded the town of Salona to the status of a *colonia*, a settlement for retired soldiers and their families, and it underwent a massive expansion programme to accommodate all of its new residents. Its full name was *Colonia Martia Julia Salona*, 'Julius Caesar's Military Colony of Salona', but it appears that hardly anyone back then referred to it by this long-winded title.[54]

A more prominent settlement located only two-and-a-half miles away from Salona was Spalathos (modern-day Split, Croatia). Spalathos, named after a type of thorn bush that grows in the area to this day, was originally a Greek trading outpost founded in the sixth century BC that

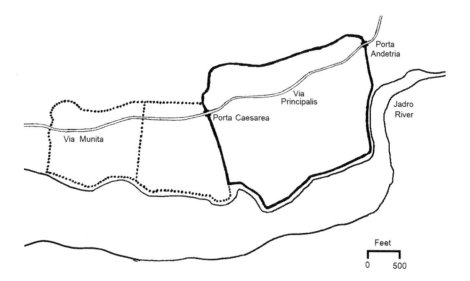

Figure 10: Map of ancient Salona. The solid line represents the old stone walls of the city that were in existence by the late first century BC, while the dotted line represents a second series of walls that were constructed much later when the city had expanded substantially in size. At first, the only major road that passed through the city was the Via Munita, which formed the *via principalis* or 'main street' within the city itself. Later, new roads were constructed linking Salona to other settlements. (*Illustration by the author*)

had grown to substantial size due to continued connections with the Greek homeland, other Greek colonies, and with the native Illyrians. When the Romans took over Illyria, the town was renamed Spalatum. Salona was built up and made the provincial capital, while neighbouring Spalatum was almost neglected. It would not be until the latter years of the Roman Empire's existence that Salona would fall by the wayside and Spalatum would again rise to prominence.

Although the Romans attempted to the best of their abilities to maintain constant control over the city of Salona, it periodically fell into the hands of the native Illyrians. The Romans had to fight hard to take it back from them: in 78 BC it was retaken by Casconius; in 39 BC it was retaken by Asinius Pollio; and in 33 BC it was taken by Gaius Octavianus, later to become Caesar Augustus. After obtaining control of the city, Octavianus reconfirmed its status as a *colonia* and expanded the city's walls so that they encompassed the entire city.

He also improved the fortifications by adding large stone towers at regular intervals along the walls.[55]

Because Salona had been occupied for so long, and successive periods of building, destruction and rebuilding had occurred, very little of the city's structure dating to the time of Caesar Augustus has been found. The clearest evidence of what Salona looked like during the BC–AD years are the fortifications that were built on Augustus' orders. These have lasted largely due to their sheer massive size, which makes them more likely to survive the ravages of both man and time than smaller or more delicate buildings. The base of a giant gate called the *Porta Caesarea*, 'Caesar's Gate', has survived along with sections of walls and towers, and it was this gate that served as the main gateway of Salona during the time of Caesar Augustus. It was built in the form of a triple-arcaded triumphal arch, with one large central arch in the middle for carts and a smaller doorway on either side for pedestrian traffic. On either side of the gateway was a massive octagonal tower, but they are unusual in that they face inside the city, not outside, and it has been hypothesized that they were actually a pair of giant water towers, reservoirs for the city's aqueduct.[56]

The city was still growing. In the late first century AD during the reign of the Flavian Dynasty, an amphitheatre and baths were built, the ruins of which can still be seen. During the second century AD, the city of Salona had expanded so much that a new set of walls had to be built around it. The height of Salona's power was during the late third century AD during the reign of Emperor Diocletian, when it was one of the largest cities in the entire Roman Empire. After this it began to go into decline, and by the fifth century AD following attacks by Goths, Huns and rebellious Roman generals, it was a crumbling second-rate slum town.[57]

Based upon archaeological evidence from the time of Rome's early occupation of the western Balkans, the process of cultural replacement was not a smooth transition. Instead, the Romanization of Illyria occurred at an uncomfortable, sporadic jerky pace. The Illyrian settlements along the Adriatic coast were the first to undergo the process of Romanization.[58] It made sense to do it this way for a few reasons. Firstly, many of these coastal towns and cities, especially those in the south, had been Hellenized centuries earlier. Rome was also heavily steeped in Greek culture, as is evident from their architecture and to some extent their dress and even their language. To both the Romans and the Illyrians who lived in these coastal settlements, there probably wasn't that much 'culture shock' when the Romans moved in. Yes, there were a few minor differences, but the outward appearance of many of these Illyrian coastal settlements would have appeared to the Romans as almost thoroughly Hellenic. The Romans would have little trouble in imposing their Roman way on a culture that was already so similar to their own.

Secondly, these coastal towns and cities were the hubs of important maritime trade routes. The Illyrians had essentially dominated the Adriatic Sea for much of their existence. You had to have been completely stupid not to realize the immense economic potential of controlling these port-cities. If the Romans could get a hold of these places, many of which had recently been Greek colonies, then Rome could get very rich very quickly.

Thirdly, once the Romans controlled the main settlements along the coast, the ones that had the greatest influence in the region, then the smaller and less powerful coastal settlements located nearby would come under Rome's control and thus a sort of domino effect would occur in theory. Controlling these coastal towns and cities acted almost like the beach-head for a cultural invasion inland. Once maritime trade centres were taken, the Romans could extend further and control the inland trade routes extending from the coastline into the interior of the then-uncharted western Balkans. These trade routes mostly followed the paths of rivers or mountain valleys. Using these pathways, Rome could locate new sources of economic potential in the interior. To this day, the western Balkans have large amounts of mineral ore including gold and silver, and I'm sure the Romans were eager to locate where the sources of all of this wealth were located. Yes, you could do business on the docks, but why not go directly to the source deep in the mountains, deep in the heart of Illyria? The Romans would turn these crude pathways into an efficient system of modern paved Roman roads as soon as they felt that the province was more secure. These roads would also almost certainly help the Illyrian rebels during the Great Illyrian Revolt of 6–9 AD, which would explain why the rebellion spread as rapidly as it did during that time.[59]

Understandably, the Roman presence would be felt the most where Rome felt its best interests lay. It made practical sense to control the coastal cities and the interior trade routes, so Rome began to make its presence felt in these areas very early on and with great force. As for other areas in the Balkan interior, which may have been nothing more than forested mountains and where the Romans saw no immediate economic concerns, they were less willing to press themselves and their culture upon the landscape and its people. Roman merchants and those seeking a new life in a new part of the realm flocked to these cities for the lure of opportunity and wealth. Since the Illyrians lived in cities with stone buildings and paved cobblestone roads, the transition from living in a Roman town to an Illyrian town was probably an easy one. The Romans were also willing to exploit the Illyrians as auxiliaries in the Roman army. Their prowess in battle was well-known, and Roman generals assuredly made a point of recruiting as many Illyrians into the ranks as possible. With the addition of these tough mountain fighters, Rome's military power was further strengthened, enabling it to press further into Europe and elsewhere and open up new markets and trade routes. Due to their expertise in ship construction and sailing, large numbers of Illyrians also served in the Roman navy. Many of them were stationed at the naval bases of Misenum (located on Italy's west coast) and Ravenna (located on the east coast).[60]

In terms of language, Latin had gained little headway in the western Balkans. Greek was far more common due to the large numbers of Greek settlers that had been living along the Adriatic coast for centuries, and so the Romans and Illyrians almost certainly spoke to each other in the one language that both parties could understand. Latin slowly crept its way into the western Balkans but inscriptions found in the region, especially deep in the interior far away from the highly-populated and highly-Romanized coastal cities, show a cruder form of Latin. Many times, the words are spelled differently and there are numerous grammatical mistakes. This shows that the native Illyrian people did not speak Latin fluently and though they tried to copy it, it shows a definite lack of linguistic understanding. Instead you have the creation of a regional dialect which can be called 'Illyrian Latin', fusing the Roman language with the language of the native people.[61]

However, the Romans were more concerned with the flow of wealth and goods rather than the progress that Roman culture was making in the region, but don't get the impression that the wealth only flowed in one direction; Roman trade worked for the Illyrians as well. As in many cases with imperial powers, the conquered supplied the raw materials while the imperial power supplied manufactured and prestige goods. Strabo says that Illyrian merchants used to travel to the northern Italian city of Aquileia on a frequent basis. Located close to barbarian lands on the northern tip of the Adriatic Sea, Aquileia was originally built as a frontier fortress to keep out enemy tribes, but its potential as a vital trading hub was soon realized. Here, the Illyrians would sell cattle, leather and slaves. They may have also been willing to offer up gold, silver, copper and salt to the Romans in exchange for luxury items. In exchange for Illyrian goods and slaves, the Romans sold or traded large casks of wine and olive oil. They may have also sold textiles and pottery. Items that were identifiably Roman would have been eagerly grabbed by local kings and tribal chiefs. As a result, both the Romans and the Illyrians became rich. It was a system that worked for both sides.[62]

Considering that the Illyrians had all this new-found wealth, one thinks that they would have realized on which side their bread was buttered and would have been eager to go along peacefully with the Roman system. If the Romans also thought this, then they were in for a big shock. In 58 BC, just one year after Illyricum became a province, the Dalmatians and other Illyrian tribes, who were by now very prosperous, attacked and seized the city of Promona, which was a city of the Liburnian tribe; like many Illyrian settlements, it was a heavily-fortified mountain stronghold surrounded by steep jagged terrain. The Liburnians appealed to Julius Caesar, who happened to be nearby, for help. Caesar ordered that the Illyrians should hand the city of Promona back over to the Liburnians. When they refused, Caesar sent a large force to attack the Dalmatians. Regrettably, the exact number of men that Caesar sent forward is not given. However, it was the Illyrians who emerged victorious and completely destroyed Caesar's army. For Caesar, such a crushing defeat was almost unheard-of and it must have affected him profoundly. He didn't bother sending in a second army because he was too busy fighting against his rival Pompey, but I also like to think that he became wary of attacking the Illyrians again.[63]

Ten years later in 48 BC, Julius Caesar crossed with a large army into Illyria with the purpose of defeating Pompey's forces. His army was divided into three parts. Caesar led one part, and his trusted subordinate Marcus Antonius commanded a second part; the strengths of both of these forces are not recorded. A third part was led by Aulus Gabinus, who commanded fifteen infantry cohorts (7,200 men) and 3,000 cavalrymen. Usually, when military forces are listed, standard Roman forces are listed in terms of legions or legionnaires and the supporting auxiliaries are listed as cohorts. This is because in the Roman military, Roman citizen-soldiers were standardized at the legion level, but auxiliaries had no legions; they were organized at a cohort level. So it is in all likelihood that Gabinus was the one who commanded the auxiliary forces while Caesar and Antonius commanded the regular Roman legions.[64]

While Caesar and Antonius' forces landed on the Illyrian coast by sea, crossing the Adriatic from their base camps in Italy, Gabinus' forces marched overland around the Adriatic. Perhaps aware that Gabinus' force was the smaller of the two main Roman forces and was also isolated away from the larger force commanded by Caesar and Antonius, the Illyrians focused their full attention on Gabinus' army. They completely obliterated Gabinus' force at the Battle of Synodium. According to Appianus' record of the event, the Illyrians were merciless, killing every single soldier in that army except for the commander Gabinus and a small group of others who managed to take refuge in Salona, and also captured a large amount of plunder. It is said that Gabinus died shortly afterwards. What is interesting is that later on, Appianus states that only five cohorts were destroyed, not fifteen, and that their standards were captured. This is either an error in translation, confusing fifteen with five, or perhaps Appianus himself made the mistake and is actually speaking about a later incident that occurred when the Illyrians destroyed five legionary cohorts in 44 BC. I shall speak about this event later.[65]

The defeat at Synodium must have been a serious blow to Caesar's plans and strength, but he continued anyway with his war against Pompey. In 45 BC, one of Caesar's subordinates named Publius Vatinius fought several battles against the Dalmatians, but was never able to bring them to surrender. After Pompey was assassinated in Egypt, and after the last of Pompey's loyalists were defeated, Caesar returned to Rome as the sole ruler of the republic. Straight away, he began to make preparations for two wars: one minor war in Thrace against the Getae barbarians, and a second massive war against the Parthian Empire. Since the Illyrians were on his marching route, they were afraid that Caesar would attack them as well. So they sent messengers to Rome to ask pardon for what they had done earlier, professed their friendship and offered to fight as Rome's allies in battle. Caesar replied that the Illyrians would never be forgiven for the deaths of so many Roman soldiers, but he would grant them an official pardon if they would send an annual tribute and give peace hostages. The Illyrians agreed. Caesar sent three legions into the country, commanded by Publius Vatinius, to enforce the terms and collect the hostages and tribute. Caesar was generous, though; the amount of tribute that the Illyrians were expected to pay each year was small.[66]

The Dalmatians believed that their arrangement had been with Rome for as long as Julius Caesar was in charge. When Caesar was assassinated in 44 BC, the Dalmatians thought that with Caesar now dead, they were no longer subject to the terms of the treaty. Therefore when General Publius Vatinius requested that the Dalmatians once again pay their annual tribute, they refused. When Vatinius attempted to use force on them, the Dalmatians attacked and destroyed five legionary cohorts, approximately 2,500 men. Among those killed was the five cohorts' commanding officer, a man of senatorial rank named Baebius (named by Stipčević as Balbius). General Vatinius retreated with the rest of his force to Epidamnus, while the Dalmatians seized control of the city of Salona.[67]

Publius Vatinius was stripped of command for this embarrassing defeat, and the Senate handed command of the army over to Marcus Brutus, one of Caesar's assassins, who was in command of the provinces of Illyricum and Macedonia. However, since Brutus and his fellow conspirators were at that moment at war against the loyalist forces of Marcus Antonius, they did not have the time, numbers or resources to engage in punitive measures against the Illyrians. It was not until 39 BC that the Romans could once again turn their attention to the persistently obdurate and troublesome Balkan tribes.[68]

Octavianus Fights the Illyrians

Following Julius Caesar's murder on the Ides of March, a civil war erupted between the anti-Caesar and pro-Caesar factions. The anti-Caesars consisted of Caesar's assassins and their supporters, notably Brutus and Cassius. The pro-Caesar side consisted of those who wanted to avenge Caesar's death, among them Julius Caesar's right-hand man Marcus Antonius and Caesar's grand-nephew, who at that time was in his early 20s: Gaius Julius Caesar Octavianus, the man who would later become Rome's first emperor.

The war between the pro-Caesars and anti-Caesars was surprisingly short, lasting for only two years. However, during those two years much blood was shed on both sides. At last, Brutus and Cassius were crushed at the Battle of Philippi in late autumn of 42 BC. Almost all of the anti-Caesar forces had been destroyed. Marcus Antonius emerged as the hero of the hour, with Octavianus playing second fiddle to Antonius' fame and prowess. Officially the two shared power, but it was obvious that Antonius was hamstringing his partner's efforts to govern effectively.

A series of political and social blunders served to damage Octavianus' reputation even further with the Roman military and the Roman people. Still, the war wasn't over yet. Although the anti-Caesar land forces had been destroyed, the anti-Caesar fleet commanded by Sextus Pompeius was still somewhere out there in the Mediterranean. Sicily was Pompeius' centre of operations, the last place where the anti-Caesars still held some power, but Pompeius and his warships were nowhere to be found. Marcus Antonius ordered his lieutenant Octavianus to take Sicily and destroy the last surviving remnants of the anti-Caesar forces. Meanwhile, Antonius began entertaining the idea of fulfilling Julius Caesar's dream of conquering the Parthian Empire, and he decided that it would be best to secure Egypt before pushing further inland.[69]

Octavianus' task was easier said than done. His tarnished reputation led to many people joining sides with his enemy Sextus Pompeius. Octavianus couldn't rely on Marcus Antonius for help because by now he had fallen madly in love with Cleopatra and was completely preoccupied with affairs in the east. His campaign against the Parthians got off to a very bad start: Syria and parts of Anatolia were quickly seized by the Parthians and Antonius' forces were retreating. Octavianus was forced to use strict measures when it came to maintaining control. Grumbling soon erupted into open hostility when Lucius Antonius, Marcus Antonius' brother, refused to recognize Octavianus' authority and waged his own private war against him. So it was that the victorious pro-Caesar faction dissolved into fighting among themselves. Marcus Antonius considered coming to his brother's aid, but he couldn't leave the eastern provinces knowing that the Parthians would swallow them whole. In 40 BC, a cease-fire was declared at the southern Italian city of Brundisium. With the civil war over, at least for a while, both Octavianus and Marcus Antonius could now devote their time to other matters.[70]

Marcus Antonius wanted to get back to fighting the Parthians, but he was distracted by affairs in Illyria. One tribe called the Partheni (no relation to the Parthians), which dwelt near Dyrrachium, was raiding throughout the province of Macedonia and had captured the city of Salona. In 39 BC, Antonius dispatched eleven legions to put an end to the troubles there; some would think this a rather heavy-handed response. His objectives were not just to defeat the Partheni, but also other tribes that refused to recognize Rome's authority over Illyricum. Gaius Asinius Pollio, who was known more for his poems and oratory skills, commanded part of the army and marched out from the port-city of Aquileia. His force was bound for Salona, which was still under Illyrian occupation:[71]

> The Dalmatians for the most part lived in the forests, whence they frequently made predatory raids. Marcius the consul had already crippled them by burning Delminium, their capital; afterwards Asinius Pollio – the second greatest of Roman orators – had deprived them of their flocks, arms and territory.[72]

Pollio recaptured Salona and conquered the Partheni tribe. In commemoration of the event, he named his son Saloninus and, being the literary muse that he was, he used the captured loot to fund the construction of Rome's first public library.[73] Pollio's expedition was a foreshadowing of things to come. The Romans were going to devote a great deal of attention to Illyria in the near future. Antonius had struck the first blow, but it would be Octavianus who would do most of the fighting from now on. If the Illyrians expected the same old see-saw routine of attack and counter-attack, then they seriously under-estimated what Octavianus was capable of.

In 36 BC, after two years of fighting and fiascos, Gaius Octavianus' troops finally defeated Sextus Pompeius and took control of Sicily, thus eliminating the last stronghold of the anti-Caesar forces. Now he undertook a grand campaign against the Illyrian tribes. Unlike other commanders who attacked the tribes piecemeal, Octavianus desired to bring the entire Balkan region under Roman authority and therefore declared war on *all* of the Illyrians. The purpose for Octavianus' grand war against the Illyrian tribes had more to do with politics than actual military threats. Both Octavianus and Antonius were engaged in a contest where both sides wanted to elevate their own image and degrade the other's. Every time one accomplished something, the other tried to outdo it. So when Antonius achieved his objective in defeating the Partheni and other malcontents, Octavianus decided to do one better and conquer the entire region of Illyria, from the Adriatic to the Danube, from one end of the Balkans to the other.[74]

Octavianus' war to subdue all Illyria was launched in 35 BC. According to Appianus, the war got off to a roaring start. In just the first campaign season, Octavianus conquered eight tribes by military force. He also compelled six tribes who had previously been subdued by Rome to once again pay their annual tributes, which they had failed

Figure 11: Marble bust of Caesar Augustus. This particular bust shows him wearing a 'civic crown', an award given to someone who saved the life of a Roman citizen. (*Capitoline Museum, Rome. Public domain image. Wikimedia Commons*)

to do for a long time. Two other tribes voluntarily surrendered to the Romans out of fear. He completely exterminated the Meliteni tribe and the entire population of Corfu Island in response to their repeated acts of piracy, killing all of the young men and selling off the others as slaves, and destroyed the Liburnians' navy. Then he turned his attention to the Japodes, who inhabited the eastern Alpine areas. Two of the Japode tribes surrendered at his approach and a third fled in terror, abandoning all of their settlements and surrendering soon afterwards.[75]

The coastal tribes were easily subdued, but those that lived in the interior were much harder to defeat. By the end of the campaigning season of 35 BC, the rift between Octavianus and Marcus Antonius had widened to the point where things could never be fixed. According to Cassius Dio, Marcus Antonius 'became more than ever a slave to the passion and the witchery of Cleopatra'.[76] War between Rome and Egypt was now unavoidable, and Octavianus now had to deal with the situation in Africa. He couldn't afford to be bogged down in the Balkans, so Octavianus made a hasty peace with the various tribes there, stating that any tribes not conquered by him during the war were still independent. Some of the Illyrians and Alpine tribes that had caused him a great deal of trouble got off lightly. Many of the tribes, however, probably felt that the war was concluded only due to the emergency in Egypt. Once Antonius and Cleopatra were out of the picture, Octavianus would surely return to settle unfinished business and continue his conquest of the Balkans and the Alps. The Illyrian warriors had the foresight to use the cease-fire to stockpile resources, especially large amounts of salt, preparing themselves for when hostilities recommenced.[77]

Octavianus went to Sicily, intending to sail to northern Africa. However, after being detained on the island due to bad weather, he gave up his plans. It was just as well because the Salassi tribe of north-western Italy and three Illyrian tribes – the Japodes, the Liburnians and the Taurisci – took this opportunity of Octavianus' absence to openly rebel against Roman rule. We are told that these tribes had already been treating the Romans with considerable disrespect for some time, they had stopped paying their tributes to Rome and they had periodically attacked neighbouring districts.[78]

When Octavianus heard about the trouble in Illyricum, he returned to the Balkans, even though he was short on manpower. He led his forces against the Japodes, and gave instructions to his subordinate commanders to have their respective forces attack certain tribes assigned to them in order to complete the war quicker; Marcus Corvinus defeated the Salassi and Gaius Vetus continued his attacks against the other Alpine tribes.[79] Octavianus' campaign into the mountains pushed the Roman military to its tactical and logistical limits. The tribes impeded the legions' approach through the use of obstacles and occasional surprise attacks. The long dragging assault against the Japodes' capital settlement of Metulum very nearly exhausted Octavianus' fighting ability, and Octavianus himself was severely injured in one of the failed attempts to storm the city. Eventually, when it appeared that the Romans would gain the upper hand, the defenders of Metulum committed a mass suicide and burned down the town rather than allow it to fall to the Romans. The hardy Japodes had been defeated, but at the cost of thousands of Roman lives.[80]

Octavianus, having supposedly recovered from his injuries, now turned his attention to conquering the Pannonians, even though Cassius Dio protests that the Pannonians had done nothing to provoke the Romans. He morbidly and macabrely states that Octavianus' war against the Pannonians was 'to give his soldiers practice'[81] and to supply his men with the plunder taken from them. He especially wanted to take control of the city of Segestica, their largest and most important settlement, because it would serve as an important base for staging future military campaigns in the north, especially against the Dacians of modern-day Romania who occasionally raided into Roman territory. As the Romans advanced northwards, the Pannonians abandoned their villages. At first, the Romans didn't destroy or pillage their settlements because Octavianus wished to turn them into Roman subjects, but eventually the Pannonians stopped retreating and they began harassing the Roman column as it advanced towards Segestica. Faced with resistance, Octavianus ordered the country to be devastated and to take whatever plunder his men could find. Then the Roman legions arrived at the city. Surrounded and with no hope of aid, the Pannonians realized that they were going to lose the battle sooner or later, and they surrendered after a thirty-day siege. After Segestica surrendered to the Romans, the rest of Pannonia surrendered as well. Octavianus left one of his subordinate commanders, Fufius Geminus, in charge of holding the city with a small garrison and returned to Rome the victorious hero. He was awarded a triumph by the Senate, but he refused to accept it.[82]

Peace did not last. In 34 BC, Octavianus' ally-turned-rival Marcus Antonius invaded and quickly seized the kingdom of Armenia, annexing it into the Roman Republic. Fearing that Antonius' star was climbing too quickly, Octavianus knew that he had to do something spectacular to boost his public image, so he planned to emulate his predecessor Julius Caesar by launching an invasion of Britain. He was already advancing his men through Gaul when he received word that all of Illyria had risen in rebellion, that the legionary garrison at Segestica had come under attack by rebel forces, and Fufius Geminus, the commander that Octavianus had left in charge of Segestica, was driven out of the city. However, the report that reached Octavianus' ears was incorrect. What actually happened was this: Chief Verzo (also called Versus) of the Dalmatians had captured the town of Promona from his enemies, the Liburnians, just as they had done almost twenty years earlier. Knowing that the Romans would retaliate, he placed 12,000 warriors within the town to defend it and smaller parties of men upon the jagged hills surrounding it. When Octavianus heard the report, he abandoned his objective of conquering Britain and hastily moved to Illyricum, ostensibly to teach the rebels a lesson and to bring this region firmly under his wing.[83]

Octavianus rendezvoused with his old battlefield comrade Marcus Vipsanius Agrippa and together they planned their offensive. Their first objective was to take back the town of Promona. Octavianus, as usual, was precise and methodical. When the legions came near, the Roman army first seized the heights surrounding the town, and then Octavianus turned his attention towards laying siege to the town itself. Illyrian reinforcements led by a warlord named Testimos were repulsed by the Romans. Running short on men and food, Chief Verzo was forced to surrender. This opening victory enabled Octavianus to penetrate into the very centre of Dalmatian territory. Meanwhile, Testimos, the leader of the Illyrian relief party who had fortunately escaped, now took it upon himself to harass the Roman column as it advanced. However, Octavianus refused to allow himself to be lured into an unfavourable situation and his army continued on as ordered, capturing the towns of Synodium and Andetrium. When the Roman army reached the town of Setovia, they found a large Dalmatian army encamped just outside the walls. In the massive battle that followed, Octavianus was wounded in the knee by a flying sling-stone. Unable to walk, he handed over command of the army to one of his subordinates named General Titus Statilius Taurus. The Dalmatians were defeated, but they were able to retreat into the town. After resting in his tent for a few days to recover from his wound, Octavianus left for Rome in late autumn while General Taurus laid siege to Setovia. The siege lasted for almost a year. In 33 BC, Octavianus (who was now in his second consulship) left Rome and returned to Setovia to find that Taurus and his troops were still encamped around the town and had not made any progress in capturing it. Rations were dangerously low, and so too were discipline and morale, and so Octavianus reinstituted the punishment of decimation: the systematic killing of every tenth man in a military unit. Usually, this punishment was instituted when an entire unit as a whole had shown cowardice in battle, but Octavianus used it as a punishment for desertion. Typically, the punishment for desertion was to be beaten to death by their fellow squad-mates. Unknown to the Romans, the Dalmatian defenders were now suffering from lack of food and the siege would surely be over soon. It is reported that when the rebels saw Octavianus reappear on the battlefield, they realized Rome's dreaded resolve in seeing them crushed and they decided that the time had come to surrender.[84]

When Setovia fell, all of southern Illyria came firmly under Roman control. It had taken Rome nearly two centuries to get the job done. Rome imposed crushing conditions on the Illyrians to chasten their rebellious spirit: a high tribute had to be paid to Rome, they had to surrender the legionary eagles which they had captured, and they were to hand over 700 children to the Roman government to serve as peace hostages. At the end of 33 BC, Octavianus and his officers returned to Rome to bask in their battlefield glory. With Illyria subdued, he could once again turn his attentions towards the increasingly troubling matters surrounding Antonius and Cleopatra, as well as to conducting a massive public works project to restore areas of the Eternal City that had been left run down. As an example of this, General Taurus funded the construction of Rome's first stone amphitheatre, and Octavianus himself used his war plunder to fund another public library in Rome (Pollio had founded the first), which was named, not surprisingly, the Octavian Library. In 31 BC, Antonius and Cleopatra were defeated at the epic Battle of Actium and Gaius Octavianus became Rome's sole ruler. Four years later in January 27 BC, Octavianus handed over control of the province of Illyricum to the Roman Senate. That same month and year, Gaius Julius Caesar Octavianus was awarded the title *Augustus*.[85]

The Conquest of Pannonia, 12–9 BC

Before we get into a serious discussion of Romano-Illyrian affairs in the early stages of the empire, I wish to provide a short vignette as to what sort of man Rome's first emperor was. Gaius Julius Caesar Octavianus, now known as Caesar Augustus, was not a physically imposing or intimidating man. According to the ancient accounts, he was short, thin, pale and sickly. He had a handsome face (numerous busts attest to his

Hollywood heart-throb chiselled features) with short blond hair and serious deep-set eyes.[86]

Like most ruling families, Augustus was conscious that the behaviour of himself and his kin was supposed to set an example for the behaviour of the rest of society. Keeping that in mind, Augustus maintained a 'common man' persona, partly to curry favour with the Roman peasants by identifying with them, partly to show that he was not an extravagant spendthrift, and partly out of his own lack of concern for his appearance. He preferred to wear ordinary home-made wool tunics rather than the expensive garments worn by the Roman elite. He was a family man who enjoyed being around children, he exercised regularly, and his favourite hobby was fishing. He was religiously and socially conservative in almost all aspects, which endeared him well to the ruling class. As examples of this, he was financially frugal, ate lightly and drank moderately. A typical breakfast for him was only bread and cheese.[87]

Like all male members of the Roman elite, he had received a rounded education involving Latin and Greek literature, but Augustus didn't take well to studying Greek and struggled with the subject. Even so, despite his handicap in studying foreign languages, he was a bookish person by nature, far more comfortable in a school or library than on a battlefield or within a royal palace. No wonder that he used his war booty to fund the establishment of a library. Augustus probably would have been an author if he had not been an emperor. He loved reading and writing, and dabbled in composing histories and poems. All of his speeches were written beforehand and recited; he *never* ad libbed anything.[88]

Augustus was not the hardiest of men. He hated cold weather, often wearing multiple tunics, and never went outside without wearing a hat to protect his pallid skin from the glaring sun. His cautious attitude towards the cold can be explained by his often poor health. He was especially susceptible to chills and chest congestion. Yet, in spite of the fact that illnesses beset him for much of his life, he was a man of massive energy and pushed through with his duties. He might not have had an iron constitution but he did have an iron will, and this in no small part helped to keep the empire under his control for the better part of forty years.[89]

It seems that there are two ways in which people think about Caesar Augustus. One image of Augustus is of an intelligent kind sage sitting comfortably in the palace dispensing justice and wisdom to his officials and subjects. The other image of him is as a brutal narcissistic adventurer and obsessive micro-manager who had no qualms about solving a seemingly never-ending cascade of problems and crises using the quickest and often bloodiest methods available. Personally, I lean towards the second option, as you may have already guessed.

One of the matters of government that Caesar Augustus attended to was figuring out how to better consolidate the province of Illyricum. Remember that at this time only the southern half of Illyria had been incorporated into the Roman Empire as a province. The northern half, Pannonia, extending from the Sava River to the Danube, was still independent though under a great deal of Roman influence. After the various campaigns waged by Augustus in Illyria prior to his accession as Rome's first emperor, Augustus needed to find homes for the veterans who fought beside him. During his reign, he undertook a policy of settling large numbers of Italian-born citizens and subjects within the coastal settlements of the Illyrian shore. *Coloniae* were established in Iader, Narona and Salona, and possibly elsewhere. However, unlike the veterans' colonies set up by Julius Caesar, Augustus' colonies were meant for civilian settlement. The colony at Narona is of particular interest because the civilian population that relocated there had an unusually high proportion of ex-slaves. Augustus must have felt that this area, which was a hostile zone for so many decades, was now sufficiently pacified to undertake a serious commitment to civilian plantation. Also, now that Illyricum was coming under increasing attention with regard to civil matters as opposed to military matters, some of the people who already lived there were beginning to see the benefits of being under Roman rule. In particular, the Liburnian tribe appears to have been singled out for preferential treatment. Members of the Liburnian aristocracy were granted perks by the Roman imperial government and found themselves in privileged positions, unlike the elite class of other tribes in Illyria. One man named Lucius Tarius Rufus, who was a Liburnian that obtained Roman citizenship, was made a Senatorial consul in the year 16 BC.[90]

In terms of government, Augustus realized that he couldn't attend to every matter personally, but he nevertheless insisted on constantly inserting his opinions and commands onto his provincial governors. In this way, Augustus bears the appearance of a boss who is officially-speaking 'hands off' but in reality is an irksome micro-manager. His attitude towards government was mirrored in his attitude towards military affairs. Although he had a lot of battlefield experience behind him, Augustus was not a particularly adept or inspiring military commander and so he preferred to appoint generals who would lead his armies in his place.[91]

One of those who would lead the Roman Army was Caesar Augustus' own stepson Tiberius Claudius Nero. The *gens* Claudia were of patrician stock, descended from the Sabine tribe, one of Rome's neighbours which it conquered in its very early history. Tiberius was the oldest son of Augustus' second wife Livia. He had a background as a lawyer and civil magistrate, but although he was a member of the imperial family and was therefore expected to take a leading role in the empire's bureaucracy, Tiberius was not really suited to administrative and government duties. He felt more at home among the grit and sweat of the legions rather than among the perfumed aristocrats of the Roman elite. He was first and foremost a fighting man by profession and by nature, and it would be on the battlefield that he would find his true calling.[92]

His first taste of combat was during the campaign against the Cantabrian tribe of Spain as a tribune (in a modern military, he would have held the rank of major). Afterwards, he commanded an army in the empire's eastern provinces and restored the ousted King Tigranes back on the throne of Armenia; Tiberius personally crowned him. While in the east, he collected the lost Roman eagle standards that had been captured by the Parthians during the Battle of Carrhae. Then he journeyed to Gaul, which was suffering from barbarian raids as well as violent feuds between the various subjugated Gallic tribes. In the year 16 BC, the Pannonian Illyrians as well as their western neighbours, the Norian Celts, invaded and overran the Istrian Peninsula at the head of the Adriatic Sea. The impetus for this was the lack of a Roman military presence in the region, since the legions were occupied fighting the Alpine tribes of what is now northern and north-eastern Italy. In response to these attacks, Publius Silius advanced upon the Pannonians and forced them to agree to peace, which left the Norians to face the Roman legions alone. They were easily crushed by Tiberius, who conquered the whole land of Noricum, which today corresponds to eastern Austria, and made it a Roman province. The following year, he and his younger brother Drusus conquered the neighbouring regions of Rhaetia and Vindelicia, comprising western Austria, southern Germany and eastern Switzerland.[93]

Tiberius' next chance for battlefield glory would come in Pannonia. This region had been considered part of Illyria for centuries, but since the Roman acquisition of the coastal regions, Pannonia and the province of 'Illyricum' were classified as separate entities. Many years before, Augustus had invaded and subjugated this land, but he hadn't conquered it; he simply beat up the Pannonians and expected them to be subservient

Figure 12: Marble bust of Tiberius Claudius Nero, British Museum, London, United Kingdom. (*Photograph by Simon Speed, 22 August 2009. Public domain image. Wikimedia Commons*)

to Rome from now on. It didn't work. For years, the people of northern Illyria had been a troublesome nuisance. They had caused disturbances in the region in the year 16 BC and again in 14 BC. As long as the Pannonians remained independent, they would always cause problems. It was time to teach them a lesson once and for all.[94]

There were concrete reasons for launching a large-scale military operation in Pannonia right away. The civilian colonies established by Augustus only a decade or so earlier in southern Illyria were under threat. So too were Rome's communication and trade routes that connected Illyricum to Italy, and also those routes that extended from the Illyrian interior to the Adriatic coast. Simply, a lot was at stake, and this time, after so much work had been put into the region, Augustus could not afford to let the northern Illyrians ruin all of that hard work. Also Augustus likely saw the advantages of pushing Rome's reach to the Danube River and controlling the various tributaries of it, such as the Sava and Drava Rivers.[95]

Caesar Augustus originally ordered that his reliable-but-aging warhorse Marcus Vipsanius Agrippa should go to Pannonia, a land 'which was eager for war',[96] according to Cassius Dio, and crush the Pannonian tribes into complete and total submission. The emperor granted Marcus Agrippa a great deal of power in order to get the job done. Joining Agrippa on the expedition would be Marcus Vinicius, a close friend of Augustus who had been made the governor of Illyricum and who was serving as a consul of the Senate that year; later, he would be made the military governor general of Germania Magna. In 13 BC, Agrippa and his troops got under way. When the Pannonians learned that Agrippa was marching against them, they immediately begged for peace. Without shooting a single arrow, Agrippa had forced the Pannonians to back down. Satisfied, he returned to Italy, but fell gravely ill soon after coming home and died shortly thereafter. When the Pannonians learned that Agrippa had passed away, they immediately renewed their plans to make war upon the Romans.[97]

With Agrippa dead, Tiberius became the second most powerful man in the whole Roman Empire. Caesar Augustus' first duty was to further ensure that Tiberius' position as the number two man in the empire was strengthened. Tiberius had been married to Vipsania Agrippa, the daughter of Marcus Vipsanius Agrippa, and he was deeply devoted to her. Agrippa himself had been married to Augustus' daughter Julia and that had made him the heir to the throne, but when Agrippa died, a new heir was needed. So, for political reasons, Tiberius was forced to divorce his dear wife and marry Julia, who he couldn't stand being around. Augustus' second task for Tiberius was for him to take Agrippa's place as the commander of the Roman troops stationed on the Danube.[98] The Illyrians, although under Roman dominance, were still edgy, and Danube defences were weak.

For decades, the Dacians, who lived on the other side of the Danube in what is now Romania, had launched raids into Roman territory. Troops had been deployed along the border to deter them, but it was a flimsy defence and the Dacians could easily exploit the empty gaps in between the military border posts. After so much time behind the lines without seeing any action, Tiberius could see his men becoming soft and lazy. For a hard blood-and-guts commander like himself, this was intolerable. He needed to get his men back into fighting shape quickly, and he knew *exactly* how to do it: the Roman legions would attack and conquer a foreign tribe in order for Tiberius to give his soldiers some much-needed 'practice'.

For his campaign to conquer Pannonia and incorporate it into the existing province of Illyricum, Tiberius employed a pincer movement. Earlier, he had suppressed the Scordisci, a Celtic tribe that inhabited central Illyria and had been frequently employed as mercenaries by the Dacians. Now, Tiberius intended to use these people in his planned attack. While Tiberius and his men attacked from the west, the Scordisci would attack from the east, trapping the Pannonians in between.[99] Even though the plan looked fine, Tiberius still needed the reassurance of the gods that things were going to go well. On his way to Illyricum, Tiberius stopped off at the Italian city of Patavium to consult an oracle there, the same oracle that had predicted that Julius Caesar would emerge victorious at the Battle of Pharsalus. Tiberius was ordered to throw some golden dice into the Fountain of Aponus and when he did so, the highest possible score came up; a good sign.[100]

Tiberius must have assumed that the Pannonian campaign would be a cakewalk, an easy brief affair taking only a few months, like his previous campaigns against the Norians, Rhaetians and Vindelicians. However, the Pannonians were not to be taken lightly. When the Romans launched their invasion in the year 12 BC, the Pannonians resisted ferociously. Tiberius must have been shocked to see how much spirit and fight the Pannonians had in them. The war dragged on for three blood-soaked years, and the Pannonians made the Romans pay dearly for every inch of ground that they conquered. Paterculus described the conflict as *magnum atroxque*, 'great and atrocious'.[101]

Unfortunately, details of the Pannonian War are scant. Gaius Paterculus' description of the whole war consists of just one paragraph:

> Shortly after, the Pannonian war, which had been begun
> by [Marcus Vipsanius] Agrippa in the consulate of your

grandfather, Marcus Vinicius, was conducted by [Tiberius Claudius] Nero, a war which was important and formidable enough, and on account of its proximity a menace to Italy. In another place I shall describe the tribes of the Pannonians and the races of Dalmatians, the situation of their country and its rivers, the number and extent of their forces, and the many glorious victories won in the course of this war by this great commander; my present work must keep to its design. After achieving this victory Nero celebrated an ovation.[102]

Cassius Dio's chronology of events for the war can at times be a bit difficult to follow. A lot was going on during these years, and the events that took place during Tiberius' conquest of Pannonia are mixed in among details of other events and they are spread out over several chapters. For the opening campaign season of 12 BC, Cassius Dio relates:

Tiberius subdued them [the Pannonians] after ravaging much of their country and doing much injury to the inhabitants, making as much use as possible of his allies the Scordisci, who were neighbours of the Pannonians and were similarly equipped. He took away the enemy's arms and sold most of the men of military age into slavery, to be deported from the country. For these achievements the senate voted him a triumph, but Augustus did not permit him to celebrate it, though he granted him the triumphal honours instead.[103]

Tiberius could probably be forgiven for thinking that he had managed to crush the Pannonians in a single campaign season. He had accomplished a lot, and to all appearances the region appeared to have been pacified. However, scarcely had he put his sword back in the scabbard when the following year in 11 BC, the Dalmatians of southern Illyria rebelled against Roman rule. Tiberius was forced to move his troops southwards, leaving only a small number of his men behind in Pannonia to maintain security in the newly-subjugated lands. Seeing the small number of troops in their country, the Pannonians rose up again. Cassius Dio wrote:

Tiberius subdued the Dalmatians, who began a rebellion, and later the Pannonians, who likewise revolted, taking advantage of the absence of himself and the larger part of his army. He made war upon both of them at once, shifting now to one front and now to the other.[104]

As a result of this, control of the province of Illyricum was transferred from the Senate to Caesar Augustus. It was also now accepted by the Roman government that a permanent military force always needed to be stationed in the region due to the numerous revolts and uprisings that were occurring there.[105]

It was also during this time that Tiberius' younger brother Drusus Claudius Nero had begun his grand campaign to conquer Germania. After defeating the Pannonians and Dalmatians, Tiberius ordered that they should pay a tribute to Rome as a mark of their submission, and then went with Caesar Augustus to Gaul. However, while he was there, the Dalmatians, angry at having to pay tribute to Rome, rose up in defiance and so once again, Tiberius was forced to go there with an army and suppress them. I imagine that he was becoming increasingly tired of having to do this.[106]

The Roman military strategist Frontinus provides a description of one of the battles in which Tiberius' legions fought:

In the campaign against the Pannonians, when the barbarians in warlike mood had formed for battle at the very break of day, Tiberius Nero held back his own troops, and allowed the enemy to be hampered by the fog and be drenched with the showers, which happened to be frequent that day. Then, when he noticed that they were weary with standing, and faint not only from exposure but also from exhaustion, he gave the signal, attacked and defeated them.[107]

The writer Publius Florus writes of how the war ended:

Caesar [Tiberius] sent Vinnius [sic] to subdue them, and they were defeated on both rivers. The arms of the conquered enemy were not burnt, as was the usual custom in war, but broken to pieces and hurled into the current, that the fame of Caesar [Tiberius] might thus be announced to those who were still resisting.[108]

In 9 BC, after three years of battle, Pannonia was finally declared 'pacified'. The newly-conquered land was incorporated into the province of Illyricum. Caesar Augustus lauded this victory in his list of accomplishments, the *Res Gestae*, which adorned his tomb:

> The tribes of the Pannonians, to which no army of the Roman people had ever penetrated before my principate, having been subdued by Tiberius Nero who was then my stepson and my legate, I brought under the sovereignty of the Roman people, and I pushed forward the frontier of Illyricum as far as the bank of the river Danube.[109]

The famed nineteenth-century German historian Theodor Mommsen described Tiberius' Pannonian campaign as a small war with big consequences. Rome's legions pushed north beyond the Sava River and Roman control over all of Illyricum had been attained, from the Adriatic coast to the Danube River. Rome could now look northwards to a possible conquest of southern Germania.[110]

Chapter Three

Outbreak

The Myth of the 'Pax Romana'

Certain scholars of ancient history, beginning with the eighteenth-century British historian Edward Gibbon, have described Caesar Augustus' reign as the beginning of the so-called *Pax Romana*, the 'Roman Peace'. According to Gibbon and others, Rome underwent a transition during this period from civil wars and internal strife to a unified land of order and control, when the empire as a whole was largely in a state of peace and free of crisis. It's a lie. Anyone who knows the history of what the newly-created Roman Empire was like under the reign of Rome's first emperor will know that there was nothing 'pax' about the time that Caesar Augustus was in charge! Fire, blood, disaffection and insurrection were everywhere.

Some have an image of Caesar Augustus as a mostly bureaucratic ruler who was busy trying to reorganize and manage the empire and had very little time for military activity. Again, this is false. The Roman Army was very busy during these years conquering new lands, expanding the empire's domain and quelling uprisings. Take the following examples. In 19 BC, the Romans conquered the Cantabrians of northern Spain. In 17 BC, three Germanic tribes declared war upon the Romans, attacked a body of Roman soldiers led by Marcus Lollius and captured the 5th Legion's eagle, the greatest of all dishonours. The following year, the Romans conquered Noricum, and the year after that they conquered Rhaetia and Vindelicia. In 11 BC, General Drusus Claudius Nero launched his famous conquest of western Germania. From 12–9 BC, the Romans fought in Pannonia, eventually conquering the territory and incorporating it into the province of Illyricum. In 4 BC, the Jews revolted against Roman domination of Judea. From 1 to 4 AD, several Germanic tribes revolted against Roman rule. Clearly, this was a busy and bloody time, hardly the image of the 'Pax Romana' that we think of.

It isn't just military expeditions, campaigns of conquest and foreign attacks and rebellions that give cause to scoff at the idea of the Pax

Romana. During Augustus' reign, things were tense on a social level as well as a military level. The Roman people were on edge and saw dire portents all around them. Cassius Dio reports that there were many evil omens that accompanied the reign of the recently-crowned Caesar. There was a partial eclipse of the sun, which was never a good sign. The bad omen proved, well, ominous. During the space of only one year, during the consulship of Cornelius and Valerius Messalla, Italy was struck by a series of devastating earthquakes and floods. The bridge that spanned the Tiber River was swept away by the flooding waters, the low-lying sections of the city were flooded (remember, Rome was famously built atop seven hills), and Cassius Dio states that for seven days, people travelled through those areas by boat, the streets having turned into Venetian canals.[1]

Cassius Dio doesn't go into details, but we can get some idea about the true human cost of these natural disasters by looking at other historical events. Katrina, which struck in 2005, was the largest and most devastating hurricane to have ever hit the United States. It was most famous for flooding and nearly destroying the city of New Orleans, but its effects went far beyond southern Louisiana. Damage was spread across the Gulf Coast from Texas to Florida, it resulted in over $100 billion of damage and the death toll numbered more than 1,800.[2] In 1908, the city of Messina, Sicily was struck by a massive earthquake, completely levelling large areas of the city, followed by enormous tidal waves that smashed into what was left. It is estimated that as many as 150,000 people died during that event. Many of the bodies were washed out to sea, and fishermen often found human remains inside the stomachs of sharks.[3]

Not only was the Roman public anxious and worried, but there were also grumblings among the legions. During the BC-AD transition, there were seventeen legions stationed throughout the empire (this number was increased to twenty-five legions at the beginning of the year 6 AD). The big problem was that Augustus didn't have enough money to pay and support all of the armed men that he possessed. As a result, the soldiers complained that their wages had not been paid to them in a very long time, and that many of them had been kept in the military long after their enlistment contracts had expired.[4] So in the year 6 AD, Augustus proposed the creation of the *aerarium militare*, a permanent fund within the imperial treasury that would be used to pay the soldiers' retirement pensions.[5]

As if all this wasn't bad enough, famine had broken out in Italy. Augustus was forced to institute food rationing, ordering that each person was to be given a fixed amount of grain and not a single crumb more. He furthermore forbade public banquets in order to preserve whatever food remained. Then, another disaster: a large fire broke out in Rome, destroying a significant portion of the city. There was little that Augustus could do to remedy that situation. He did, however, institute the 'night watchmen', a sort of combination of a city police department and a city fire department, who were organized into seven divisions and were overseen by a member of the Equestrian Order.[6]

For those who were superstitious, I can imagine that they were having near-constant panic attacks. Ever since Augustus came to power, Rome had suffered through one calamity after another: earthquakes, floods, famine, fire, a distressed population, almost constant warfare and an army on the verge of mutiny. I'm not sure if there were such people as 'doomsday preppers' in those days, but if these things happened today, I'm sure that we would see a lot of people frantically building shelters in their back yards and stockpiling food, medicine and weapons.

The fire that ravaged the city was the last straw. The ordinary people, distressed by the heavy taxes that they had to pay, by the famine and by the fire, were on the brink of violence. Cassius Dio states that they openly discussed plans for a revolution and flooded the city with seditious pamphlets urging people to rise up and overthrow the emperor. Augustus demanded that an investigation be made as to who was responsible for all this treasonous behaviour and issued rewards for the arrest of the ringleaders. This unrest ceased when the famine came to an end and large amounts of grain once again came back to the city's markets.[7]

Well, things might have been bad at home, but what about abroad? If the Pax Romana did not cover things happening within the Eternal City, did it at least cover the overall state of the empire? Surely, the empire as a whole was strong and secure, right? Not really. Cassius Dio states that during this period there were many wars. Firstly, pirates were causing havoc throughout the Mediterranean.[8] Secondly, the island province of Sardinia had no governor administering it for several years and was being run by the Roman military. The Romans repeatedly treated the inhabitants of this island rather harshly, demanding large amounts of grain and tribute. Uprisings and revolts were numerous.[9] Thirdly, several cities had rebelled against Roman authority, though Cassius Dio doesn't state their names.[10] Fourthly, the Isaurians of southern Turkey launched attacks on Rome (whether by land or sea isn't stated). At first they launched only minor raids, but they soon became bolder and unleashed all the horrors of war, as Cassius Dio puts it, upon the Romans. The Isaurians probably played some part in the pirate epidemic during this time; they were notorious seafaring raiders. The Isaurians had been conquered in either 76 or 75 BC by Publius Servilius Vatia, who was later given the *agnomen* Isauricus. The region was incorporated into the province of Cilicia.[11] Fifthly, the Gaetulians of Northern Africa revolted against their Roman puppet king Juba. Not content merely with revolution and perhaps out of further anger at Rome's overlordship of their country, their warriors attacked the neighbouring Roman provinces. Cassius Dio states that when Roman troops were sent in to crush the rebellion, the Gaetulians killed many of them, until General Cornelius Cossus marched a second army in and at last subjugated them. So great was the effort in bringing this one tribe back into submission that General Cossus was awarded a triumph for his deed, something that was usually reserved only for major victories in major wars, and he was also awarded a title but it isn't stated if it was an *agnomen* or some other title.[12]

In the first years after the birth of Jesus Christ, Augustus would have to confront one of the biggest crises of his life, and one that would have severely tested any national leader in any age. It would force him to postpone one war in order to fight another. It would require Rome to muster one of the largest armies that it had ever dispatched. It would practically bankrupt the imperial treasury. It would be responsible for the destruction of countless villages, towns and cities, and would result in an incalculable number of dead. Yet in the end, after all that effort, pain, fire and blood, Rome had hardly anything to show for it.

This is how it happened.

The Stage is Set

It appears from the records that the revolt in Illyria was not a planned or prearranged event, but was instead something that happened on the spur of the moment. According to the historian Gaius Paterculus, in the year 6 AD, Rome *was* preparing for war, but not against the Illyrians. They were about to begin a war against a Germanic tribe called the Marcomanni. The name means either 'the border men' or 'the forest men', since *marc* could be a variation of the Norse word *mark* meaning 'woods' or 'forest', but it could also mean *march*, meaning 'borderlands'. The Marcomanni were the strongest and most powerful of all of the southern Germanic tribes during the age of Caesar Augustus, and might have been the mightiest of all of the Germanic tribes in general.[13]

The Germans were nothing new to the Romans; they had been fighting against each other on and off since the late second century BC. The war against the Teutons and the Cimbri is especially infamous, for this massive horde of barbarians destroyed several Roman armies before they were destroyed and defeated in turn. During his war against the Gauls in the 50s BC, Julius Caesar fought against a large army of Germans led by Chief Ariovistus of the Sueves at the Battle of Vosges. After defeating them, Caesar crossed the Rhine and explored Germania for a couple of weeks before heading back into Gaul. Julius Caesar's exploration of Germania is the first recorded instance of a Roman military presence in the area, and it wouldn't be the last. During the reign of Caesar Augustus, the Romans and Germans were having an increasing number of problems with each other: Roman merchants and settlers were squatting on German territory, and the Germanic tribesmen were conducting raids and attacks on Roman settlements in Gaul. In 13 BC, Caesar Augustus' nephew Drusus Claudius Nero was tasked with conquering the Germans. Throughout 12 BC, Drusus conducted pre-invasion reconnaissance missions, and from 11 to 8 BC, he and his legions slaughtered and burned their way from the Rhine to the Elbe, subjugating and re-subjugating one tribe after another, until Drusus suddenly died from an accident-related infection. His older brother Tiberius Claudius Nero, who had just finished conquering the Pannonians the year before, was now ordered by Caesar Augustus to hurry north to finish the job of conquering the Germans. However, rather than seizing new territory, Tiberius consolidated the lands that were currently in Rome's possession, preferring to further strengthen the lands that the legions controlled rather than overreaching himself. After Tiberius made the western Germanic tribes agree to a peace treaty in 6 BC, the territory of 'Germania Magna' lay under the authority of a series of military commandants who were entrusted to maintain law and order in the region and to work on building up this occupied territory into a 'proper' province.[14]

The Marcomanni tribe had been spared Drusus' and Tiberius' wrath during Rome's invasion and conquest of western Germania because their chief had been friendly to Rome. The tribal leader was King Maroboduus (his name may have been pronounced as Maroboduwoz), who, as far as I can tell, is the only Germanic tribal leader that the Romans actually addressed as *Rex*, 'King', as a sign of both the man's power as well as his close connections to the Roman Empire. According to the historian

Strabo, he was a German who held Roman citizenship. When he was younger, he lived in the Eternal City, possibly as a peace hostage, and 'enjoyed the favour of Augustus'.[15] Paterculus wrote of him as 'a man of noble family, strong in body and courageous in mind, a barbarian by birth but not in intelligence'.[16] When he got older, he left Rome and returned to his lands to act as Rome's vassal. The Marcomanni were originally much smaller in number and occupied lands that lay much further to the west, so when Maroboduus returned to assume his position of power, he ordered a mass relocation of the tribe into Bohemia (modern-day Czech Republic), a land previously occupied by the central European Celts called the Boii. In fact, the name *Bohemia* is a modernized version of the Germanic name *Boiohaemum*, 'the home of the Boii'.[17]

For a long time, relations between the Roman Empire and their Marcomannic vassal had been cordial, but when Maroboduus returned to his lands, things immediately began to turn sour. It started when he embarked on a campaign of conquest to bring his Germanic neighbours into subjugation. In order to do this, he needed an army. Using knowledge of military drill and tactics gained from the Romans, and possibly even using Roman mercenaries fighting under his banner (although I have absolutely no evidence to back up that claim), Maroboduus managed to forge a solid strong kingdom in the mountains of south-central Germania and forged an equally solid strong military force to defend it. In fact, the Marcomanni was the only Germanic tribe during this time that possessed a professional military modelled closely on the Roman army, numbering 74,000 warriors strong: 70,000 infantry and 4,000 cavalry.[18]

This scared the Roman imperial government, who may have considered that these heavily-armed well-trained men would come marching down out of the hills, but what worried them even more was King Maroboduus' increasing disregard for his relationship towards Rome. Rome had allowed King Maroboduus to reign over the Marcomannic people and had allowed his kingdom to retain a certain degree of sovereignty, provided that he always acknowledged Rome, and more specifically the Roman emperor, as his master. Yet this master-subject relationship deteriorated rapidly. Roman criminals who were running from the law would cross the border and seek asylum within Marcomanni territory. Roman envoys who came to King Maroboduus' court, presumably to ask for him to extradite criminals as well as other matters of business, were required to address him as if he was Caesar Augustus' equal, not his vassal. Faced with the growing power of King Maroboduus' army and his increasing uppity behaviour, the Romans had become more and more worried about their northern Germanic neighbour. King Maroboduus was becoming more assertive and was acting with a greater degree of pushiness towards the Romans. For a long time, the Romans had tolerated the Marcomanni as long as they didn't cause any trouble, but now Caesar Augustus was becoming concerned that the Marcomanni were a looming threat. The Romans needed to launch a pre-emptive strike before the Marcomanni became too powerful to handle or before they could turn on their imperial master and launch an invasion and so, in the later stages of 5 AD, the Romans began planning for war.[19]

And what a war it would be, too, if we look at how the Romans prepared for it. A massive number of troops were gathering for the expedition. Bohemia was a natural fortress, a massive ring of rugged jagged peaks and crags laced with thick pine forests. The Romans knew that this land would be a nightmare for military operations because they had fought in treacherous mountainous landscapes before: in central Italy, in Spain, in southern Gaul, in Rhaetia and in Illyria. They expected a hard fight against both the environment and against King Maroboduus' 74,000 professionals.

The general who was ordered to command this mass invasion of the Marcomanni kingdom was Tiberius Claudius Nero, who was not happy about being called into military service yet again. After he had finished the conquest of western Germania in 6 BC, Tiberius had given up the military life and went into a self-imposed exile on the island of Rhodes. However, when Caesar Augustus' grandsons and heirs Gaius and Lucius both died, Tiberius was regarded as the only one left into whose hands the emperor could place the difficult task of running things. In the year 4 AD, Tiberius returned to Rome, and was officially adopted by the emperor as his true son and heir.[20]

Tiberius' first job was to take command of the troops in Germania. A couple of years earlier, the tribes had risen in revolt and the incumbent military commandant Marcus Vinicius was struggling to put the rebellion down. Tiberius would immediately head north and take charge of things. Under Tiberius' command, the Germanic uprising was crushed in less than a year and peace was made with the rebellious tribes. Marcus Vinicius was fired, Gaius Sentius Saturninus was appointed in his place as the new governor general of the territory and Tiberius returned to Rome. The Marcomanni had stayed neutral during this rebellion, which is telling. As Rome's vassals in the region, they might have been expected or even ordered to lend a hand in suppressing the hostile tribes, but their obvious lack of involvement shows the increasing hostility that they themselves were showing to the Romans. It was around this time that Caesar Augustus began seriously thinking of conquering the Marcomanni.[21]

Tiberius, now placed in charge of the planned conquest of Marcomannic Bohemia, devised a standard pincer offensive. While Tiberius himself led an army upwards from the south, a second army led by General Gaius Sentius Saturninus, the military commandant of Germania Magna who Tiberius had appointed as his second-in-command for the operation would advance downwards from the north-west. In late 5 AD, Tiberius finished setting up his winter headquarters on the Danube River and had brought up his legions to within five days' march of the Marcomanni border. The invasion would begin the following year in 6 AD.[22]

Tiberius' base camp, the jumping-off point for the invasion, was the town of Carnuntum, located about twenty-three miles east of the modern city of Vienna, Austria (known in ancient times as Vindobona).[23] Carnuntum was an army town, being heavily fortified, heavily garrisoned and stocked to bursting with weapons and supplies. It began its life as a mediocre-sized Celtic settlement on the southern shore of the Danube River. The name means 'stone town', or more likely 'a walled settlement of stone', since *carn* might be a version of the Celtic word *caion*, meaning 'enclosure' or 'fenced-in place'.[24] However, once the Romans took over control of this region following Tiberius' conquest of Pannonia during the war of 12–9 BC, it began to truly grow and prosper. At first, Carnuntum was nothing more than an army base with a small civilian population, but its strategic and economic importance led it to expand more and more from the early first century AD onwards. At the height of its power in the middle second century AD, it had grown into a major city of 50,000 people, complete with an arena and a gladiator school. In its history, the city was attacked and destroyed twice, the first time in 166 AD during the Marcomannic Wars and the second time in 374 AD by the Germanic Quadi tribe. The city never recovered after this second act of destruction, and it quickly fell into ruins.[25]

In June 2014, Austrian archaeologists from the Ludwig-Boltzmann Institute for Virtual Archaeology announced that they had discovered the remains of a large Roman military camp located just outside the western gate of Carnuntum's town walls. Professor Wolfgang Neubauer, the head of the institute, stated that the camp was dated to the early first century

AD and might possibly be the very camp that was set up by Tiberius immediately preceding his campaign against the Marcomanni.[26]

Surely King Maroboduus would have become aware of an ever-growing build-up of Roman troops near his border. Yet despite the size and condition of his Germanic army, the historical records make no mention at all of any outright provocative or aggressive actions on Maroboduus' part towards Rome. In fact, Paterculus states that Maroboduus promised that he would never start a war with Rome, but if Rome chose to start a war against him, he would fight them with every bit of strength that he could muster. His words would soon be put to the test.[27]

The Explosion

It was now 6 AD. The long-awaited invasion of the Marcomannic kingdom was going to begin. Knowing that this war would lead to many troops being pulled away from their usual stations and leaving large sections of the empire open and defenceless, Caesar Augustus authorized the creation of eight new legions, bringing the total number of legions in the empire from seventeen up to twenty-five.[28] The legions were spread throughout the empire at strategic locations and were headquartered in fortified strongholds. Even with this increase in manpower, there were still large areas of the empire that had little or no military presence. Due to the vast space of the empire and the relatively low number of troops that were available to defend it, there were often huge swathes of land that had no protection whatsoever. Areas that were deemed more important had more troops on hand to defend them, such as Spain, Africa, Egypt and Syria. In the province of Illyricum, the majority of Roman military bases were located along the Danube River, which separated the province from the barbarian territories of the Germans, Dacians and Sarmatians. There were only a few handfuls of troops within the Illyrian interior or along the Balkan Adriatic coast.[29]

The invasion was about to begin. A rendezvous point was established along the border for any additional recruits to collect before moving off into Marcomanni territory. Tiberius' able lieutenant Gaius Sentius Saturninus, the military commandant of Germania Magna who would command the northern arm of the grand pincer attack, received his orders from his commander to move his troops into position for the opening offensive. When the 'first shots' were fired, it was expected that it would only take a few days for Saturninus' men to cut their way through and link up with Tiberius' troops in the south.[30]

Tiberius needed as many men as he could get his hands on for the great expedition against the Marcomanni. He contacted Marcus Messallinus, the *proconsul* (a provincial governor who was an ex-consul) of Illyricum, and ordered him to come with his soldiers to provide aid for the invasion. Marcus Valerius Messalla Messallinus, Governor of Illyricum, was the son of the famous orator M.V.M. Corvinus. He was a member of the Senate and had served as one of its consuls in the year 3 BC and again in 3 AD. He was also highly-connected to the imperial family; he was married to one of Caesar Augustus' nieces. In the future, when Augustus died and Tiberius was made emperor, Messallinus proposed to Tiberius that the people should swear an oath of allegiance to Tiberius every year in order to reaffirm their loyalty. This was important because the Roman soldiers didn't swear their loyalties to the Roman Empire or to its emperor but to Caesar Augustus personally, and when Augustus died in 14 AD the legions were no longer beholden to anyone. As a result, several legions mutinied. To prevent such a thing from happening again and to continuously re-instil loyalty to Tiberius, a yearly oath of allegiance seemed like a good idea. After all, in spite of his martial prowess, Tiberius was *no* Augustus! The historian Paterculus held Messallinus in high regard, stating that he 'was even more noble in heart than in birth, and thoroughly worthy of having had Corvinus as his father'.[31] Tacitus claimed that Marcus Messallinus was a good speaker, which was an important quality in ancient societies, and he was a friend of the poet Ovid.[32]

As soon as he received his instructions from Tiberius, Messallinus marched off to join Tiberius on the borders of Bohemia. He took with him the majority of the Roman soldiers that had been stationed in Illyricum, leaving only a small skeleton security force behind. This left the province woefully under-protected, but Messallinus believed that the province was secure. He had no reason to suspect any trouble.[33]

According to Peter Swan, there were five legions posted in Illyricum at this time: the 8th Legion *Gemina*, the 9th Legion *Hispania*, the 14th Legion *Gemina*, the 15th Legion *Appolinaris* and the 20th Legion *Valeria Victrix*.[34] The ancient historian Paterculus confirms that the 20th Legion was in Illyria at that time but it was only at half-strength, numbering at around just 2,500 men.[35]

Before he left, Messallinus ordered the native Dalmatians of southern Illyria to provide as many warriors as they could to serve as auxiliaries

in the upcoming war against the Marcomanni. The Dalmatians had no
choice but to obey the governor's order. The tribes selected groups of
warriors and sent them on their way to join the Roman forces; their total
number isn't recorded. I assume that they travelled with their armour,
weapons and equipment, as will soon become evident. For a long time, the
natives of Illyria had chafed under the boot of Roman domination, and
in particular resented the tributes that they had to pay to the Romans.
Ever since the Romans conquered Pannonia and incorporated it into the
province of Illyricum, Romanization had come in more forcefully than
ever before. Taxes were levied, Roman laws were enforced and native
culture was being progressively replaced by Roman culture. However,
in spite of their hatred, they had kept their mouths shut and grudgingly
obeyed their orders.[36]

A point must be made here. During the early years of the Roman
Empire, the vast majority of the empire's male population were not
citizens. By law, all free-born males in Italy were citizens, and there
were smaller numbers of citizens scattered here and there throughout
the remainder of Rome's provinces.[37] This means that the overwhelming
majority of the men in the province of Illyricum were not citizens. As
such, they were not allowed to join the regular legions but could only
enlist in the auxiliary battalions. It would not be until 212 AD when
Emperor Caracalla extended citizenship to all free-born men throughout
the entire empire.

Because the legions' ranks could not be filled by the local native
Illyrians, all of Rome's legions that were stationed within Illyricum had
to be raised from elsewhere (mostly in Italy) and then transferred to
the western Balkans. The fact that there were no professional 'home-
grown' legions within Illyricum was a significant flaw both strategically
and logistically. When the Great Illyrian Revolt erupted and all of the
professional troops within Illyricum were gone, the Roman government
had to frantically divert troops from elsewhere in order to suppress the
revolt. Of course, transferring the troops away from their posts to deal
with the Illyrian rebels would open up huge gaps in Rome's defences
and set the stage for other enemies to take advantage of the borders'
weaknesses.

When all the Dalmatian warriors from the various tribes gathered
together at the designated assembly point (it isn't stated where), all of
them presumably heavily armed, they saw just how many of their own
number they were. According to Cassius Dio, it suddenly came into their

minds that with such large numbers as theirs, they could easily overpower the Romans:[38] 'Under the vehement urging of one Bato, a Desidiatian, at first a few revolted and defeated the Romans who came against them, and then the rest also rebelled in consequence of this success.'[39]

It isn't stated if Bato of the Daesidiate tribe was present at the assembly point and was in fact the primary instigator in urging his fellow warriors to attack and overpower the Romans, or if the attack happened first and after hearing about it afterwards he urged the remainder of his countrymen to join in the fighting.

What sort of a person was Bato? No Roman historian describes their enemies' leaders in great detail. They commonly wrote down only vague cursory descriptions of the commanders who fought against the legions. Vercingetorix the Gaul was described as possessing great energy. Arminius the German was described as handsome, brave and intelligent. Queen Boudicca of Britannia has a somewhat more precise description, though by modern literary standards it feels incomplete: tall with long red hair, and with a harsh intimidating voice. All three of these famous native resistance fighters against Roman conquest have monumental bronze statues erected to them in their honour. Yet these are largely the product of nineteenth-century Victorian Romanticist imagination and are not meant to be taken as exact accurate depictions of their appearance.

The Illyrian rebel leader, Bato the Daesidiate, is no exception to Roman brevity in describing their enemies' leaders. We have no idea how old Bato was at the time of the rebellion (despite numerous modern sources of questionable quality which state that he was born in 35 BC – why certain people arbitrarily selected this year for his birth confounds me – which, if true, would make him 41 years old during the outbreak), we have no information about what he looked like, we have no information about his family, and we have next to nothing about his life before the rebellion. All we have to go on is one passing phrase given by Paterculus which reads '*Cuius immensae multitudinis, parentis acerrimis ac peritissimis ducibus.*'[40] This translates as 'Which of an immense multitude, he was the most clever and most experienced leader who was given obedience.'

The Latin phrase is more complex than the translation suggests. The word *ducibus* is derived from the Latin word *dux*, meaning 'military leader' or 'warlord'. The word *parentis* is also worth looking at. True, it is often translated into English as 'parent', but the word itself does not mean 'one's mother or father'. Instead, the word means 'someone who is given obedience', since one's mother and father were expected to be obeyed. Army commanders were referred to as *parentis*, and so too was the emperor in all likelihood. Both of these words show that Bato was a leader of warriors, and a rather prominent one too since his men listened to him. Peter Swan hypothesizes that Bato might have been an auxiliary commander like the German warlord Arminius[41] and this is almost certain, but auxiliary unit leaders were sometimes Roman citizens. However, there is no mention in the records of Bato possessing citizenship. The word *acerrimis* is translated as 'sharpest', derived from the word *acer*, meaning 'sharp'. In this case, the word can be read both literally and figuratively. Bato, therefore, must have been intelligent, clever and very quick-witted. The Latin word *peritissimis* derives from *peritus*, which means 'to become skilled or experienced after undergoing tests and trials'. This implies that Bato already possessed military expertise and had combat experience before the rebellion broke out in 6 AD. Unfortunately, Paterculus does not give any further information to elaborate on his statement. We will likely never know what sort of martial exploits Bato undertook prior to the year 6 AD, nor will we be able to determine just how engaging and sagacious he was, nor will we know exactly how many warriors he commanded.

Cassius Dio stated that the Dalmatians 'defeated the Romans who came against them'.[42] This is almost certainly one of the small handfuls of soldiers that Governor Messallinus had left behind, presumably at the rendezvous point. No ancient source gives an exact date or a precise location for when this sudden outburst of violence occurred. As far as the question of 'when' is concerned, we know that the uprising began in the year 6 AD but can we refine the date a bit further? The most likely answer is very early spring, probably mid or late March. Throughout ancient and medieval times, military campaigns were almost always conducted in spring. By this time, the weather was getting warmer, the snows had thawed and the ice had melted, opening up travel routes that would later become invasion routes used by armies. The Romans were about to invade Bohemia, and they had to get all of their men in position when the spring thaws first came. Taking that into consideration, Tiberius and his subordinate commanders must have begun mobilizing for the campaign against the Marcomanni well beforehand to get everything ready for the scheduled invasion. The Dalmatian auxiliaries would have been called up in late February, maybe. It would have taken them a while to assemble and get things organized, not to mention march towards the rendezvous point.

That leads me to the question of 'where', which is a lot harder to answer. It's certain that the rendezvous point could not have been the city of Carnuntum because that's where Tiberius himself had gathered with all of the legions under his command. If the Illyrians revolted there, they would have been immediately slaughtered. I also highly doubt that the Illyrian auxiliaries were rendezvousing at the provincial capital of Salona and went on their rampage there. Salona was located on the coast of the Adriatic Sea. Such a location would be ideal for launching a *naval* expedition somewhere in the Mediterranean, but it's very unsuitable as a forward base for launching an *overland* invasion of a landlocked country. Salona was simply too far away. The Marcomanni territory lay far to the north, and it would make much more sense to have a northern city as the major assembly point for the amassing Roman troops rather than a city located far away from the front. Furthermore, the provincial capital was heavily fortified and well-garrisoned. Salona served as the headquarters for the 11th Legion *Claudia*. With such a prominent unit stationed nearby, it certainly would have made a great deal of news and commotion if it had been defeated, although the 11th Legion may have been withdrawn from the city to prepare for the upcoming war against the Marcomanni. Therefore, I don't believe that the provincial capital of Salona was the location for the beginning of the revolt.

The most likely rendezvous location, and by extension the location for the revolt's outbreak, was located somewhere in the northern part of the province, so that there would have been minimal marching time from the Illyricum border. All Cassius Dio says is that the Illyrians 'defeated the Romans who came against them'.[43] That's not much to go on. Does he mean Roman soldiers, or ordinary Roman civilians who took up arms to resist the Illyrian aggressors? It is almost certain that each town and city had its own garrison. Local militia might have been the first target, or it could have been other Roman soldiers, be they legionnaires or auxiliaries, who had also rendezvoused at that location. It's likely that this location, in order to accommodate or at least attempt to accommodate the large numbers of heavily-armed men that entered its gates, possessed some type of military base and a permanent garrison. In other words, this was a location where Roman troops were permanently stationed.

So what options do we have to choose from? Most of the northern cities and towns that you'll find on maps of Illyricum, such as Sabaria and Aquincum, which would appear to be ideal locations for gathering large numbers of troops together, were founded decades after the

Great Illyrian Revolt and therefore they cannot be the right places. I believe that the city of Segestica was the location where the Great Illyrian Revolt erupted. Granted, I have no direct proof whatsoever of this, but I do have some pieces of circumstantial evidence that make Segestica the most likely contender.

First, Segestica was located in the northern part of Illyricum. This would have made it an ideal place for Tiberius to establish his administrative headquarters prior to the invasion, and to collect his Illyrian auxiliaries together before moving off to join the rest of Tiberius' forces at Carnuntum. Granted, it was still a long hike from Segestica to Tiberius' base camp. In a straight line, Segestica and Carnuntum are approximately 180 miles from each other, but with the winding Roman roads, it would have been longer. Considering that Tiberius needed his auxiliaries to arrive at his base camp in a hurry, this sounds like a very long distance to walk and it is, but this may have been the only option. Second, Segestica would have been a good place for the Dalmatian recruits to gather. Remember, Governor Messallinus had ordered the *Dalmatians* of southern Illyria to assemble at a certain point, not the *Pannonians* of northern Illyria. The Dalmatians were, for the most part, a coastal people while the Pannonians dwelt in the deep interior, and Segestica was located on the border area between Dalmatian and Pannonian territories. It would not have been difficult for the Dalmatian auxiliaries to gather together at the northernmost Dalmatian city. Third, Segestica was a fairly large city, and as such would have been a good place for assembling large bodies of men and provisioning them. Fourth, Segestica had a large military garrison. A legionary fort was constructed nearby, though the actual number of men garrisoning the fort at the time was probably small. As I said earlier, no ancient historian would have been able to ignore the event of a legion being defeated, so the fort would not have had its full garrison during the outbreak. Fifth, when the time came for the Romans to take command of the situation and to fight off the Illyrian rebels, Tiberius made absolutely certain that he seized control of the city of Segestica first, even though there were many other places of equal importance that needed to be retaken as well. Therefore the city must have had great importance tactically and strategically, but maybe also symbolically. It would be a great blow to the rebels' morale if the centre of their uprising was taken by the Romans.

Is there any hard archaeological evidence within Segestica, modern-day Sissek, for this uprising? There have been many Roman artefacts found within the western Balkans that can be dated to the reign of Caesar Augustus or to the first half of the first century AD, including helmets, weapons, pieces of armour and coins. However, when it comes to specifically placing these artefacts within the context of the Great Illyrian Revolt, that is much more difficult. It is easier to place the dating of Roman artefacts in Germany, because we know of specific instances in which the Romans ventured into the land beyond the Rhine. Artefacts found there can be accurately dated because we can establish a connection between the artefact and a date of known Roman activity within Germany. It is far harder to do that in the land that is still called 'Yugoslavia' by a lot of people. The Romans occupied this region continuously for approximately 170 years prior to the revolt, and occupied it continuously for another 470 years afterwards. While broad date ranges can be applied to a Roman artefact found in the western Balkans, establishing a narrow and precise date is very difficult, and ascertaining whether or not a specific artefact definitely and unquestionably was involved in the Great Illyrian Revolt is practically impossible unless it bears an inscription saying something like 'This belonged to Gaius who fought against the Illyrian rebels.' Therefore, while it is likely that these artefacts *could* be connected with that dire three-year-long war, it is also equally likely that these artefacts date to either the years immediately before the war or immediately after it.[44]

So, based upon what has been discussed thus far, I believe that the opening phase of what would become known as the Great Illyrian Revolt occurred in the city of Segestica sometime during mid to late March of 6 AD. The historical records do not state if the rebels actually seized control of the city or if they just went on a rampage through it and killed all of those who came against them. However, I am inclined to think that the rebels under Bato the Daesidiate actually did, in fact, take possession of the city of Segestica. Remember, the Illyrians were not your standard common or garden barbarians. Others, like the Celts and the Germans, may have been satisfied with loot and pillage, and then moved on. Many Romans criticized the barbarian tribes for lacking strategic thinking, which is why they reacted so strongly when faced with the likes of someone like Arminius who had a knack for military strategy. The Illyrians were not like the Celts or Germans; they had professional armies with generals and strategists. They knew the value of seizing targets and holding on to them as opposed to just plundering them and moving on to the next destination. Furthermore, the fact that Tiberius would later seize control of Segestica must mean that the Illyrians had taken control of it first. So I say that the rebels not only attacked Segestica, but actually captured it and claimed it as their own, and also routed a Roman military unit that had been stationed in the area. Not bad for one day's bloody work. One wonders if they slaughtered the city's population, as was customary (actually, almost a requirement) in those days. The authors don't make any mention of it, but the rebels very well might have done it in order to better secure their hold on the city. If they had, it would have added all the more to the growing sense of crisis in the region.

The First Big Battle: The Battle of the Dravus River

As serious as the Dalmatian uprising was, it would have been considered a local problem, not a threat to the empire as a whole. It certainly would have immediately grabbed the attention of all the local town and city magistrates, who would have been desperate to take measures to protect their settlements, not to mention saving their own skins. The rebels would have been considered a problem, but the Roman government officials and army officers in the area may have felt that if it was dealt with promptly and swiftly, it could be managed. After all, there had been numerous uprisings and revolts in this region before and they had been dealt with. Why should this newest one be any different?

However, things moved much faster than the Romans had anticipated. After the mass uprising of the Dalmatian auxiliaries in Segestica (again, it's only a hypothesis, but since I think it's the most plausible, I'm running with it), eventually seizing possession of that city, and after they scored first blood against the Roman army by destroying a small unit stationed in the nearby fort, the rebellion spread. Others who heard about the outbreak of violence were other Illyrian tribes in the area, and one of them was a Pannonian tribe called the Breucians. Led by a man named Bato (no relation to the other Bato who was leading the rebellion in the south), they conducted a simultaneous uprising in the north. In fact, the historian Festus, who wrote a brief history of Rome in the fourth century AD, actually stylized Bato the Breucian as 'King of the Pannonians'.[45] Now things were getting very serious: another tribe had joined in the revolt and the hostility was spreading. If something wasn't done right away, the entire Balkans would be overrun.[46]

One can never be sure about the time span between various events recorded in ancient history unless it is specifically stated in the records.

I won't be so bold as to propose a certain number of days or weeks that may have passed between the Dalmatian and Pannonian uprisings. The Spartacus-like revolt within the city must have made big news, and word of it would have travelled fast. Some of those who heard about it would have been the people living in nearby villages, towns and cities, and I imagine that the magistrates had to use all of their power to prevent a state of panic from breaking out in the areas that they controlled.

One of the first people to respond to the growing threat was Aulus Caecina Severus, the governor of the province of Moesia. This province corresponds roughly to modern-day Bulgaria, with its capital city in Sardica (modern-day Sofia, Bulgaria). This region had been acquired by the Romans years earlier, but it had remained little more than a territory under military occupation until recently. Moesia was a frontier province, wedged between the vassal state of Thrace to the south and the wild and woolly barbarian north. To the north of Moesia were the Dacians and Sarmatians, who occasionally crossed the Danube River and raided into Roman territory, as attested by the Roman poet Ovid.[47]

We don't know that much about Aulus Caecina Severus before the events of 6 AD, but we certainly know about him afterwards. He was born to an eminent family from Tuscany and served as a *consul suffectus* (a man who was made a consul because the original Senatorial consul had died or had been removed) in the year 1 BC. By 6 AD or possibly earlier, he had been made governor of Moesia. He took part in the Great Illyrian Revolt of 6–9 AD, the mutiny of the legions in 14 AD, and in the war against Arminius and his German rebels following the Battle of Teutoburg. Tacitus says that he was married and had six children.[48]

It is not known how Governor Severus learned of the rebellion, nor is it known if he was aware of just how extensive it was by this point. If it is true that the rebellion erupted in the city of Segestica, how long would it have taken information to reach Severus in his headquarters in Sardica? Messengers must have been desperately sent out in all directions, informing people of the situation and asking them for help. It surely took several days for the information to reach Severus, although it may never be known precisely how long it must have taken for a dispatch rider to arrive at the governor's house in Sardica, telling him of the growing disaster.

With Tiberius being in command of a powerful force gathered to the north, one would suspect that he would have been one of the first to act. Yet every available record of this war shows that he acted slowly. In fact, he only committed himself after the rebellion was well under way and the rebels had already done a great deal of damage. Could it possibly be that word of the rebellion simply did not reach Tiberius until much later than expected? I don't buy that. He must have been concerned when the Illyrian recruits that he had been promised didn't arrive. In a straight line, the distance between Segestica and Tiberius' base at Carnuntum is about 180 miles. By contrast, the distance between Segestica and the Moesian provincial capital of Sardica is almost 400 miles, more than twice the distance to get to Tiberius and his legions. Given that Tiberius was closer and was in possession of a much larger military force at hand, why didn't Tiberius respond sooner? Why did another man, with a presumably smaller military force and who was located much further away, respond to the crisis in the Balkans first?

In order to come up with possible answers to these questions, we must enter the hazy realm of conjecture. As stated earlier, the Marcomanni tribe possessed a large professionally-trained and professionally-armed force. Rome had become very wary of the Marcomannis' power in recent years and began to fear it as a growing force in the region. Besides, Romans had always had a certain bogeyman-like phobia of the northern tribes.

Tiberius was also becoming more and more cautious as he grew older. Granted, he was never one of those mighty sword-wielding heroes of ancient lore, but he had sufficient boldness to enable him to be an adept military commander and had carried out several successful wars. However, Tiberius appeared to lose his taste for fighting as the years passed. The historian Suetonius, who wrote a biography of the general-turned-emperor-turned-tyrant, says that Tiberius' dash had faded, and that he was becoming much more private and introverted. Perhaps Tiberius was not far from hanging up his sword permanently. Due to his increasingly cautious nature, Tiberius might have been unwilling to tackle the Illyrian rebels, believing that his force, as large as it was, was still not yet big enough to resist the rebels, and so he waited for more troops before taking the offensive. After all, Saturninus was due to arrive in a short while with more men from Germania and Tiberius' strength would be significantly bolstered by these new arrivals. Another possibility is that Tiberius was afraid that if he turned his whole army around, the Marcomanni might launch an attack upon his men from behind. This would explain why he kept his troops in position at Carnuntum while the province of Illyricum went up in smoke. It wasn't until much later, when he presumably felt assured that King Maroboduus would not attack, that he finally agreed to mobilize his troops.

While Tiberius waited, the rebels were rampaging across Illyricum virtually unopposed. Since Tiberius had no intention of doing anything until he felt sure of his strength, someone else had to take the initiative. That certain someone was Aulus Severus, Governor of Moesia. Governor Severus knew that he had to do something immediately. He quickly cobbled together as many men as he could get his hands on and sent them westward. I imagine that the troops were marching flat out during that whole time. How long would it have taken Governor Severus to get his men together and march to meet the rebel threat? Under optimal conditions, on flat ground in good weather with no unforeseen problems or distractions, the average marching pace is twenty miles per day, but in an emergency you can easily push your men to march faster than that, even double-pace. It is probable that he would have picked up other small units of soldiers along the way, gathering them together as he marched.

However, keep in mind that this was in the mountainous landscape of south-eastern Europe. If it's true that the war erupted in the springtime before the spring campaign season began, then it would have been chilly. The temperatures for this region in the months of March and April are typically between 40–50 degrees Fahrenheit (5.5 to 10.5 degrees Celsius). Imagine being pushed double-time… in the mountains… in 45-degree weather. It isn't unusual for it to snow in March, and sometimes even in April, in that region. Typically, the area around modern-day Sofia gets five inches of snow in March. I haven't the faintest idea what the exact temperature or the exact weather was like at the time of Severus' march, but I'm sure that they were not the 'optimal conditions' that I mentioned beforehand.

Which units were likely to have accompanied Severus on his mission? There were three legions stationed in Moesia during this time: the 4th Legion *Scythica*, the 8th Legion *Augusta* and the 11th Legion.[49] I highly doubt that he would have brought in everyone; he needed someone to guard the home front. After all, Moesia was a frontier province and prone to frequent attacks by the horse-riding barbarians of Eastern Europe. There's no way whatsoever of knowing how many men Severus gathered under his command for this mission, and any numbers that I were to spit out would be entirely unsubstantiated guesswork. If I were in his shoes, I would think that it would be safe to take one-third of the soldiers with me, and certainly no more than half. So at most, I would have had one and a half legions marching with me. I would have likely had a sizeable force of auxiliaries accompanying me as well, and I might have even taken the rather desperate measure of press-ganging men from the local population to march with me, outfitted with whatever weapons and gear they could get their hands on.

While Governor Severus and his men raced to face the rebels, the rebels had pressed the offensive. The Breucians attacked the Roman town of Sirmium (modern-day Sremska Mitrovica, Serbia), located on the north side of the Sava River where it converged with the Bacuntius River (now known as the Bosut or the Bosset River). Sirmium was originally a settlement of the Amantini tribe, until the Romans seized control of this town during the Pannonian War of 12–9 BC. Sirmium was deep in the Illyrian interior, approximately 160 miles away from the hypothetical epicentre of the revolt in Segestica. The fact that the rebels were launching an attack here shows just how quickly the revolt had spread throughout the province. It is not recorded when the rebels' attack on Sirmium began, nor does it state how long the town was under siege, but the rebels were unable to break into the town. During the siege, Governor Severus and his troops arrived, like the cavalry coming to the rescue in so many Wild West movies.[50]

Governor Severus must have been informed of the attack on Sirmium while en route to meet the Illyrian rebels. Sirmium is located approximately 250 miles north-west of Sardica in a straight line. The actual route in reality was not a single straight line at all, so considerable mileage must have been added to the travelling distance and travelling time. According to a map that I saw of Roman roads in Eastern Europe, this was Severus' most likely route. After departing from the Moesian provincial capital city of Sardica (Sofia, Bulgaria), he and his men travelled north-west until they reached the city of Naissus (Niš, Serbia). From there, they continued marching north-west but at a slightly more northern angle, until they reached Margus, also called Horreum Margi (Ćuprija, Serbia). After this, they turned north until they reached the Danube River city of Viminacium (Kostolac, Serbia). Travelling westwards along the route of the Danube River, they reached Singidunum (Belgrade, Serbia). It was probably at this stage that they heard about the rebels' attack on Sirmium, if not before. After this stop, they marched east until they hit Sirmium. The angular route adds at least fifty miles onto the journey for a total trip of 300 miles. The undulating nature of the landscape adds more miles to that.

Normal marching pace for infantry has been traditionally set at twenty miles per day. In the mountains, in chilly weather, even if you were pushing your men hard, you'd be lucky to break past fifteen miles per day. If Severus and his men were marching at this rate, it would have taken him and his men fifteen whole days to reach Sirmium after departing from Sardica. The fact that it would have taken his men at least two weeks to complete their march means that they must have been prepared to set up camp for the night. At the end of each marching stage, a camp would have been laid out and tents arranged in rows for various men to sleep in. The following day, everything had to be hastily packed up and the army would move on.

So far, the only contact that the rebels had with the professional Roman army was a small unit that had been stationed near Segestica; that unit had been quickly overwhelmed and slaughtered. The next big fight between the Illyrian rebels and the Roman legions would come now, and it would take place at the Dravus River.

The Dravus River of antiquity is almost certainly the Drava River of modern times. It is one of the major tributaries of the Danube, and it forms a large section of the boundary between modern-day Croatia and Hungary. The Drava River is located forty or so miles to the north-west of Sirmium, so this must mean that the arrival of Severus and his men forced the rebels to quit their siege of Sirmium.

Although Cassius Dio states that Severus and his men arrived at the city of Sirmium while the siege was in progress, I would caution against believing this. If the Roman army *had* arrived on the scene while the Illyrians were still in the process of laying siege to the city, then a big battle would have taken place just beyond the city walls. Since there is no record of the Romans actually fighting the Illyrians on the spot, this means one of two things: the sudden sight of the Romans led the Illyrians to hastily abandon their siege and run for their lives, or the Illyrians were informed in advance of the Roman army's approach and decided to abandon the siege and withdraw to another location before Severus and his reinforcements arrived. Personally, I believe the second of these two options. If the Illyrians saw the Roman forces appear on the horizon, it would give them only a short time to pack up their necessary gear and get out of there. By the time they got under way, the Romans would have been very close behind. If the Romans pursued, it would have only taken them a short time to close the gap and Severus and his men would have attacked the retreating Illyrians long before they would have been able to reach the marshes of the Drava River. So this suggests that the second option is the correct one. While the Illyrians were laying siege to Sirmium, their intelligence network was made aware of the approach of a large Roman force from the south-east. Knowing that they couldn't handle the city garrison and Severus' reinforcements at the same time, the Illyrians decided to abandon the siege and fall back to a more defendable location where the odds were a bit more in their favour.

The rebels fled northwards and the Romans pursued, chasing them for at least two days before finally catching up to them. As to what happened next, it's a bit confusing. We have several options to choose from:

1. The terrain where the Drava River connects with the Danube River is very marshy and swampy. Today, much of this site is the property of the Kopački Rit Nature Preserve in north-eastern Croatia. This would have been a good place for an ambush or just to make a general stand, since the heavily-armoured Romans were not as likely to fight so well in marshy terrain. The Illyrians were not idiots. They knew that word of the attack on Sirmium would get out sooner or later and that the Romans would retaliate. In that eventuality, they needed to be prepared to meet the Roman threat, and so they made a 'plan B' to withdraw and fight the Romans in the swamps where they would have the advantage.
2. The Illyrians had their backs to the Drava River and couldn't retreat any further. Cornered and with nowhere to run, they turned around and attacked the Romans.
3. The Romans chased after the rebels until they finally caught up with them at the Drava River and attacked them there.
4. On the south side of the Drava River was the town of Mursa (modern-day Osijek, Croatia). This town had a bridge that spanned the river. Controlling this town, and especially controlling the bridge, was vital, so the battle had to be fought there.[51]

I wish to discount the fourth option right away. With the rebels possibly making their way towards the town of Mursa and its bridge, it may mean that this town had already fallen under rebel control. However, there's a problem. The ancient records state that the rebels and Romans fought at the river, not at the town of Mursa. In fact, the town of Mursa, which *did* possess strategic importance, is surprisingly never mentioned in any of the available sources on this rebellion. This must mean that the Illyrian rebels were not racing to get to the town of Mursa, but may have been trying to escape into the marshes that lay east of Mursa. The swamps would have been a formidable place to fight a battle and one that favoured a defensive position.

It appears that out of the four possible scenarios listed earlier, the first is the most likely. As Severus and his men continued to march to Sirmium's relief, the Illyrians began making plans as to how they could destroy the oncoming Roman forces and fell back to a more favourable position deep in the swamps that lay along the Drava River.

Time was pressing. If Severus allowed the Illyrians to escape, they could board boats and row up the river, getting further into the Illyrian interior. If the Illyrians were in the swamps, Severus had to fight them there before they could get a chance to flee. Mostly likely, the Illyrians had hunkered down in the marshes, wishing that Severus would be stubborn enough and stupid enough to fight them there, despite all of the self-evident hazards. They got their wish.

As an interesting annecdote, there is a village called Sarvaš, also called Szarvas, which is located just south of the Drava River within swampy terrain. It is possible that this village is named after Governor Severus, which would indicate a historical memory of the location of the battlefield. However, records of this village's existence only go as far back as the thirteenth century, which makes the idea that this place's name is somehow connected with the battle that Severus fought here back in the first century AD rather unlikely.

No records survive of the actual fighting along that river, but Cassius Dio provides two clues about the battle's aftermath: first, Governor Aulus Severus and his men defeated the rebels; second, the Romans suffered heavy casualties in the process.[52] The Battle of the Dravus River was a Pyrrhic victory for the Romans.

Rome asks the Thracians for Help

The Romans wanted to end the rebellion quickly, but they also realized that they couldn't afford such costly victories as the Battle of the Dravus River. With the rebels greatly outnumbering the legionnaires that were immediately at hand, the Romans knew that they needed to rapidly increase their numbers. So they sent word to their allies and vassal states, requesting aid. Among those who were contacted was Thrace.[53]

Ancient Thrace encompassed eastern Greece, most of southern Bulgaria and the European part of Turkey. The people who inhabited this land were called Thracians, and may have been related to the Dacians, their northern neighbours, who dwelt on the opposite side of the Danube River in modern Romania. The ancient Greeks knew the Thracians very well; the historian and geographer Herodotus, writing in the fifth century BC, discusses them in detail in his *Histories* when he was describing Shah Darius' invasion of Europe. The name almost assuredly descends from the name of one of their tribes, the Trausi; this name would have been ascribed to all of the Thracians by outsiders such as the Greeks. Herodotus states that the Thracians were divided into many tribes, with most following a similar culture.[54]

Thrace did not exist as a unified country until the mid to late 400s BC. For the preceding hundred years, the Odrysae tribe had been expanding their territory and gaining power. Then in the mid-fifth century BC, King Sitacles of the Odrysae proclaimed himself 'King of the Thracians' and proceeded to conquer all of his neighbours, and even fought against the kingdom of Macedon. However, the unified Thracian kingdom was short-lived. After Sitacles' grandson died in 358 BC, Thrace split apart once again. Thrace became a target for invasion and became incorporated into one dominion or another for many years. It wasn't until the reign of Caesar Augustus that Thrace was once again unified, not as an independent kingdom but as a vassal state, more commonly known as a client kingdom; Thrace had its own laws, government and ruler, but it still had to acknowledge Rome as its overlord. King Rhoemetalces I, the son of Chief Cotys of the Astae tribe, was the first ruler of this new united Thracian kingdom. King Rhoemetalces I reigned from 11 BC to 12 AD. His capital city was located at Bizye (Vize), which lay exactly halfway between Byzantium and Hadrianopolis. It was the home of an important Thracian holy site and at least one royal tomb consisting of a burial mound containing gold, silver and bronze objects. He had a brother named Rhascyporis, who would fight alongside him during the Great Illyrian Revolt. Thrace would become a Roman province in 46 AD during the reign of Emperor Claudius.[55]

By the time of Caesar Augustus, the Thracians had been very heavily Hellenized. Thracian coins had inscriptions on them in Greek. King Rhoemetalces, as he is called in the Roman sources, is listed as *Basileos Roimhtalkou* on Thracian coins. His actual name, based upon a combination of Greek and Roman variations of it, might have sounded like 'Rowim-hetalkos'. Rhoemetalces' wife was Queen Pythodoris, who we only know about due to her image on Thracian coins. Many of these coins reflected the Thracian kingdom's relationship with Rome. On one side of the coins is a picture of Rhoemetalces' profile beside that of his wife, while on the opposite side is a profile portrait of Caesar Augustus, with the accompanying inscription *Kaisaros Sebastou*.[56]

Blood, Fire and Destruction

Bato the Breucian and his Pannonian warriors had been defeated by the Romans (just barely) at the Battle of the Dravus River. Meanwhile, further to the south, Bato the Daesidiate led his forces in an attack on Salona, the capital city of the province of Illyricum. I'm certain that this attack had both strategic and symbolic importance. However, Bato the Daesidiate had just as much luck taking Salona as his counterpart had in taking Sirmium. Marcus Messallinus, the governor of Illyricum, was not in the capital city during the attack; he had already gone north to meet up with Tiberius and had taken most of the soldiers in the area with him. The lack of military protection helped the Illyrian rebels gain control of the countryside with relative ease.[57]

However, gaining control of the fortified city proved to be much harder. During the attack on Salona, Bato was badly wounded when he was struck by a sling stone, which prevented him from taking part in the attack and in fact removed him from command. Getting struck by an ancient slingshot was not a minor injury, as the story of David and Goliath well attests. Football-shaped lead missiles the size of a large marble would be flung out with the speed and impact force of a bullet. An expert slinger might be able to hit a human-sized target at a range of 130 yards.[58] With their leader down and with the city too formidable to take, the Dalmatians were forced to abandon their assault on the city.[59]

Even though Bato the Daesidiate was recovering in his bed, he ordered his subordinates to lay waste to all Roman settlements along the Adriatic coast. Cassius Dio states that the Dalmatian rebels 'wrought havoc along the whole sea-coast as far as [the city of] Apollonia'.[60] Cassius Dio also says that after the Dalmatians were defeated at Salona, they fought another battle against the Romans at an unnamed location and this time the Dalmatians were victorious.[61] Gaius Paterculus gives a more detailed description of this, saying 'A considerable detachment of veterans, stationed in the region which was most remote from the commander, was exterminated to a man.'[62] It isn't surprising that Roman authors go into detail on Rome's victories but give few details on Rome's failures. Neither Paterculus nor Cassius Dio nor any other ancient source states where or when this battle took place, how many troops were involved or who the Roman commander was.

With Severus' men now in no position to resist the Illyrians after the mauling that they had received at the Dravus River, there was nothing to stop the rebels. They grew exponentially in strength and cut a swathe of destruction throughout the land wherever they passed. Paterculus gives some statistics on the rebels' military strength during this time. He says that the Illyrian rebels totalled a jaw-dropping 800,000 in number, including 200,000 infantrymen trained in Roman military tactics as well as 9,000 cavalry. Such large numbers are absurd exaggerations. The idea of 200,000 professional Illyrian infantry troops, presumably auxiliaries, is utterly ridiculous and laughable, and owes more to Roman attempts to convey fear and terror in the minds of their readers concerning the rebel threat rather than to provide accurate descriptions of events. Danijel Dzino hypothesizes that the total rebel strength might have been only one-tenth to one-eighth of this high number, with the rebels numbering, at most, 100,000 participants.[63] The rebels divided their force into three parts: one-third of their force would invade Italy; a second would invade the province of Macedonia; and a third would stay behind and protect the rebellious provinces from attack.[64] I'm certain that the attack on Macedonia had great symbolic significance for the Illyrians since the ancient kingdom of Macedon had been one of the Illyrian tribes' traditional enemies for centuries.

The rebels achieved a great deal of success in the initial stages of the revolt. Paterculus states:

> No nation ever displayed such swiftness in following up with war its own plans for war, and in putting its resolves into execution. Roman citizens were overpowered, traders were massacred, a considerable detachment of veterans, stationed in the region which was most remote from the commander, was exterminated to a man, [the entire province of] Macedonia was seized by armed forces, everywhere was wholesale devastation by fire and sword. Moreover, such a panic did this war inspire that even the courage of Caesar Augustus, rendered steady and firm by experience in so many wars, was shaken with fear.[65]

Rome Responds

The war had not gone well for the Romans. In the opening stages of the revolt, the city of Segestica had been captured and Roman soldiers stationed in the area had been defeated. The Romans managed to score a victory against the Illyrians at the Battle of the Dravus River, but they suffered high casualties in the process. After a failed attack on Salona, the Illyrians spread out, destroying settlements and slaughtering the population. Another military unit stationed in the southern part of the province of Illyricum was completely exterminated. Finally, the rebels had managed to seize control of the whole province of Macedonia, and were preparing to launch an invasion of Italy.

The reality was plain to everyone: the Romans were losing.

In Rome, the situation in the western Balkans was no longer regarded as a crisis, it was now a catastrophe! The people living in the Eternal City were especially apprehensive about an Illyrian invasion of Italy. They imagined a massive horde of heavily-armed and professionally trained Illyrian soldiers descending down the peninsula and burning Rome to the ground. Visions of Hannibal must have abounded in their thoughts and fears. In fact, the historian Suetonius says that the Great Illyrian Revolt was the greatest threat to Italy since the wars with Carthage.[66] Such a claim is in all likelihood an exaggeration, and considering how formidable the Carthaginians were in their time, I'm certain that the Illyrians would have been greatly flattered if they had heard of them compared in such a way. However, regardless of historical parallels, there was no denying that the rebellion in the Balkans posed a significant threat in three ways.

First, Romans had been living in the region of Illyria for more than two hundred years. Many towns and cities had been established in that region, with populations of some settlements numbering in the thousands. All of these settlements and the people living within them were now targets. Lives were at stake. Indeed, according to Paterculus, the rebels were already killing every Roman that they saw.[67] The Illyrians weren't interested in taking prisoners this time, they wanted blood.

Second, there was the risk that the rebels would control the road networks that led in and out of Illyria. If they did so, they could easily send their hordes of warriors north-west around the northernmost tip of the Adriatic Sea and invade Italy. Moreover, they could spread their warriors along many of these roads, which would result in a speedy and blood-soaked takeover of the region, not just the province of Illyricum, but the neighbouring provinces as well. Bato the Daesidiate had already ordered his Dalmatian warriors to do this. In accordance with his command, they destroyed countless settlements and slaughtered countless people, and had even taken control of the entire province of Macedonia. I'm sure some Romans of Hellenic descent must have envisioned large parties of these rebels continuing their march southwards into Greece and burning Athens to the ground as the Persians had done nearly five centuries earlier.

Third, the rebellion could lead to severe economic repercussions. For centuries, the Illyrians had dominated the Adriatic Sea, dictating trade policy. What if such a thing happened again? Many of the cities in the Roman province of Illyricum were located on important trade routes and contained a great deal of wealth. If the rebels managed to permanently gain control of the region, the overland trade routes connecting Western and Eastern Europe would be shut down, and if the Illyrians managed to regain control of the sea, that made matters all the worse. Trans-Adriatic trade would either be severely limited or come completely to a halt, especially if the old threat of fleets of Illyrian pirates once again raised its fearsome head.

To prevent such calamities from happening, the empire needed to act quickly. If the Romans didn't do something substantial *right now* to combat the rebel threat, then the rebels would assuredly win the war. Caesar Augustus made a speech in the Senate House stating firmly and desperately that unless immediate measures were taken, the rebels would appear within sight of the Eternal City within just ten days. The government immediately organized a draft. From all over the empire, the retired veterans were called back to active duty. The rich were ordered to furnish as many freemen as they could to serve in the army. Knights and senators were ordered to muster themselves for battle. Legions that were posted in other provinces were dispatched to fight in the Balkans.[68]

Yet who would lead this massive host of armed men? The Senate stated that there was only one man who was capable enough to deal with this crisis: the famous war hero Tiberius Claudius Nero. Augustus agreed, and he made his stepson the overall commander of the Roman forces sent to crush the revolt.[69]

Tiberius Claudius Nero was still on the northern border preparing his army to invade and conquer the Marcomanni kingdom. He must have been worried when the Illyrian recruits that he had been promised didn't arrive. Then he was told what had happened. Yet for weeks and possibly months, Tiberius did *absolutely nothing* while who knows how many towns and villages in the Balkans were raided and destroyed, and who knows how many thousands of people had been killed. It was only when a threat to Italy, to the Roman heartland, had manifested itself that he realized that procrastination is a fatal vice in war. Paterculus states: 'It did not seem to Tiberius a safe course to keep his army buried in the interior of the country and thus leave Italy unprotected from an enemy so near at hand.'[70] Paterculus' choice of words here is very interesting. He specifically states that Tiberius only got his men moving when Italy herself was threatened with attack. This means that he was either minimally concerned or completely unconcerned with how other areas of the empire handled the Illyrian uprising.

If Tiberius had immediately turned his whole army around, swung southwards and attacked the Illyrians when the rebellion first broke out, he might have been able to break the revolt within a few months. Now the Illyrian rebel force, which at first had been small, had mushroomed beyond imagining and had grown in power. Tiberius' delay and caution had proved extremely costly. He knew that if he didn't do something right now, the Eternal City itself might be the next place to be burned to the ground. At last, he called his army to march. He ordered his entire army to abandon its campaign against the Marcomanni – they could always fight against the Germans some other time – and instead turned southwards to fight the Illyrian rebels. Marcus Messallinus, the governor of Illyricum, had joined up with Tiberius, taking most of the Roman troops that had been stationed in Illyricum with him. That decision had left Illyricum virtually defenceless and now the Romans were paying for that mistake. Now Tiberius ordered Messallinus to go back with his men and retake what had been lost. Messallinus and his men would be acting as a vanguard, while Tiberius brought up the remainder of the army. Under his command, Messallinus only had the soldiers of the 20th Legion, which at that time was only at half-strength, about 2,500 men. Perhaps Tiberius felt that such a force would be of sufficient size to deal with any problems that occurred. In theory, it was large enough to hold its position in the event of a heavy attack, holding long enough for Tiberius and the rest to arrive. Tiberius was taking a calculated risk. His problem was that he was not fully aware of just how serious the rebel threat was.[71]

Bato the Daesidiate was still lying in bed, still recovering from the injury he had received during the failed attack on the city of Salona.

Then he was informed that a large Roman army was approaching from the north-west. Tiberius was coming. Although he was not yet fully recovered from his wound, Bato resolved to rise from his bed and face the Romans in battle.[72]

There are two records of the fight that occurred soon afterwards. Paterculus states that both sides fought in one single large battle and that the Romans emerged victorious. Cassius Dio, writing nearly two centuries later, states that Bato and his Dalmatian warriors fought against Messallinus in two engagements: in the first fight the rebels defeated the Romans, but later the Romans ambushed the Dalmatians, and Bato and his warriors were forced to retreat.[73]

Paterculus provides some details about the ensuing battle. According to his version of the events, Messallinus led his small force of 2,500 men forward and was sucked into a trap. He was immediately surrounded by a much larger rebel army. Cut off from any help, he ordered his troops to take the offensive. Despite being massively outnumbered by about eight to one, Messallinus won a great victory, forcing 20,000 rebels to flee for their lives. For this impressive victory, he was awarded with the ornaments of a triumph in lieu of an actual triumphal parade.[74]

The fact that the Romans were surrounded probably contributed to their ferocity. Armies that are completely cut off will fight ferociously to escape or even just to survive. A good general knows that enemy armies will fight all the harder if they are surrounded. Knowing that they will either be massacred or taken prisoner, the enemy forces will fight with great tenacity to survive. Therefore a good general will always leave a pathway of escape, no matter how small, for the enemy force. Knowing that they have an opportunity to get out, the smaller enemy force will usually abandon its position and flee rather than fight to the last man. Once the enemy side panics and routs, then the general can send out his cavalry in pursuit and hack them down while they run. It seems that Bato did not do this, and we will never know his reasons. Perhaps Bato intended to overwhelm the Romans through sheer brute force. If that was his plan, he failed.

Scoring a great victory despite being immensely outnumbered by enemy forces is nothing new in Roman history. As an example, Gaius Julius Caesar, commanding an army numbering 40,000 men, defeated a massive Gallic horde numbering 250,000 at Alesia. Still, it must be said that Caesar's men were fighting in a well-prepared defensive position, and that his men were professional heavily-armed and heavily-armoured legionnaires fighting against a massive horde of local tribesmen, many of whom did not have body armour and were not drilled in military tactics. Marcus Messallinus did not have such tactical advantages. The rebels that his small force fought against were just as well-armed, well-armoured, well-equipped and well-trained as his own men. By the book, Bato's rebels should have scored an easy victory but they didn't; in fact, they were forced to retreat. How could Messallinus have possibly beaten off such odds? In my opinion, the Romans just 'wanted it' more. I admit that it isn't much of an explanation, but you'd be surprised at what people are capable of when they are motivated hard enough, and there is no greater motivation than facing the prospect of death.

The Rebel Alliance

Although all of Illyricum was in uprising, the revolt was not a united one. There were in fact two simultaneous uprisings within the same region, one led by the Pannonians and one led by the Dalmatians. In order for the revolt to be a success, the two separate rebel forces would have to unite. After his embarrassing defeat by Governor Messallinus, Bato the Daesidiate decided that he should meet with Bato the Breucian and discuss the possibility of combining their forces to achieve a common goal. Although no record is given as to the location or details of this meeting, the desired objective was attained: the two uprisings were now a single united revolt aimed at destroying the Roman presence in Illyricum forever.[75]

This new alliance would soon be put to the test, because the Romans were assembling a massive force to crush the revolt. Tiberius had already sent Governor Marcus Messallinus forward with a small vanguard of soldiers to clear the path; Messallinus and his undersized 20th Legion had accomplished that goal. Tiberius himself was soon to follow with an absolutely massive army, but it would still take some time for his men to reach the border.[76]

Rome's allies were also lending contingents of native warriors to aid the Roman forces. One of them was King Rhoemetalces of Thrace, one of Rome's vassals. Earlier, the Thracian king had been contacted with regard to sending aid. Rhoemetalces accepted (as Rome's vassal, he really didn't have any choice in the matter), and marched off to battle with a large number of cavalry. The Thracians had a reputation for fine horsemanship, and their cavalry would certainly be put to good use.[77]

In addition to Tiberius' army approaching from the north near the German border, a second large Roman force was about to invade Illyricum, this time by sea, although it isn't stated from where these soldiers were coming. This force was led by the two Senatorial consuls: Aulus Severus (the governor of Moesia) and Marcus Plautius Silvanus. The army consisted of five legions (a maximum of 24,000 men on paper, although probably much less than that) and an unknown number of auxiliary cohorts.[78] One of the units that was brought in from elsewhere was the 7th Legion *Claudia*, which had previously been posted in Galatia ever since Augustus had come to power. Now it was being sent westwards to fight in the Balkans.[79]

It is clear that the Roman strategy was a pincer movement. Tiberius would invade Illyricum by land, attacking from the north. The second Roman army, commanded by Severus and Silvanus, would launch an amphibious operation, presumably attacking from the south and landing their troops on the rebel coast. According to this plan, the rebels would be trapped in the middle, smashed by two large Roman armies advancing upon them from the front and the rear simultaneously. It seemed like a good plan.

However, as any veteran or student of military studies knows, something always goes wrong. The timing of the operation was more than a little off; the two Roman attacks were not synchronized to attack on the same day. The amphibious army of Severus and Silvanus landed much sooner than expected, and Tiberius' forces did not get under way until well after the seaborne troops had already landed on the beach. However, I should state that having coordinated attacks, especially ones occurring hundreds of miles apart, was almost impossible until radios were used on the battlefield.

When word arrived that Roman troops had landed on the coast and were advancing inland, the Illyrians appear to have been caught off guard. They had been preparing to repel Tiberius' attack from the north and they were confident that no new Roman troops would advance upon them from the west, but they were not expecting an attack across the Adriatic Sea. A group of rebels hurriedly took a stand at the nearest location that they thought would be defendable and would give them slightly better odds against the oncoming troops: a hill called Mount Alma.[80]

The Battle of Mount Alma

Aulus Severus and his seaborne army had already landed on Illyricum's shores and were advancing into the interior. He sent King Rhoemetalces and his Thracian cavalry ahead of the Roman force as a vanguard, presumably to scout the area. Eventually, the Thracians made contact with the Illyrian rebels stationed atop Mount Alma and prepared for battle.

Unfortunately, you won't find Mount Alma listed on any modern map. The name means 'fertile/fruitful mountain'. Some historians and archaeologists say that the Mount Alma of ancient times is called Fruška Gora today,[81] and with good reason. Despite its name, Mount Alma was not a mountain, but was instead a low grassy hill without any of the fortifications common to Illyrian hilltop forts.

Considering that no ancient author or geographer describes this location in detail, how can we possibly know what Mount Alma looked like? My first reason for making my claims comes from the historic records, or rather the lack of them. Cassius Dio is our only source for this battle and he never mentions Mount Alma as having any defensive fortifications whatsoever, unlike other mountains in Illyria. Many times, Greek and Roman writers explicitly testify when the Roman army was forced to lay siege to or assault an Illyrian fortified settlement, and they often describe the fortifications in detail. The lack of any description of walls, towers, stockades, trenches or indeed any defensive fortification of any sort leads me to think that Mount Alma was unfortified.

My second reason for surmising what Mount Alma looked like comes from those who were involved in the upcoming battle itself. According to Cassius Dio, the force that attacked the Illyrians atop Mount Alma was made up entirely of cavalry. You *cannot* use cavalry to storm a fortified defensive position. True, the horsemen could have dismounted and fought on foot, but King Rhoemetalces and his Thracians were *light* cavalry, who were either lightly armoured or completely unarmoured, and armed primarily with javelins. Such troops rely on mobility and quick manoeuvres, showering their enemies with missiles from a distance and using the speed of their horses to escape when the enemy attacks. If you were to take such troops off their mounts and have them fight on foot, they would, quite frankly, be sitting ducks, especially if they have to fight uphill.

In addition to being unfortified, Mount Alma wasn't steep or rocky either. It is specifically stated that cavalry were the only attacking forces involved in this battle – no infantry at all – and they were almost certainly javelin cavalry. Cavalry cannot advance up steep rocky terrain. If the land was rocky and steep, the Thracians would have dismounted, but if they did that they would have been slaughtered. Mount Alma, therefore, could not have been one of those impressive rocky crags that Roman writers talk about with a castle perched atop its pinnacle. It was just a big grassy hill, similar to the one located on the golf course a few miles away from my house.

The site that is regarded by many as the same as Mount Alma, Fruška Gora, has many of the qualities that we are looking for. Although large parts of it are now overgrown with small trees and shrubs, these are 'secondary growth' plants, and I dare say that the hill would have been much more open and grassy. It isn't unusual to see flocks of sheep along its slopes. The Latin name, 'fruitful or fertile mountain', hints that the hill may have been used as a sheep pasture or possibly for the production of wine in ancient times.

Mount Alma may not have been fortified, steep or rocky (which certainly would have been advantageous), but perhaps the Illyrians making their stand atop it were comforted to a slight degree by the knowledge that their enemies would have to advance *uphill*. When fighting in elevated terrain, like on a hill or mountain, the army stationed on the top will almost always be at an advantage, especially in pre-gunpowder warfare when fighting is mostly conducted hand-to-hand. The defending force stationed atop the hill has the ability to dig in, if it chooses. They do not need to wear themselves out by marching and as such can be well-rested, a crucial advantage in an age when fighting relied primarily upon one's physical strength. If the defending force has archers, the increase in elevation will enable the archers to shoot at their intended targets from longer distances. By contrast, the attacking force is at a distinct disadvantage. They will be forced to advance uphill, which will make the troops tired even before they make contact with the enemy soldiers.

A parallel to the Battle of Mount Alma could be the Battle of Hastings in 1066. Here, in the opening stages of the battle, Norman cavalry needed to launch an uphill assault to attack a defensive infantry position. The hill in question was not particularly steep and it was grassy, not rocky. Yes, advancing up it would have been slightly more difficult for horses, but not that much more.

The Thracians had arrived on the scene. One would think that they would send word back to Severus to quickly bring up the rest of his army so that they could overwhelm the position through force of numbers. However, King Rhoemetalces didn't do this. Instead, he did something that many military commanders today would find foolish and reckless: he ordered his light cavalry to sweep up the hill and attack the Illyrians alone without waiting for the rest of the army to arrive.[82]

What chance did this unit of Thracian cavalry have against the Illyrian defenders? What kind of soldiers were they? The Thracians were regarded by the Greeks and Romans as being thoroughly barbaric. Tacitus states that the Thracians were savage people living like wild animals up in the mountains and were completely undisciplined, and then states that they only obeyed their chiefs when they chose to do so. This shows that the Thracians practised what is known to anthropologists as 'bottom-up' leadership, in which the ordinary people dictated to the leader what had to be done and if the leader asked the people to do something that the people didn't want to do, then the people would simply not follow that chief any more. They chose their war-leaders, and would flatly refuse to fight under the command of anyone of whom they personally did not approve.

Strabo and Polyaenus write of how the Thracians would break truces:

> Ephorus says that the Thracians, after making a treaty with the Boeotians, attacked them by night when they, thinking that peace had been made, were encamping rather carelessly; and when the Boeotians frustrated the Thracians, at the same time making the charge that they were breaking the treaty, the Thracians asserted that they had not broken it, for the treaty said 'by day,' whereas they had made the attack by night; whence arose the proverb, 'Thracian pretence'.[83]

> The Thracians fought against the Boeotians by lake [sic] Copais, and were defeated; then they retreated to Helicon, and made a truce with the Boeotians for a certain number of days, to give time for agreeing the terms of peace. The Boeotians, who were confident because of their recent victory and the truce that followed it, celebrated a sacrifice in honour of Athene Itonia. But at night while they still were intent on the ceremony, and engaged in festivities, the Thracians armed, and attacked them; they cut many of them to pieces, and took a great number

prisoners. When the Boeotians afterwards charged them with a breach of the truce, the Thracians replied that the terms of the truce expressed a certain number of days, but said nothing concerning the nights.[84]

The Greek military historian Polyaenus describes a battle between the Thracians and the Greeks led by Clearchus during the Persian Wars. After encamping in the mountains, the Greek leader expected that the Thracians would attack his position during the night, which shows that night attacks by the Thracians were fairly common; later on, Polyaenus writes that the Greek soldiers were always afraid of night attacks. Clearchus ordered his men not to take off their armour and posted watch sentries in shifts throughout the night. During the night, while most of the soldiers were asleep, in order to test his own men's readiness for battle, he secretly selected a few of his men, took up position beyond the encampment and then began banging their weapons together. Polyaenus says that the Thracians used to do this in order to intimidate their enemies. Believing that these men were actually Thracians, the Greek soldiers immediately drew themselves up in battle formation. However, Clearchus did not have time to congratulate his men on how well prepared they were, because at that moment the Thracians really did attack! They had been stealthily creeping towards the Greeks' camp, and had expected to take the Greeks completely by surprise when they were startled by the sudden noise. The Thracians were slaughtered.[85]

The Thracians, especially the eastern tribes, had been heavily influenced by the steppe nomads of central Asia which had settled in the lands north of the Black Sea, including the Scythians and Sarmatians. The warriors of these tribes were primarily cavalrymen, mostly armed with bows and arrows. The poet Ovid states that the warriors of the Getae tribe who lived around the frontier town of Tomis would ride their horses through the streets. All of them carried a quiver full of arrows, all of which had their heads dipped in a poisonous concoction of snake venom, human blood and human excrement. The arrowheads had a ring of small thorns around their base to shred the flesh as they entered and which would also make the arrowhead difficult to extract (likely ripping the flesh as it did so, making it almost impossible to cleanly sew up and as such would likely not heal) and possibly even break off inside the body, causing great bleeding and eventually death.[86]

Thracian warriors fought both on foot and from horseback, and were equally good at both. The most common weapon used by Thracian warriors, either infantry or cavalry, was the javelin. The ancient Greeks called Thracian infantry javelineers *peltasts*. The name comes from the type of shield that these men used: a crescent-shaped shield made of wicker and covered with leather called a *pelte*. The English verb 'to pelt' means to hit someone or something by throwing something at him/her, which may be derived from the *peltast* javelin-throwers that the ancient Greeks fought against.[87]

The Thracians were famous for the high quality of their cavalry. Thracian horses were bred for speed. Thracians didn't like wearing body armour, preferring to be light and mobile rather than be protected but encumbered under so much weight. The only heavy troops, those that actually wore armour, were the members of the king's bodyguard.[88] Eastern Thracians, like the Getae tribe, preferred to fight as cavalry archers, much like their Scythian and Sarmatian neighbours. Ovid, residing in Tomis, had first-hand experience of dealing with these people: he saw them, he fought them and was even shot at by them, if we believe his verses.

It is unknown what the strengths of both sides were as they gazed at each other across the grassy slope of Mount Alma. The Thracian cavalry must have been sufficiently numerous to feel bold enough to attack the Illyrian position alone without any additional aid from Severus' army. I dare say that the lure of plunder and personal glory played some part in King Rhoemetalces' decision as well. Therefore the number of men involved on both sides may have been equal or nearly equal.

The signal was raised, the command was given and the Thracians spurred their horses up the slope of Mount Alma. We can imagine the Thracian cavalry charging up the hill, perhaps only a handful of them at a time, hurling their javelins at the Illyrian defenders and then looping around to the rear, then turning back for another charge and so on. These hit-and-run tactics were just what the Thracian cavalry were best at. Behind this initial handful of horsemen was another group, who would hurl their javelins and then turn away. Behind them was another group, and behind them, another. In this way they quickly developed a wheel of cavalry spitting out javelins every time the wheel turned to face the Illyrian ranks, like a giant conveyor belt of missiles. The Thracians overwhelmed the rebel position atop Mount Alma, and the Illyrians were either slaughtered or forced to flee.[89]

The Romans Fight their Way Inland

In a year marred by defeats and costly casualty-heavy wins, the Thracians' easy victory at Mount Alma was a much-needed morale booster for the Roman side. Considering that King Rhoemetalces ordered his vanguard light cavalry to attack an enemy defensive position without informing the remainder of the Roman force to come forward to assist him, things could have gone very badly for the Thracians that day. Tactically, ordering his light horsemen forward without infantry support was risky at best and foolish at worst. As it happened, King Rhoemetalces was lucky.

After the battle was won, the Thracians either remained in position and waited for the rest of the Roman army under the consuls Severus and Silvanus to catch up to them, or else they back-tracked and rejoined the rest of the Roman force that was still in the process of making its way forward. The first option is more likely. As the Americans who fought in Vietnam discovered, the second that you abandon a strategic position, the enemy moves back in. Why fight to dislodge the Illyrian rebels from the slope of Mount Alma, only to withdraw and give the enemy the option of reoccupying the hill? So it is almost certain that the majority of the Thracian force remained at Mount Alma, resting and regaining their energy, and possibly using the hill as a lookout position, while a few riders were sent back to inform Severus and Silvanus of what had just happened.

Severus and Silvanus, the two commanders of the Roman amphibious force, were informed that the Thracians who had been sent forward from the main army had easily defeated a small rebel force atop Mount Alma. Even so, while the small party of rebels atop Mount Alma had been turned back, the majority of rebel forces were still assembling to take on the advancing Romans. However, the victory at Mount Alma had made the Roman commanders confident, so confident that they made a serious blunder: they advanced without first sending out scouts to locate the rest of the enemy's forces.[90]

This was the second time that this army made a grave tactical mistake. Sending out scouting patrols was standard practice, and the fact that the two commanders didn't do so shows that they were either incompetent or were so confident of victory that they didn't bother to take even basic precautions. In Paterculus' account, he states 'the generals... had allowed themselves to come into contact with the enemy before they had learned through their scouts where the enemy was.'[91] Paterculus also states that the Thracian cavalry as well as the Thracian king himself were with the Romans when they came under attack.[92] What we can infer from Paterculus' statement is this. Rather than keeping the cavalry out in front to screen the army's approach and to spot any enemy forces that may be up ahead, the cavalry rejoined the Romans and they marched onwards as a single massive column. Big mistake. Lacking proper intelligence of enemy movements, the two consuls were unaware that a large Illyrian rebel force was gathering together to launch a mass attack against the oncoming Romans. When the Romans finally made contact with the bulk of the rebel force, they were caught completely by surprise. Not only that, but the rebels were far more numerous than the commanders had assumed, so numerous in fact that they completely surrounded the entire Roman force.[93]

Paterculus states that the force commanded by Severus and Silvanus consisted of five legions, an unknown number of auxiliary cohorts and an unknown number of Thracian cavalry. At full strength, that would be a minimum of 25,000 men. In order for the Illyrian rebels to surround this force, their number would have to be just as large, if not larger. With the numbers involved on both sides, the battle was a fearsome one. Regrettably, none of the ancient sources state exactly where this monumental clash took place, nor is the terrain described in any way, nor how far away this battle's location was from Mount Alma either in terms of miles' or days' travels. All that being said, it unfortunately seems unlikely that its location will ever be discovered. Yet although the battle's location and the landscape's topography are not described, Paterculus does give some information about how the fighting progressed. At first, the battle seemed in favour of the rebels: the Illyrians forced the valued Thracian cavalry to retreat, including the Thracian king's elite royal guard, as well as *all* of the cohorts of Roman auxiliaries. After the Thracians and the Roman auxiliaries fled, the rebels focused their full power on the legions. The battle was going badly for the Romans. By now, some of the legionary cohort commanders had been killed. The camp commandant and other cohort commanders had been cut off and were desperately fighting for their lives. Some of the centurions had been wounded and other centurions who had been in the front ranks had been killed. Defeat seemed inevitable, but the Roman legions themselves held firm and would not let the same panic that had overpowered their auxiliaries and allies overcome them as well. Paterculus states proudly: 'The legions, shouting encouragement to each other, fell upon the enemy, and not content with sustaining their onslaught, broke through their line and wrested a victory from a desperate plight.'[94]

Throughout history, there are many examples of battles in which one side seems to be winning at first, but the opposing side manages to regain the initiative and emerges victorious. One parallel that immediately comes to my mind is the Battle of Verneuil, fought in 1422 during the Hundred Years' War, where an English army, on the brink of defeat, took the offensive and smashed a much larger combined French and Italian army.[95]

I also believe that the Illyrians made a serious mistake in the opening stages of this unnamed battle: they completely surrounded their opponents. As I stated in an earlier section, one should *never* entirely surround one's enemy, because your enemy will know that his fate is sealed and he will fight all the harder to survive. Regardless of how much the odds are in your favour, it would be best to allow your enemy an escape route for no other reason than to provide them with the illusion of safety and escape, while your reserves wait patiently further off and then charge forward to slaughter your enemies while they frantically try in vain to run. Perhaps the Illyrians wished to slaughter the entire Roman force in one battle, mimicking the great feats of Alexander or Hannibal and they probably could have, if they hadn't surrounded their opponents. Why would the rebels make the same mistake twice? If surrounding a smaller Roman force didn't work when attacking Governor Marcus Messallinus, then why would it work now? It appears that the rebels were trying to overwhelm the Romans by sheer force of numbers and giving little thought to strategy. This, of course, flies in the face of the idea that the Illyrians were adept battlefield tacticians, employing cunning and strategy to win their fights against their traditional enemies of Greece, Macedon and Rome.

One idea that may explain why the Illyrians kept blundering when they shouldn't have is the notion that while Bato was experienced and battle-savvy, his subordinate commanders and warriors were not. This also happened to the Germanic rebel leader Arminius several years later, in which he tried to organize an effective and decisive defeat of the Roman military and eradicate the Roman presence in Germania forever, only to be repeatedly undermined either by his contrary subordinate commanders or his men who were more concerned with plunder and gaining battlefield glory than with discipline and following orders. Decades before, the Gallic leader Vercingetorix had a similar problem in which he had to constantly negotiate and compromise with the various tribal chiefs under his command, all of which were very independently-minded, in order for them to follow his banner against the legions of Julius Caesar.

A similar situation might have met Bato. Remember that the Illyrians were composed of numerous tribes, just like the Celts and the Germans. The warriors of each of these tribes were loyal only to their tribal chief and not to any overarching authority. They did not identify themselves as 'Illyrian', nor was there any sense of a pan-Illyrian nationalism motivating these rebels. 'Illyria' was not a single unified entity. In order for Bato the Daesidiate and Bato the Breucian to carry out their rebellions against Rome, they too would have to negotiate, make deals and make compromises. They would have to work with very egocentric tribal chiefs who were more concerned with their own legacy and gaining power for themselves rather than acting for the greater good. The two Batos would have to grant concessions to them due to their position and the fact that their warriors answered to the chiefs, not to the rebellion's two leading commanders. Both of these men could try to give orders, but those orders would only be obeyed if their subordinate commanders felt like obeying them. That was the greatest difference between the Illyrian rebel horde and the Roman legions. For the two Batos, orders or suggestions could be given and the subordinate chiefs could very likely issue their own orders instead. As for the Romans, if an order was given, it was followed with no exceptions. As the Great Illyrian Revolt continued, both Batos, especially Bato the Daesidiate, would become increasingly frustrated by lack of discipline among the lower ranks and back-stabbing among the upper ranks.

It may be that Bato the Daesidiate intended to attack the Roman force only on three sides, leaving one side open for retreat, but his men either took it upon themselves to surround the Romans or else their commanders gave the order themselves. This is of course just supposition and guesswork, and while it may be what happened, it is only an idea and nothing more.

For the Romans, victory had been attained when defeat seemed certain, but this victory had come at a high cost. Many high-ranking officers had been either killed or wounded, and although no actual numbers are given, casualties were likely heavy. This was the second time that Governor Aulus Severus of Moesia had won a hard-fought victory during the first months of the war.[96]

These opening conflicts were a foretelling of how the Great Illyrian Revolt would play out. Despite their poor discipline, the Illyrians were tough tenacious fighters and they would use all their strength to bleed the Romans without mercy. However, the geography of the western Balkans, with its brutal mountainous terrain and steep jagged valleys, was just as much an enemy to the Romans as were the Illyrian rebels. For the next three years, the Roman legions would scrape and crawl through these winding limestone crags and forest-covered hills, fighting hard battles all along the way, being forced to assault one mountaintop stronghold or one staunchly-defended river crossing after another, often suffering horrendous casualties in the process. I am here reminded of the famous quote given by the Second World War American general Omar Bradley when he commented on the hard fighting in Normandy: 'Beyond every river was another hill, and beyond every hill was another river', and there are *many* hills and rivers in the western Balkans.

Enter Tiberius

It was around this time that Tiberius' main army entered Illyricum. The fact that Tiberius delayed taking any action in the Illyrian rebellion, holding his army in the north while other troops further to the south fought on desperately, shows that he was still uncertain as to whether or not King Maroboduus and his 74,000 Marcomanni warriors showed any signs of launching an attack. He couldn't abruptly swing around and attack the Illyrians in the south if there was a very distinct possibility that the Marcomanni would attack him in full force from behind. It was only when the Illyrian rebellion had grown so much that the rebels threatened to invade Italy and after Tiberius' doubts about the Marcomanni were assuaged and he became confident that they would not launch an attack against him that he turned his army around and ordered them to march southwards to put down the Illyrian uprising. Paterculus states: 'It did not seem to Tiberius a safe course to keep his army buried in the interior of the country and thus leave Italy unprotected from an enemy so near at hand.'[97]

As an interesting side-note, Paterculus states that he fought in this war as a cavalry officer, and later as a legion commander, though he doesn't state which legion he led:

> In this war also my modest abilities had an opportunity for
> glorious service. I was now, at the end of my service in the

cavalry, quaestor designate, and though not yet a senator I was
placed upon a parity with senators and even tribunes elect, and
led from the city to Tiberius a portion of the army which was
entrusted to me by Augustus. Then in my quaestorship, giving
up my right to have a province allotted me, I was sent to Tiberius
as legatus Augusti.[98]

The Roman force led by the consuls Severus and Silvanus, which had
been earlier mauled but not beaten, now linked up with Tiberius' forces.
Tiberius now commanded a total of ten legions, more than seventy
auxiliary cohorts, fourteen cavalry battalions and more than 10,000 recalled
veterans, along with numerous volunteers and the surviving remnants
of the Thracian cavalry. Paterculus states that not since the civil wars
of the late republic had so many soldiers been gathered together in one
place. This single location was most likely Segestica, since this place
is mentioned by both Cassius Dio and Paterculus as the place where
Tiberius stayed. Therefore Segestica might have been the headquarters
for the Roman forces taking part in the revolt.[99]

Among those who likely entered the scene at this moment was the
Germanic prince Arminius, a young nobleman of the Cherusci tribe
who fought in the Great Illyrian Revolt under Tiberius' command. It is
possible that Gaius Paterculus, who would later write an account of this
remarkable young man, knew Arminius *personally*. Paterculus describes
the Germanic prince as brave and clever; no small praise, considering
the Romans' contempt for barbarians. Arminius was born in 16 BC, the
son of Chief Segimerus, a prominent leader among the Cherusci tribe
of west-central Germania (apparently this tribe did not have one single
chief). Arminius' younger brother Flavus (a Latin name literally meaning
'yellow', no doubt a reference to the boy's blond hair) also served in
the Great Illyrian Revolt as a scout and would later lose an eye during
one of the war's battles.[100]

Prince Arminius had been taken under Rome's care in 6 BC following
the subjugation of the western Germanic tribes; he was 10 years old at
the time. As a peace hostage, he would have been educated in Latin, been
sent to school and eventually became an auxiliary commander in the
Roman army. When he was posted to fight under Tiberius, he would
have been 22. He would see action in the Great Illyrian Revolt, likely
as an auxiliary cavalry commander, but from what we can gather of his
life from the ancient sources, his combat service was limited to scarcely

a few months during the year 6 AD. Still, during that time he performed magnificently, and as a reward for his battlefield bravery he was given a double promotion, which was an almost unheard-of honour. Prince Arminius was made a Roman citizen, which gave him the right to vote, and he was knighted, which enabled him to own land within the empire and to become involved in the workings of the Roman government.[101] Unfortunately, none of the ancient accounts say what epic feats of daring Arminius did in order to deserve such rewards.

The Romans were confident that with such a massive force behind them, they were certain to defeat the rebels. However, the men were to be disappointed. Tiberius allowed his massive army a few days of rest and then split the force apart, deeming that such a large force could not be controlled effectively. He ordered Severus' and Silvanus' reinforcements back home. Realizing that the rebels might take the opportunity to attack the reinforcements as they made their way back, he ordered his own army to escort them, and so they travelled 'on a long exceedingly laborious march, whose difficulty can hardly be described'.[102]

While Tiberius and his commanders stayed in Segestica, the Dalmatians attacked and overran the territories of Rome's allies in the area (probably the Liburnians, who by now had been thoroughly Romanized), and 'caused many more to revolt'.[103] There are two ways to interpret Cassius Dio's quote. The first is that those who now joined in the revolt were in fact fellow Illyrians who had previously been sitting on the fence, not wishing to take part in the fighting, but now decided to join in. The second option is that they were the people that the Dalmatians had defeated, and they were now forced to change sides and fight for the rebel cause. I believe that the first of the two options is the more viable one, because if Rome's allies had been forced to abandon their friendship with Rome and swear their loyalty to the rebels, the Roman authors surely would have made mention of such an act of treachery, as they would have seen it.

Now it was the empire's turn to strike back. Paterculus gives a rousing record of the achievements of Tiberius' forces during the first year of the rebellion:

> What armies of the enemy did we see drawn up for battle in that first year! What opportunities did we avail ourselves of through the foresight of the general to evade their united forces and rout them in separate divisions! With what moderation

and kindness did we see all the business of warfare conducted, though under the authority of a military commander! With what judgement did he place our winter camps! How carefully was the enemy so blockaded by the outposts of our army that he could nowhere break through, and that, through lack of supplies and by disaffection within his own ranks, he might gradually be weakened in strength![104]

If Paterculus' laudatory record of Tiberius' actions comes across as sounding rather thick, you're not wrong. After all, Gaius Paterculus wrote his *Roman History* during the reign of *Emperor* Tiberius. Of course he's going to make the general-turned-Caesar look as glorious as he possibly could. Even so, we can detect a few hints of the true conduct of Tiberius during this campaign by examining Paterculus' panegyric praise.

Paterculus specifically states that Tiberius tried to avoid a direct head-to-head clash against the full might of the rebels. Remember that the Illyrian rebel forces significantly outnumbered the Romans, and they had already proven to be more than capable of giving even large Roman armies a severe thrashing. If we take Paterculus' account as possessing a certain degree of truth, then it's understandable that Tiberius would be wary of becoming engaged in a single massive all-or-nothing fight against the Illyrians, lest he and all of his men should be pinned down and thoroughly massacred. Roman history already had its fair share of embarrassing defeats at the hands of so-called 'barbarians', and he likely didn't want his own name to be added to the list of the empire's hall of shame. So instead, Tiberius carefully avoided the massive bulk of the Illyrian rebel force and instead focused his attention on small enemy units, pounding each of them one by one. Thereby Tiberius and his legions managed to whittle down the Illyrian rebel force one tiny piece at a time.

However, the historian Cassius Dio, writing 200 years after Paterculus, tells the complete opposite version of the story. According to *his* account of these events, Tiberius actually *wanted* to attack the rebel army and destroy the whole lot of them in a single massive battle. Cassius Dio says that Tiberius took his large army on the offensive, but very little was actually done because the rebels always managed to somehow stay one step ahead of Tiberius. Bato the Daesidiate and his Dalmatian warriors continuously evaded the Roman advance, refusing to engage in a pitched battle, and instead engaged in a scorched-earth policy to cause as much devastation as they could and to deny the Romans supplies and food. Cassius Dio elaborates that due to the Illyrians' knowledge of the terrain and the lightness of their equipment, they could quickly travel from place to place and as a result Tiberius was never able to catch up with them.[105]

So which story is the right one? I'm more inclined to believe Cassius Dio's account for three reasons. First, Paterculus was writing his history during the time of Emperor Tiberius' reign, which was also the time of the reign of terror conducted by Tiberius' head of the Praetorian Guard, Lucius Aelius Sejanus. To him, criticism was the same as treason, and so it's safe to say that Paterculus' account of Tiberius' actions during the war is certainly biased in an effort to prolong his own life span as much as he could by showering Tiberius with flattery. Because Cassius Dio was far removed from the politics of the Julio-Claudian dynasty, he was able to write about things that happened two centuries earlier with little fear of retaliation. Second, Cassius Dio's account is significantly longer and more detailed than Paterculus' account, which is very odd because as a direct participant in the war, you'd naturally think that Paterculus would write a very long rendering of the saga of the Great Illyrian Revolt. Yet this doesn't happen: Paterculus whizzes through the bloody chaos in the western Balkans in eight chapters, which, in Roman literary works, are actually more like eight very lengthy paragraphs. By contrast, Cassius Dio devotes fourteen chapters to the war. Third, if the war was going so swimmingly for the Roman side, then why did Caesar Augustus send in Germanicus to help the war effort along? Both Paterculus and Cassius Dio say that Germanicus was called in to help fight the rebels. The only reason that I can think of for Augustus to do this is if he felt that the war's progress was not going to his liking, and this probably means that Tiberius was not making much headway against the Illyrians, so Germanicus was sent in to speed things along. Therefore I believe that Cassius Dio's account is the more reliable and trustworthy of the two major accounts of this war.

As suspect as Paterculus' record of Tiberius' actions in the war may be, I'd like to examine one of the things he says because it could have two meanings. Paterculus' comment that Tiberius conducted his campaigns with 'moderation and kindness' might be a reference to Tiberius' personability among his soldiers. According to Paterculus, Tiberius' soldiers loved him. A notable example is when Tiberius was sent into Germania to take charge of subduing a rebellion among the tribes in the years 1–4 AD. Paterculus beams:

> Words cannot express the feelings of the soldiers at their meeting, and perhaps my account will scarcely be believed – the tears which sprang to their eyes in their joy at the sight of him, their eagerness, their strange transports in saluting him, their longing to touch his hand, and their inability to restrain such cries as 'Is it really you that we see, commander?' 'Have we received you safely back among us?' 'I served with you, general, in Armenia!' 'And I in Raetia!' 'I received my decoration from you in Vindelicia!' 'And I mine in Pannonia!' 'And I in Germany!'[106]

Suetonius' account of Tiberius' conduct in the opening stages of Rome's revenge campaign against Arminius and the Germans following the disaster at the Battle of Teutoburg in 9 AD states very clearly that Tiberius always took care to listen to the advice and counsel of his subordinate commanders, he issued all orders in writing so that his men could easily understand them, and if anyone was uncertain about what his orders were, he gave them the freedom to come to him anytime, day or night, even waking him up from his sleep, in order to get clarification.[107]

Then again, 'moderation and kindness', especially the 'moderation' part, might also be a stealthily-concealed jab at Tiberius for not being aggressive enough, which is the very same thing that Cassius Dio stated in his own record of the war two centuries later. The historical record shows that as Tiberius grew older, he became more and more cautious in his military ventures. Even Caesar Augustus would grumble about the slow progress that Tiberius was making against the Illyrian rebels and felt compelled to call in Tiberius' nephew Germanicus, the darling of the imperial family, to add a bit more *oomph* to the war effort.

Meanwhile, Back in Rome...

When Caesar Augustus read the reports of Tiberius' lack of progress, he began having suspicions about his commander. The emperor believed that Tiberius should have easily overpowered the Dalmatians but had moved slowly rather than speedily, and became concerned that Tiberius wanted to retain control of the army longer than anticipated; the emperor was highly conscious of threats to his power. He therefore ordered that Tiberius' nephew Germanicus should go to Illyricum.[108]

Drusus Claudius Nero Germanicus was born on 24 May 16 BC. The young boy did not know his father all that well since Drusus the Elder was almost constantly on campaign during the boy's early childhood, but the boy was a beloved member of the imperial household and Augustus and other members of the family took every effort to make sure that the young Germanicus had a proper Roman upbringing. As he matured, he turned into a fine young man. In the year 5 AD, Germanicus married his cousin Vipsania Agrippina, the daughter of Marcus Agrippa and Augustus' daughter Julia. Germanicus had never commanded troops in battle before, and he had never held any major political offices. As charming as Germanicus was, sending such an inexperienced youth into a war zone like that seems odd to say the least.[109]

Cassius Dio states that Caesar Augustus' choice of commanders was limited at this stage. In fact, he only had two to choose from: Germanicus and his younger brother Marcus Vipsanius Agrippa Postumus, so-named because he was born after his father had died. Agrippa Postumus' conduct left something to be desired. Cassius Dio says that he was prone to vice, he had a hot temper and often didn't know when it was best to keep his mouth shut. Augustus had, for a time, considered him as a successor, but his poor character made Augustus change his mind. In the autumn of 6 AD, he was banished to the tiny island of Planasia, located not too far from the larger island of Elba.[110] This left Germanicus as the only option on the table.

Augustus recognized that even more soldiers were needed to combat the Illyrian rebels, and so he gave Germanicus his own army composed of citizens, freed-men and recently-freed slaves that had been taken from their masters specifically for the purpose of fighting in the war against the Illyrians; the masters were given a monetary compensation of the slave's value plus the cost of their upkeep for a period of six months. This shows that Augustus didn't expect the war to last any longer than that. He would be in for a dismaying shock. Germanicus would spend much of the remainder of 6 AD and the early part of 7 AD getting his army in shape.[111]

Augustus was having problems at home, too. The population of the city was full of anxiety due to the war and also due to a famine that had set in, and so Augustus tried to devise any methods he could to keep the population calm. Moreover, fighting the rebellion in the Balkans was severely depleting the empire's treasury, and so Augustus introduced a 2 per cent sales tax on slaves in order to replenish the imperial coffers. Moreover, he decreed that no money should be spent on gladiatorial games. The Romans, for the time being, would have to give up their blood entertainment for the sake of necessity.[112]

The War in Winter

Tiberius returned to Segestica just as winter set in, and he ordered his subordinate commanders (Paterculus states that he himself was designated to be one of Tiberius' subordinates, which was a very high honour) to take charge of the various Roman military camps in the country. Paterculus states that the winter of 6–7 AD was very harsh; whether this statement applies to Illyricum specifically or to Europe in general isn't clear.[113] Winter in the western Balkans is dreadfully harsh, and back in ancient times it was just as bad.

Governor Aulus Caecina Severus of Moesia had been one of the first to respond to the revolt and had quickly sent in soldiers to help suppress it. He had fought two large battles against the rebels and on both occasions was very nearly defeated. He and his men were battered and weary. Now he was compelled to return to his province of Moesia. The Dacians and Sarmatians, two large and powerful barbarian ethnic groups that dwelt in the north in what is now Romania and Ukraine, had taken advantage of the absence of Roman troops in Moesia, crossed the Danube River and were now utterly ravaging that province.[114]

We can get an idea of the threats posed by these two barbarian groups by looking at the writings of the poet Ovid. In the year 8 AD, he was exiled by Caesar Augustus as a punishment for an unknown offence. He was sent to the furthest fringe of Rome's holdings in Europe, to the frontier town of Tomis (modern-day Constanța, Romania), located on the shore of the Black Sea in eastern Moesia. Tomis was a Greek colony founded sometime in the 600s BC, and the Romans had made it their own. He would remain in Tomis for the rest of his life, but he only had nine more years to live.[115]

Tomis was located right on the border of barbarian territory. It was an important centre for trade, with the barbarians bringing slaves, furs and other goods in exchange for the aspects of 'civilized' society such as wine, olive oil and fine clothing. However, the nearest Roman military force was miles away, and the townsfolk were expected to defend their settlement themselves. Most of the population was Greek and Getae (a Thracian tribe) but mostly the latter. Ovid describes them as boldly walking in the streets carrying their weapons, including knives, bows and poisoned arrows. Many of these tribes did not farm but were pastoralists, migrating with their flocks in search of greener grass. A few authors comment that in the wintertime the Danube River freezes and that large numbers of men, horses and waggons could cross over it as if it were solid ground.[116]

In circumstances like this, raiding parties become a very serious threat when winter comes. Warriors who are desperate to prove their martial prowess, who are covetous of the prestigious goods that the Greeks and Romans bring and who are becoming increasingly anxious due to the shortage of food, will begin their raids and descend upon the frontier settlements like Tomis. Many tribes made their livelihood by raiding their neighbours. During the 300s AD, a Greek clergyman named Grigoris ('Gregory' in English) was preaching to the Sarmatians. He told them that they had to give up their lives of brigandage and plundering, but the Sarmatians were greatly disturbed by this. At length, their leader asked the Greek missionary how they could survive if they gave up robbing and plundering their neighbours.[117]

Ovid states that while the weather was warm, the Danube protected the people of the town because the barbarians could not cross it, but when winter came and the river began to freeze, the barbarians then descended upon them in hordes. Ovid gives chilling accounts as to how these nomadic horse warriors were perceived, how they conducted their battles and how the people of Tomis were forced to fight against them to save their lives. Even Ovid himself had to man the defences against attack.[118]

Usually when winter sets in the fighting stops, with both sides hunkering down in the camps and readying themselves for the next spring's campaigning season, but the Dalmatian rebels decided to use the winter to their advantage. Assuming that the Romans would be within their winter quarters, which they were, the rebels launched a fresh offensive and invaded the province of Macedonia for a second time. Winter offensives were extremely rare in pre-modern warfare, and this one almost certainly took everyone by surprise. There was very little that the Romans could do to stop this. Aulus Severus, who could have easily marched his men south, was preoccupied fighting the Dacians and Sarmatians who were in the process of ravaging his province. Tiberius and his forces were encamped in far-off Segestica, and by the time he mustered his men and marched the many miles through the freezing cold to help the people of that province, and with his supply and communication lines always in danger of being cut, it might have already been too late to help. Rome's Thracian allies were the only ones who were available to come to Macedonia's aid and to meet the Dalmatians in battle. King Rhoemetalces and his brother Prince Rhascyporis commanded the army that stood against the rebels. No details are given with regard to the battle's location or time, nor is there any information on the numbers of men that fought. All that we know is that the Thracians were victorious and the Dalmatian advance was stopped:

> Later, when...Tiberius and Messallinus were tarrying in Siscia [Segestica], the Dalmatians overran the territory of their [Rome's] allies.... As for these forces, now, Rhoemetalces and his brother Rhascyporis checked them by a battle; and as for the others, they did not come to the defence of their country when it was later ravaged (in the consulship of Caecilius Metellus and Licinius Silvanus), but took refuge in the mountain fortresses, from which they made raiding expeditions whenever the chance offered.[119]

Paterculus wraps up his commentary of the first year of the rebellion by taking note of the practices of the Roman army's medical corps and of Tiberius' character. Tiberius, he says, cared deeply for the soldiers that he led, and there was not one single person among the Roman force that fell ill without having Tiberius attending to that person's health as fervently as any other martial duty of his. Although his mind was preoccupied with many heavy responsibilities, he devoted himself entirely to the care of those who needed care, as though this was his primary duty. The Romans employed ambulances – horse-drawn waggons – to carry away the sick. He donated his personal litter to help carry away the sick, although Paterculus states that Tiberius very rarely used it since he preferred to ride his horse rather than be carried on a litter by servants. Also, his personal physicians, his personal cooking staff and even his bathing equipment were all given up to serve the greater comfort of the sick soldiers.[120]

By now, the Romans' repeated assaults upon the rebels had inflicted many casualties. Moreover, the rebels' morale was crumbling. Paterculus gloriously states that the rebels were no longer satisfied with their numbers and had little confidence in their abilities to inflict a serious blow upon the Romans, and they had no faith in themselves whatsoever if they were certain to face Tiberius! Indeed, the portion of the rebel force that had been fighting against Tiberius since the revolt began had been so worn down by constant attacks and constant defeats that it was on the verge of collapse. The rebels in that area knew that Tiberius would attack again. Not willing to make another stand against the legions on open ground, for they were certain that they were all going to be slaughtered if they remained where they were, they retreated to Mount Claudius (now named Moslavača Gora, located near Warasdin, or Varaždin, on the Drava River[121]) and set up a defensive position behind fortifications.[122] Cassius Dio states that from this position and other mountain strongholds like it, the rebels would launch raiding expeditions.[123] To add to their misery, a famine was now under way in Illyricum. The rebel forces now faced destruction not by the hand of the legions, which could be either merciless or merciful depending on their whims, but by the constant merciless hammer of starvation.[124]

As the winter of 6 AD changed to the winter of 7 AD, the Illyrians were no longer boastful and defiant. Their early victories had been soured and tempered by several crushing defeats at the hands of Rome and its Thracian allies. Things were not looking good and some of them began to contemplate putting an end to the fighting now, while they might still have a chance to live.

Chapter Four

The Tide Turns

The Spring Offensive: Enter Germanicus

It was now the spring of 7 AD. Quintus Caecillus Metellus and Aulus Licinius Nerva Silianus were made the new consuls for that year. The winter of 6–7 AD had been harsh. The weather had been unusually cold and the snow was heavy, and in contrast to the custom of the time, the fighting had not stopped. Instead, the Illyrians had persistently launched numerous raiding and harassment missions against their Roman enemies, and the Romans could do little to stop it. Now that the snows were thawing, full-scale operations against the Illyrian rebels could begin once again.

Now that the campaign season for 7 AD had begun, it was time for Germanicus to get his own troops moving. Late in the previous year, he had been granted a commission by his grandfather Caesar Augustus to suppress the Illyrian rebels. Germanicus had absolutely no military experience whatsoever, and now he was being asked to take charge of an entire army at the age of 21. None of the ancient sources state how many men Germanicus had under his command.

Cassius Dio says that the 'troops' commanded by Germanicus were soldiers in name only. In fact, they were nothing more than a gaggle of draftees that had been hastily cobbled together from here and there in order to create one more military unit to fight the rebels. These were not soldiers but ordinary people, presumably with no military training, like Germanicus himself, composed of citizens, ex-slaves and even slaves that had to be bought from their owners. An untested commander leading untested troops into battle. This sort of thing sounds like a recipe for disaster.[1]

However, Germanicus had three things in his favour: his charming charismatic personality, a little bit of time to prepare himself and his men, and the full unwavering support of the imperial government. Germanicus was highly skilled in rhetoric and public relations. He knew how to put on a show, he knew exactly which buttons to push, and he was able to be very persuasive and inspiring. When he spoke, other people listened. Germanicus was a natural leader because he acted like one; it was as simple as that. Over the years, he would further cultivate his public image and he would become more and more popular with the Roman people.

By the time Augustus had granted Germanicus his military commission, winter was approaching. Germanicus would not be sent into action until the campaign season next year, so he had a couple of months to give his green recruits a little bit of military order and training. Since he didn't have that much time, it was likely a crash-course affair teaching only the basics, and even then it was certainly done to a rushed schedule. Lindsay Powell proposes that since public festivals and entertainments had to be cancelled for the sake of wartime frugality, this left a lot of gladiators and gladiator trainers looking for work. Having the gladiators and their *lanistae* teaching Germanicus' would-be legionnaires the art of fighting might have been just the break that they were looking for. Germanicus, ever the charmer, had developed relationships with the gladiator schools earlier in life, and I'm certain that he was able to use his smile and a few well-placed flattering words to convince the arena fighters to train his men out of duty to their country and to their families. It's also likely that Germanicus paid the *lanistae* a few gold coins for their trouble.[2]

Finally, being a member of the imperial family and being well-liked by the emperor himself meant that anything that he asked for was at his disposal. Any type or any quantity of military equipment could have been sent to him any time that it was requested. Blacksmiths and armourers were likely working around the clock to provide enough gear for the troops, and even old unused items that had been mouldering away in storage were brought out for front-line service once more. Using every method at his disposal, Germanicus managed to get his unit in something approaching proper shape in time for the campaign season of 7 AD. His soldiers marched towards the front.

Where did Germanicus and his men march from, and where did they march to? It is fairly obvious that Germanicus' men were recruited from Italy. He could not assemble a unit anywhere in the Balkans since the entire region was a war zone. The provinces of Rhaetia and Noricum were under threat of an Illyrian attack, since a large portion of the rebels was making plans for a mass invasion of Italy and in order to get there, they had to pass either through or very near to these two regions. Gaul and Spain were too far away to provide any effective and timely means of sending troops to the front. This left the Italian peninsula as the only option to expediently send some more men into the fight.

Did Germanicus and his men march overland, or did they sail across the Adriatic and land on the Illyrian coast? All of the sources that go into detail in these matters say that Germanicus marched, and furthermore, the first target for his men was a tribe of Pannonians called the Mazaei. Because the Pannonians, and the Mazaei in particular, were a northern tribe that dwelled in the interior, that could only mean that Germanicus and his men marched north through Italy, likely picking up more volunteers and supplies along the way, arced around the northern end of the Adriatic and marched upon the rebels from the north. It is also stated, or at least implied, that Germanicus' role was not to act as an independent force but rather to assist his uncle Tiberius in defeating the rebels. Germanicus' army was probably too small to act as an effective field force that could take on the Illyrians all by themselves. Therefore Germanicus and his troops were not an independent army but were instead Tiberius' reinforcements. This means that Germanicus was fighting with his uncle stationed in the north.

Germanicus' soldiers were probably a motley bunch, likely armoured in whatever helmets and body armour they could quickly get their hands on, and equipped with a variety of weapons and shield types. It's fairly certain that his unit consisted almost entirely of infantry. No ancient source makes any mention of there being horsemen within Germanicus' ranks and besides, the Romans had to import cavalry by ordering the Thracians to send their mounted warriors into the fighting. This demonstrates a lack of available horses, not only for Germanicus' unit but for the Roman military in general. If there were any horses, then it's likely that there were only a handful reserved for Germanicus and other high-ranking officers. Even so, records of the battles in which Germanicus fought during his career showed that he preferred to fight on foot side-by-side with his infantry. No doubt this, too, was a means of cultivating favour with the soldiers by showing that he was one of them.

As Germanicus and his troops marched northwards up the Italian peninsula, it is highly likely that he regularly gathered intelligence as to what the Illyrian rebels were up to and what the sentiments of the population were like. Also, seeing armed troops marching through the towns and villages would help to boost the morale of the people as well as dissuade anyone thinking about using the chaos in Illyria to their advantage. As they neared the northern part of Italy, Germanicus and his men would act as a security force, blocking the path of any would-be invaders. Granted, their small number would not be formidable enough to deter the hordes of rampaging rebels (if indeed they were as numerous as the historian Suetonius would have us believe), but it was still something. Confident that the rebels would not push further southwards, Germanicus and his men pressed onwards, with the goal of linking up with Tiberius' army.

Severus Strikes Back: The Battle of the Volcaean Marshes

While Germanicus was busy training his men and thereafter having them march to the front, others were already on the way. Once again, the first person to take action was Aulus Caecina Severus, the governor of the province of Moesia. When the rebellion first broke out the previous year, Severus was the first person to send in troops to suppress it, but he was not successful; he managed to defeat the Illyrians at the Battle of the Dravus River, but many of his men had been killed in the process. Later on, with the help of Rome's Thracian vassals, he won another Pyrrhic victory in a battle whose location, name and date are unknown. Still, despite his losses, he continued to hold his own against the rebel forces, but he was apparently not making much progress. When winter was coming on, Severus had been forced to withdraw his troops from Illyricum and return to Moesia because the Dacians and Sarmatians had crossed the frozen Danube and were rampaging across his province. Now that spring had come, the ice that covered the Danube River had melted, which meant that the barbarians who lived to the north could no longer cross the frozen river to attack Moesia. The end of winter had ended the barbarian threat, at least for the time being.

Now that the threat from the Dacians and Sarmatians had been mitigated, Governor Severus could once again turn his attention to other matters and take the offensive against the Illyrian rebels. Ivan Radman-Livaja and Marko Dizdar say that Severus commanded three legions in the opening offensive of 7 AD.[3] Cassius Dio says that Severus and his men set up their marching camp in a place called the Volcaean Marshes, and it would be here that the first major battle of the new campaign season would take place.[4]

Unfortunately the historical sources do not state where exactly the Volcaean Marshes were and this has led to a lot of guesswork by secondary authors. Peter Swan hypothesizes that it corresponds to the lowlands of the Sava River,[5] while Ivan Radman-Livaja and Marko Dizdar say that the Volcaean Marshes were in south-eastern Slavonia.[6]

The names for this landscape that are recorded in the ancient documents are *Volcae paludes* and *Hiulca palus*.[7] The Latin noun *palus* (pl. *paludes*) means 'marsh, swamp or bog'. *Volca* might be an archaic form of *Hiulca*, which in turn may be related to another geographic feature, the *Ulca fluvius*, 'Ulca River', which, according to Byzantine sources, was located somewhere in Pannonia.[8] Bishop Ennodius of Pavia mentions an *Ulca fluvius*, but he also describes the landscape around the river as a boggy fenland. This would explain why in Sextus Aurelius Victor's *Epitome de Cesaribus*, written in the late 300s AD, he states 'near Cibale, a marsh named Hiulca'.[9] He specifically calls it a marsh rather than a river. Cibalae, also written as Cibalis, is believed to be modern-day Vinkovci, Croatia. The Byzantine writer Zosimus also makes mention of Cibalae in conjunction with swampy ground, stating:

> Cibalis, a city of Pannonia, which stands on a hill; the road to which is rugged and narrow. The greatest part of this road is through a deep morass, and the remainder up a mountain, on which stands the city. Below it extends a spacious plain, which entertains the view with a boundless prospect.[10]

The *Volcae paludes* may have been located within the territory of the Andizetes,[11] and one modern source claims that the *Volcae paludes* is actually Lake Balaton in modern-day Hungary.[12]

I wish to offer another proposal as to the location of the enigmatic *Volca paludes*. I believe that the Volcaean Marshes of ancient times were located where the Vuka River converges with the Danube, where the modern-day town of Vukovar, Croatia now stands. In ancient times, this would have been a very marshy environment. Besides, the modern name 'Vuka' might be a modern rendition of the ancient names Ulca, Huilca and Volca. The modern town of Vinkovci, Croatia, the site of the ancient fortified settlement of Cibalae, is located not far from the Vuka River, and is itself located upon a prominent bend in the Bosut River. This whole region would have appeared as Ennodius described it – a boggy fenland – with the fortified town of Cibalae standing atop a hill overlooking the marshy swampy landscape, making this settlement a well-defended position.

It specifically says in Cassius Dio's account of these events that Severus set up his camp in the middle of a swamp. Why, especially if Cibalae was located nearby (if we are to believe the reconstructed geography)? One wonders why Severus and his men didn't take Cibalae itself, considering that the settlement was situated in an ideal tactical location. As said before, it was a fortified town built atop a hill located on a prominent bend in a river and surrounded by swampland. It was an ideal location for defence. The fact that Severus chose to have his men make camp within the marshes shows two things. First, there were areas of solid ground within the marsh that would have enabled him and his men to establish a sizeable marching camp. It wasn't all water and mud. Second, Severus must have been prevented from entering Cibalae. This could only mean that the Illyrian rebels held the town at this time. Knowing that Cibalae was an important location and likely a key rebel stronghold in the area, Severus decided to direct his first offensive there. Because he couldn't invest the town itself, at least not yet, he set up his camp in the marshes just beyond the town. The river and the boggy terrain around the campsite would act as a natural moat and would hinder any attackers. He would do the same thing years later when fighting against the German rebel leader Arminius.[13]

Wherever a Roman army marched, it always set itself up in a camp at the end of the day's journey. These camps were all constructed more or less to a standard square or rectangular-shaped blueprint. A V-shaped trench about five feet deep would be dug around the encampment, and the excavated earth would be used to create an earthen wall inside. This would then be crowned with sharpened wooden stakes that the legionnaires carried with them, tied into bundles of three, which the military historian Vegetius called *tribuli* and resembled the familiar D-Day anti-tank obstacles seen at Normandy. Within the rampart, the tents were laid out in a grid pattern in a specific order, and every squad knew exactly where to pitch their tent in the line. Within the camp, there were open areas called *intervallum* which were used for quickly moving troops about as well as for keeping tents somewhat distant from any enemy missiles. There was an open square in the centre of the camp for arranging troops in formation, and there were also open streets running along the length of the rampart so that soldiers could quickly be moved from one section of the wall to the other without tripping over the tent pegs. There would be four entranceways, placed in line with a cross-intersection of two main paths that ran through the camp.

It is believed that a full-sized legion numbering around 5,000 men could be accommodated in a camp measuring thirty acres in area.[14]

Because Roman soldiers had to construct these camps everywhere that they went, they were highly-skilled construction engineers as well as battlefield warriors. I've heard it said that for each day that a legionnaire held a sword, he spent nine days holding a shovel. That may be an over-simplification, but it does illustrate that the men of the legions were required to quickly and properly construct such fortifications regularly, and to do so far more often than engaging in combat.

The dangers of assaulting the Romans while they were still encamped were evident. True, the Romans did not have the same degree of flexibility that they would have in an open field battle, but it is always a difficult matter to take a fortified defensive position. From the cover of deep trenches and steep ramparts crowned with sharpened stakes, the Roman legionnaires and auxiliaries could keep their attackers at bay while at the same time showering them with missiles. Having all of the troops in a compact area as opposed to having them spread out over a wide distance meant that it would be easier for a commander to relocate troops from one location to another in a hurry in the event that reinforcements were needed at one section of the perimeter or another. Moreover, it would be next to impossible to flank or out-flank a defensive position, since the men would be arranged in a box formation. However, a large army could be very capable of surrounding a camp and besieging it, either by blockading it or by bombarding it with artillery.

As far as we are aware, the Illyrian forces did not possess any artillery – no ancient source makes any mention of the Illyrian rebels possessing ballistas or catapults – but the rebels certainly had numbers. As said before, it is a very likely possibility that the Volcaean Marshes, to which Severus had marched his soldiers and set up his camp, is mentioned by the Byzantine historian Zosimus as being close to the hilltop town of Cibalae. This settlement was likely held by an Illyrian rebel garrison at the time of Severus' arrival. Once again, the Illyrian rebels did something that we might find stupid. Cassius Dio states that, rather than holding their position within Cibalae's walls and waiting for the Romans to come to them, the Illyrians instead decided to attack Severus and his men head-on within the swamp.[15]

At first glance, such a decision appears to be completely and utterly illogical. A large Roman force was stationed within a fortified encampment in the middle of swampy terrain. Meanwhile, the Illyrians, who may have been stationed only a short distance away at Cibalae, held a fortified town atop a hill. Coming down from their stronghold to attack through the marsh seems foolhardy. What on earth would induce the Illyrians to make such a decision?

There are two possible answers to this. The first is the threat that Cibalae would be cut off from escape if the Romans laid siege to it, therefore the Romans had to be knocked out before they could launch their attack upon the town itself. The historical sources don't mention if Severus brought any siege engines with him, such as ballistae. A full-sized legion of 4,800 men would have been accompanied by a contingent of artillery, one ballista for every century within the legion; that's sixty ballistae per legion. If Severus did indeed have three legions under his command and if all three legions were at full strength, then that means he could have brought 180 giant crossbows with him, launching three-foot-long spears and rocks the size of fists at the Illyrian garrison manning the walls.

Even if Severus didn't assault the town by bombarding it with artillery, he could still pin the rebel garrison in place by blocking off the escape routes. Many people don't realize this, but hilltop positions have one serious drawback: although they command the landscape, they can be easily cut off. If you're on top of a hill and the enemy is advancing upwards, your mobility options are drastically limited. Zosimus stated that there was only one narrow road leading up the slope to the town's gate. Severus likely didn't need to actually attack Cibalae; all he had to do was block off access in or out of the town and simply wait for the garrison inside to starve. Perhaps the rebels realized that Severus could easily do just that with the numbers he had brought with him, and therefore the Roman threat had to be dealt with before Severus and his troops actually arrived at Cibalae.

However, the idea that the Illyrians were compelled by necessity to knock out Severus' army before it could lay siege to Cibalae is only one hypothesis. A second one, and one that is just as believable, is that the Illyrians felt confident enough to tackle Severus' force out in the open. Cassius Dio states in his account that the Illyrian force which would soon attack Severus was far larger than the Romans had anticipated.[16] So perhaps the Illyrians were once again trying to overwhelm the Romans through sheer force of numbers.

How were the Illyrian rebels able to muster up the numbers that would make them bold enough to take on three Roman legions? Cassius Dio states that the two Batos joined forces for a combined massive assault on Severus' camp.[17] This demonstrates a few things:

1. Before the battle, Bato the Daesidiate and Bato the Breucian actually met each other face to face and discussed strategy.
2. Bato the Daesidiate, who commanded the rebel forces in the south, did not feel confident enough in his own strength against Severus' army, and so he had to call in reinforcements from the north. This would leave the north vulnerable, and that would explain why Tiberius and Germanicus advanced with such ease during their march during the early stages of the campaign of 7 AD: the Illyrian rebels had been pulled southwards to fight against Severus' army, which was deemed a much more serious threat.
3. The Illyrian rebels were not numerous enough to deal with both Tiberius' force and Severus' force simultaneously. Casualties that they had suffered during the first year of the war had hit them hard and had greatly reduced their strength. Therefore, the leaders of the rebellion had to shuffle their forces around to meet threats as they presented themselves.
4. Between the two Roman armies that were arrayed against them, the Illyrian rebels decided that Severus' army was the much more serious threat. Even though Severus' force was far smaller than Tiberius' army, Severus' troops had been able to push themselves into Illyria much further and faster than Tiberius' large and unwieldy horde. Besides, Severus' army, being smaller than Tiberius' army, was a much more tempting target. Maybe the Illyrians adopted a version of the Schlieffen Plan. If the Illyrian rebels could quickly destroy Severus' army right now, or even just force it to retreat back to Moesia, they would not have to fight a two-front defensive campaign. Once Severus and his legions were defeated, the Illyrian rebels could do an about-face and concentrate their full strength upon Tiberius.

It has been hinted that Bato the Daesidiate might have had military experience prior to the outbreak of the Great Illyrian Revolt, possibly serving as an auxiliary commander. If this is true, then this should mean that he would have been fully aware of the dangers of assaulting the Roman forces within their camp, especially one that was located within difficult terrain. The fact that he chose to assault Severus and his men while they were within their camp would have gone against his better judgement. One of them might have been persuaded or pressured by the other to attack the camp. If so, it's likely that Bato the Breucian (who, as far as we can tell, didn't have any military experience of any kind prior to the outbreak of the rebellion) goaded his colleague Bato the Daesidiate into launching an attack on the Roman camp, perhaps out of a hunger for glory and plunder and partly in the belief that it would be an easy victory. In later years, the Germanic rebel leader Arminius would have the same trouble with his subordinate commanders, notably his uncle Inguiomerus, who insisted on assaulting the Romans head-on rather than waiting for more appropriate circumstances.

After joining their forces together, both Batos launched a direct mass assault on Severus' camp. Cassius Dio relates that the attack was completely unexpected. Severus had not prepared himself for facing so many people. He likely knew that there was an Illyrian force up ahead, but he may not have known that the force was as large as it was. The sentries that were posted beyond the ramparts to guard the camp were so terrified at the large rebel army now barrelling towards them that they fled back into the camp. However, from within the protection of their ramparts, the wavering legionnaires mustered up their courage and arrayed themselves upon the walls, ready to repel anyone who attempted to storm the camp. The Illyrians charged the Roman position, hoping to take possession of it through sheer brute force, likely launching human wave attacks. Despite the impressive size of the enemy force, which likely surrounded their position, and the ferocious tenacity with which they threw themselves at the defences, the men in the camp stood their ground. In the end, with no progress being made, the Illyrians were forced to withdraw. The historical accounts do not make any mention of the Illyrians being able to break into the camp, so the perimeter must have held firm. The scene that day must have been truly gut-wrenching to behold, as thousands of corpses lay heaped upon each other in the swamp.[18]

Once again, Governor Severus had just barely scored a victory. It is not stated if the Romans pursued or if they were content to simply let the Illyrians go. I'd wager the second option. As long as the Romans were protected behind their fortifications, they were okay. Once they left that protection they were targets, and Severus couldn't afford to lose any more men.

Burn All, Kill All, Destroy All

The recent near-defeat that Severus had suffered at the Battle of the Volcaean Marshes may have convinced Tiberius that a change of strategy was needed. Ever since the war had begun the previous year, the Romans had been seeking pitched battles with their Illyrian opponents. While they were largely successful, they had been so severely mauled in the process that it should have been clear to them that if they continued the war in this fashion, they would soon exhaust all of their military capacity. Something else had to be done.

As is the case so many times throughout history, from ancient to modern times, when one army faces very hard resistance from an opponent, the generals resort to attrition. If they could not exact decisive blows upon the enemy in the open battlefield, then they would take the war to the home front, steamrolling over the country, burning and looting farms and villages, taking everything of value and destroying the rest, crushing the enemy's capacity and will to fight on.

Cassius Dio reports that to better carry out this policy, Tiberius took his large and unwieldy force and split it up into several smaller forces, fanning them out over the land, with orders to kill and destroy everything in sight. One of these detachments was commanded by Tiberius' nephew, Drusus Claudius Nero Germanicus:

> After this the Romans were divided into detachments, in order that they might overrun many parts of the country at once; most of these detachments did nothing worthy of note, at least not at that time, but Germanicus conquered in battle and harassed the Mazaei, a Dalmatian tribe.[19]

Who were these people? Strabo calls the Mazaei a Pannonian tribe living in southern Pannonia, while Cassius Dio calls them Dalmatian. According to Pliny the Elder, the Mazaei were one of the more powerful tribes in the region, stating that the territory they occupied was divided into 269 districts.[20] Lindsay Powell states that the Mazaei were a Celtic tribe that lived in the land located between the Una and Bosna Rivers.[21]

For Germanicus' ragtag unit of slaves, ex-slaves and citizen-soldiers, it was a remarkable victory, and one that definitely helped to boost their morale. The fact that Cassius Dio states that this was the only event worthy of note for that campaign season shows that even the Romans thought this feat was impressive. The Mazaei occupied a sizeable portion of territory within central Illyria. Cassius Dio implies that Germanicus and his men only fought one battle against the Mazaei tribe. 'Harassing' is likely referring to the piece-by-piece assault upon their land, sweeping into and burning down one village after another, slaughtering anything they came across.

So we can likely infer from this account that Germanicus and his men, previously untested in action, fought one major engagement against the much larger and much more powerful force of Mazaei Illyrians and emerged victorious. After this victory, the Mazaei were thrown on the defensive and were forced to continuously pull back while Germanicus' troops advanced further and further into their domain, methodically looting and destroying their settlements one by one.

Such tactics have several goals. First, such wanton attrition destroys the enemy's home base by depriving them of lodging, food and supplies. Second, these actions may also serve to gain much-needed supplies for one's own forces. Thirdly, and most importantly, it is meant to induce fear. This is, in some respect, psychological warfare. As your army burns and destroys its way through an enemy country, every little victory is a constant reminder of just how powerless the enemy is to stop you. The message is clear: *All of this can end if you surrender.*

Now, with the tide turning against them, many Illyrians were thinking of doing just that.

The Rebel Alliance Begins to Break Apart

When the revolt kicked off in the spring of 6 AD, it appeared that the Illyrians were unstoppable. They had scored many victories against the Romans and had seized control of a large amount of territory. However, in the second half of 6 AD, the Romans got a second wind and they began to push the Illyrians back. Battles against the legions and Rome's Thracian allies resulted in high casualties for the Illyrian rebels. They could not afford such losses as those that Severus had inflicted upon them at the Battle of the Volcaean Marshes. Tiberius and Germanicus were pushing down from the north-west, while Severus was pushing in from the east.

Now the rebels were squabbling and intriguing among themselves. Bato the Breucian, the leader of the Pannonian uprising, received an offer: if he betrayed his co-commander Pinnes, he would attain the right to rule over all of the Pannonian tribes. Bato immediately seized the opportunity to do away with his rival and become the sole leader of the Pannonian rebels. The records stated that Pinnes was not killed, so he must have been imprisoned somewhere. Bato the Breucian was now in complete control, but Pinnes was popular with the men and Bato became

concerned about the loyalty of the tribes that he commanded. So Bato
went to each of the tribe's lands and demanded that they hand over peace
hostages. I assume he threatened that if these tribes wavered in their
loyalty or even flatly refused to follow him, he would kill the hostages as
an example. Such was a common practice in those times.[22]

It seems that both Bato the Daesidate as well as General Pinnes were
more concerned with the big picture, while Bato the Breucian was using
the war as an opportunity to win glory as well as to exercise personal
power. That would explain why Pinnes was imprisoned rather than
murdered, and that would also explain why Bato the Breucian questioned
the loyalty of the people that he now ruled over and demanded that they
hand over hostages to keep the peace. Pinnes was evidently a popular
commander and if he was executed, it might spark an uprising. As long
as Pinnes was still kept alive but in bondage, and as long as a potential
threat existed to murder him if the people rose up, the threat of a coup
would be neutralized. However, there was still a lot of grumbling and
dirty looks. Knowing that the people supported Pinnes more than him,
Bato the Breucian ordered the tribes to hand over hostages.

When Bato the Daesidiate heard about Bato the Breucian's actions,
he decided that he had had enough of his Pannonian colleague. Bato
the Daesidiate, the leader of all Dalmatian forces as well as the *de facto*
leader of the Illyrian rebellion as a whole, immediately marched his men
northwards. Pinnes could be relied upon to rally his men to fight the
Romans, but Bato the Breucian might cause just as much damage as the
Romans. Bato the Breucian had to be eliminated and Pinnes had to be
restored to a position of command.[23]

Bato the Daesidiate likely wanted to get this operation over and done
with in one quick bloody move since a protracted conflict within the
alliance would only distract the Illyrians from fighting the Romans and
with casualties mounting, their fighting strength would continue to
deteriorate. The result was just as Bato the Daesidiate intended: quick
and bloody. In a surprise attack, his warriors ambushed the Pannonian
leader and his men, and defeated the Pannonians in a battle. None of
the sources state where this battle took place, nor do they state how
many people were involved in it. Regardless of the details, the rebels
were now fighting *each other* instead of fighting the Romans.[24] The
casualties suffered in this battle were ones that the rebel alliance could
ill afford, since every death meant one less warrior available to fight off
the legions.

Bato the Breucian fled to the protection of a nearby stronghold, which is unfortunately unnamed in the sources. However, when Bato the Daesidiate approached with his army, Bato the Breucian was immediately handed over to the Dalmatian warlord by those inside. Bato the Breucian was presented before the whole rebel army, was publically condemned to death and was executed right there.[25]

The Pannonians Surrender

With Bato the Breucian dead, General Pinnes (who by now was presumably released from his imprisonment) was placed in command of all Pannonian forces. Straight away, Pinnes began a fresh offensive. This shows two things. First, Pinnes was a charismatic fighting man who was able to immediately rally his forces to launch a new attack upon the Romans. In this way, Pinnes sort of resembles an Illyrian version of Germanicus. Second, this shows his dedication to the rebel cause. No matter what, defeating the Romans was the foremost priority. Knowing this, it becomes easier to understand why Bato the Daesidiate made Pinnes his right-hand man during this stage of the war.[26]

Unfortunately General Pinnes' offensive failed: he was checked by the Roman commander Marcus Plautius Silvanus, who had fought alongside Aulus Severus the year before. The ancient sources do not state how much damage Pinnes and his troops managed to cause before they were defeated, nor do the sources state where the showdown between himself and Silvanus took place. It is also not clear if the Pannonians were defeated in one concise engagement or if they were gradually worn down little by little and their advance was finally stopped.[27]

After General Pinnes and his men were defeated, Marcus Silvanus and his men conquered the Breucian tribe. This was likely a very severe blow to the rebels' morale, since the Breucians had been one of the major players in this revolt. Their defeat likely signalled to many that the Great Illyrian Revolt was failing. After the Breucians fell, some other Pannonian tribes submitted voluntarily to Rome without offering any further resistance.[28] There could no longer be any doubt that the war was now definitely going in the Romans' favour.

When Bato the Daesidiate heard about the dire circumstances happening in Pannonia, with the Romans gaining much territory, with one tribe conquered and many others laying down their weapons without a fight, he gave up on Pannonia. Realizing that Pannonia was doomed to be overwhelmed by the legions sooner or later, he stationed his warriors in the mountain passes leading to Dalmatia, his homeland, to try to stall the Roman advance while other bodies of armed men continued to ravage the Roman settlements in southern Illyria. With Pannonia being overwhelmed by Silvanus' legions, in the summer General Pinnes offered to surrender both himself and all rebel forces in Pannonia.[29]

Something must have happened for General Pinnes to make such a drastic decision. It must be stated that the war in Pannonia had not been going well for the rebel side. Rome had inflicted one defeat after another upon them. Hundreds and perhaps thousands of Pannonian rebels had died the previous year. At the present rate of destruction, the rebel forces in Pannonia would be wiped out before the year was over.

Perhaps General Pinnes believed that continued resistance to Rome was futile. He had suffered many losses, his army had lost a lot of territory and reinforcements didn't seem forthcoming, so a counter-attack was out of the question. All he could hope to do was to hold his ground and be gradually pushed back mile by mile, and all the way the route would be marked by piles of rebel bodies killed by Romans on one nameless battlefield after another. Rather than face certain extinction, General Pinnes surrendered, perhaps believing that if he surrendered, he and his men would be granted mercy.

Another possibility is that Tiberius himself proposed such an offer. This war was a costly one and had distracted him from carrying out the war against the Marcomanni. The sooner he could have this war ended, the better. That way, things would get back on schedule. So Tiberius might have sent a secret message to the Pannonian rebels stating that the war was all but over and that Rome was certain to crush the resistance, but if they surrendered, they would be shown mercy. Tiberius may have even offered some type of bribe to sweeten the deal, either a pardon or an actual bribe in cash. The reason why I say this is because it says in the historical sources that Pinnes was defeated by Marcus Plautius Silvanus, but instead of surrendering to him, Pinnes surrendered to Tiberius. Wouldn't it make better sense that Pinnes surrender to the general who had defeated him? Not necessarily. Not if Tiberius was the one who actually persuaded Pinnes to give up, especially if Tiberius' terms were preferable.

Another distinct possibility was the environmental factor. The winter of 6–7 AD had been very bad and the year 7 AD did not improve things. Throughout that year, much of southern Europe underwent a crushing famine and this included the western Balkans. Faced with food shortages, the warriors simply might not have had the will or even the physical strength to continue fighting.[30] Regardless of the reasoning, General Pinnes decided that he would surrender. It was over.

The official surrender of all rebel forces in Pannonia took place on the banks of the Bathinus River in the summer of 7 AD. According to the *Fasti Antiates*, the exact date of the surrender was 3 August. General Pinnes led thousands of his warriors to this location, surrendered himself and his men to Rome, and then laid down their weapons on the ground. They all then either knelt or lay down on the ground in submission. Paterculus states that these thousands of warriors who had boasted not so long ago that they would conquer all of Italy now surrendered themselves ignominiously to Tiberius. The historical records do not state what the fate of Pinnes and his men were. It is likely that they were sold into slavery.[31]

Never Surrender: The Story of the Pannonian Partisans

The news of the Pannonians' surrender to Tiberius in early August must have come as a severe shock to Bato the Daesidiate. Half of the entire rebel force had laid down their arms and pledged to submit themselves to Rome, including the Pannonian commander General Pinnes, a man in whom Bato had confidence to carry out the war for as long as possible. Bato and his Dalmatians must have been in a state of panic. It must have also been a severe blow to their morale. How could they possibly win in their war against the Romans now that the Pannonians had surrendered?

However, Cassius Dio notes that not all of the Pannonians were willing to give up as easily as General Pinnes and his men had done. Small bands of Pannonian warriors were determined to continue the war against the Romans until death, regardless of the official surrender. They carried out their own private war against the Romans for a long time afterwards.[32] This sort of fighting is known as partisan or guerrilla warfare. No concrete information is given about these underground resistance groups as to their location, numbers or activities. I assume that they continued to harass the Romans for the duration of the war, which would last for two more years. Their continued involvement would explain why it would take the Roman troops two more years to push into Dalmatia. By carrying on the war, it not only served to keep the Roman legions engaged and slow down their advance into southern Illyria, but it also helped to maintain Illyrian pride. General Pinnes' surrender earlier that year had been a devastating blow to the rebels' morale, but these little bands fighting on doggedly against the Roman invaders helped to preserve their country's honour.

In order to see what sort of tactics these guerrilla bands would have used, we need to take a look at similar circumstances that have occurred at other places and times in Roman history. Notable examples include the Spartacus Revolt as well as the Roman invasions of Spain, Gaul and Germany. Sextus Frontinus claimed that the Germans excelled in ambush tactics: 'The Germans, in accordance with their usual custom, kept emerging from woodland-pastures and unsuspected hiding-places to attack our men, and then finding a safe refuge in the depths of the forest.'[33]

The preceding quote definitely describes partisan or guerrilla operations: emerging from some secret hideout to attack or harass the enemy and then quickly retreating to some place where they could conceal themselves. The Pannonian partisans, too, would have engaged in a strategy of stealth and surprise, attacking quickly and then vanishing. Using such techniques, they would whittle down the Roman presence in Illyria one by one and cut crucial supply and communication lines. Roman units would be regularly and continuously harassed by small armed bands roving through the countryside and then disappearing. Guerrilla operations thrive in wars that involve over-extended enemy forces, formidable terrain and a supportive local population, and all three of these factors were definitely in play in the rugged mountainous land of Illyria during the first years of the first century AD.[34]

All guerrilla-based wars have certain similarities. First, guerrilla forces cannot sustain themselves without local help, so the local people have to support the rebel side. To do this, the guerrillas work hard to build up the loyalty of the population. Second, a small core of specifically-selected targets is attacked that are designed to both weaken the enemy as well as demonstrate to the people that the enemy forces are not as strong as they appear. These carefully-chosen targets include destroying key military installations as well as the methodical assassination of military personnel and government officials. Third and finally, the guerrillas cease their clandestine operations and engage in open field warfare against the enemy force.[35]

In order to carry on their operations, guerrilla forces need to relocate away from urbanized areas and establish secret camps far removed from the prying eyes of military or government forces. Here they can find refuge, build up their strength or recuperate from losses.

Guerrilla operations also exact a psychological toll in addition to a militaristic one. Modern militaries that have had to fight against guerrilla forces, such as the British redcoats in the Thirteen Colonies, Napoleon's Grande Armée in Spain, the Nazis in Yugoslavia, the Americans in Vietnam and the Russians in Afghanistan, all relate that a distinct atmosphere of fear and uncertainty pervades any operations conducted in those theatres. You never know when you will be stabbed in the back, step on a land mine or have your head taken off by a sniper's bullet.

Would the Roman military have launched counter-insurgency operations? I doubt it. Their strategy for dealing with guerrilla fighters was simply to destroy every living thing that they saw and burn down every settlement that they came across. There was no ancient Roman version of the US Army Special Forces or the British SAS. Many times, the opposing military force will turn their aggression upon the ordinary people to dissuade them from providing any assistance to the guerrilla forces as well as provoking the rebels into abandoning their places of concealment and coming out into the open where they can be easily destroyed by the military's superior force.

Guerrilla forces seemed to be predisposed to suffering unusually high casualty rates. Their limited numbers, their limited strength and logistical capabilities, as well as the enemy's drive to thoroughly destroy them usually mean that partisans suffer heavy losses, but the enemy finds it difficult or even impossible to completely destroy them. Such may have been the same for the Pannonian partisans. This would also explain why the Romans had to deploy so many troops to this region. In order to deny the partisans any territory for recruitment or refuge, every single piece of ground would have to be held. In order to do that, thousands of troops would have to be brought in to provide a sizeable amount of security. Small detachments would be easy pickings for partisan forces, as the Romans would find out in Germany.

Aside from these small bands of fanatics, Pannonia was out of the war. All that was left was the subjugation of Dalmatia. Tiberius named one of his subordinates, General Marcus Aemilius Lepidus, as the commanding general of all Roman forces operating within Illyria, at least until the start of the next year's campaigning season. Tiberius also designated his aide-de-camp Magius Celer Velleianus, Paterculus' brother, as his second-in-command (Tiberius would actually have Velleianus decorated due to his conduct in the war). In autumn, the army marched proudly back to their winter quarters and awaited the coming offensive against the Dalmatians.[36]

Chapter Five

A Long Hard Slog

The Rebels are on the Defensive in Dalmatia

It was now the year 8 AD. Marcus Furius Camillus and Sextus Nonius Quinctilianus were made the new consuls for the Senate. Caesar Augustus stayed in the Adriatic city of Ariminum (modern-day Rimini, Italy), so that he could receive news of the revolt faster than if he stayed in Rome.[1]

The campaign of 8 AD got off to a late start. Usually, the campaigning season began right after the spring thaw, but in this circumstance Rome's forces didn't start moving until the beginning of summer.[2] One wonders why. No explanation is given within the ancient accounts as to why the Romans launched their operations so late in the year, but considering what had happened towards the end of the previous year's campaign season, we can make some guesses.

First, the Romans had made some substantial advances into rebel territory. They likely needed time to consolidate their positions even further before pressing onwards. Second, although the Pannonians had officially surrendered, small groups continued to wage an underground resistance campaign against the Roman occupation forces. These guerrilla bands were likely harassing Rome's supply and communication lines in the area, as well as attacking targets of opportunity. These partisans would have hampered Rome's war effort. Third, in order to destroy or just neutralize the guerrilla threat, Rome had to bring in large numbers of troops to act as security forces, manning every individual station so that the rebels could not locate and exploit any easy targets. It would take a staggering amount of manpower in order to make sure that every inch of the reclaimed zone was sufficiently defended, and it would take a lot of time to get such numbers of troops into position. This would also validate claims given in the ancient sources as to the large numbers of troops that Rome employed to suppress this rebellion.

This delay in operations gave Bato the Daesidiate and his Illyrian rebels a few months' head start to make all necessary preparations to resist the Roman advance. Following General Pinnes' surrender the previous

August and with the subjugation of most of the Pannonians, Bato had decided that it was no longer feasible to defend all of Illyria, especially the northern region of Pannonia where the rebel presence was too low and the Roman presence was too high. Yes, there were small guerrilla operations going on there, but he correctly deduced that it would not take the Romans long to isolate and destroy each of these rebel bands one by one. So he withdrew all surviving rebel forces under his command southwards to defend his home region of Dalmatia. Pannonia's landscape was mostly flat, and it was easy for the Roman army to advance across it with relative ease. By contrast, Dalmatia's terrain was much more rugged and treacherous, and much better suited to the defensive campaign that Bato was now trying to wage against the ever-advancing legions. Trudging up and down mountains and steep forest-covered river valleys was sure to wear the legions down. Every rock and every tree stump would be defended, and he would make the Romans pay dearly for every inch of ground that they took. Bato would turn Dalmatia into his own version of the Gothic Line, and would make each battle fought here like an ancient Roman version of Monte Cassino.

A Delayed Start

Once summer had begun, General Marcus Lepidus and his troops marched from their winter camp to aid Tiberius in the war to the south. Paterculus states that Lepidus and his army had to struggle not only with the difficult rugged terrain, but also with the constant attacks by the ferocious natives. The legions ventured into the territories of various tribes that had not yet been attacked by the Romans during the revolt. These tribes had not suffered defeats and their morale was still high, and as such they were in high spirits when it came to killing the legionnaires.[3]

Regrettably, our information for the whole campaign season of 8 AD is aggravatingly slim. Only two authors, Gaius Paterculus and Cassius Dio, provide any information about the fighting during this year, and both of them relay only generalized facts about General Lepidus' campaign against the Dalmatians. So we are forced to fill in a lot of the details ourselves.

Before we go into the particulars of this offensive (or more accurately, the *hypothetical* particulars since there is hardly any information for the campaign season of 8 AD), it's important to establish a little biographical information concerning our man of the hour so that we can get a better idea of why the campaign progressed in the way that it did. Marcus Aemilius Lepidus came from one of the oldest patrician families in Rome. He was a prominent senator, a gifted lawyer and had imperial connections: he was the brother of Lucius Aemilius Paullus, the husband of Julia the Younger, Caesar Augustus' granddaughter. In the year 6 AD, he served as a Senatorial consul.[4] Therefore it was during his administration that the conflagration in the province of Illyricum erupted.

If there ever was a paragon of the Roman ideals of *virtus* (manliness), *dignitas* (dignity) and *severitas* (sticking to one's principles no matter what the consequences may be), then Marcus Aemilius Lepidus must have been regarded as such a person during his time. Paterculus described Lepidus as 'a man who in name and in fortune approaches the Caesars, whom one admires and loves the more in proportion to his opportunities to know and understand him, and whom one regards as an ornament to the great names from whom he springs.'[5] Tacitus was more simplistic in his praise, calling him noble and wise.[6] Marcus Aemilius Lepidus was therefore a prime example of *exempla*: a role model of proper behaviour that is supposed to be copied by others.

In keeping with this conservative principled image, General Lepidus' conduct in this stage of the war was stereotypically Roman. He not only inflicted heavy losses on the tribes that attacked him, but also burned their houses and farms and slaughtered many of the people who lived in that region as a punishment for siding with the rebels.[7]

However, impressive as these records are, there are many aspects about this campaign that the historical documents do not mention. For example, it was earlier stated that at the end of the campaign season of 7 AD, Tiberius designated Marcus Lepidus as the commanding general of all Roman forces engaged in the Illyrian uprising and named his aide Magius Celer Velleianus as his second-in-command, which I find to be a rather odd choice. This leads me to ask the following question: where was Tiberius? If he named another man as the supreme commander of all Roman forces within Illyria, that naturally implies that Tiberius himself was not in Illyria during the winter 'recess'. My guess (and it is only a guess) is that he went south to Ariminum to keep Caesar Augustus apprised of the situation and to get a little rest and recuperation in Italy before heading back east again to beat up the rebels. For the commanding general, going back to Rome during the winter lull was a common occurrence. Indeed, Cassius Dio states that in early spring of 9 AD, Tiberius returned to Rome.[8] So when the winter season of 7 AD began to set in, he was presumably on his way south to Italy and he put Lepidus in charge of things while he was gone.

With Marcus Lepidus now in command of all Roman troops in Illyria, where would he himself have been stationed during the winter? Any number of places within north-western Illyria could be a probable answer. The sources say that when he got his men moving, Lepidus joined up with Tiberius' forces. So if we know where Tiberius and his men were stationed, then we might be able to make a guess as to where Lepidus and his men were stationed.

Since Lepidus was put in charge of Roman troops within the region, and since Tiberius was presumably nowhere to be found, and since there was still a resistance movement going on in Pannonia, I would say that it's fairly reasonable that Marcus Lepidus was headquartered somewhere within Pannonia so that he could maintain command and control over all of the Roman troops operating within that region, who I imagine were busily engaged that winter in patrols hunting for the Pannonian guerrilla fighters. Because Tiberius was away, the city of Segestica seems to be the most likely place where Marcus Lepidus would establish his headquarters. It lay on the border between the regions of Pannonia and Dalmatia. From here, Lepidus could keep apprised of the efforts of the Roman occupation forces to the north, while at the same time remain close enough to the rebel forces in the south to keep an eye on them.

Moreover, there does not seem to be an adequate number of Roman bases located within Pannonia itself to provide any workable option. Archaeology and historical records show that many of the Roman sites within northern Illyria were constructed *after* the Great Illyrian Revolt took place. Only a few Roman settlements were located within the region, none of which appear to have been sizeable enough to support a large military presence. There were only a small number of forts, most of them being forts for Roman auxiliaries, and nearly all of them are constructed along the Danube River frontier. This may have been just fine for guarding against attacks by the Germans and Dacians who were located on the opposite bank, but it was inadequate for guarding against any Illyrian rebels that were already in the area. The largest military base within northern Illyria, the fort at Vindebona, was almost at the furthest northern edge of Illyria, and would have been of absolutely no use whatsoever in acting as a headquarters for military operations because the action was too far to the south by this time. So, since Segestica seems to be the only reasonable option, it is likely that Marcus Lepidus was stationed there.[9]

Since it says in the records that Lepidus and his troops linked up with Tiberius and *his* troops during the campaign, it is obvious that these groups of soldiers were separated from each other when the campaign season of 8 AD began. There were, therefore, two Roman armies marching into south-central Illyria at the same time. Since Lepidus was likely headquartered in Segestica during the winter, and since the majority of the troops under his command were there and to the north in Pannonia, and since Tiberius was away (presumably in Italy) during the winter lull, and since more troops were needed to be brought in for security and to provide ever-greater manpower when it came to carrying out the war, then it is therefore possible that Tiberius had been busy recruiting men in Italy and then led them into the war zone, possibly by marching along the coast. So we would have Tiberius driving in from the east, and we also have Lepidus and his men driving down from the north-east.

This would also explain why the campaign of 8 AD got off to a late start. If Tiberius' intention was to have a two-pronged assault into central Illyria, he needed a sufficient number of men to do it. Aulus Caecina Severus couldn't be called in once again because his troops had already fought hard and had suffered much. Besides, he needed to defend his own province. As for the large number of Roman troops that were already within northern and western Illyria, the vast majority of those were tied down trying to keep the Pannonians in line and hunting for the partisan groups. So Tiberius would have to raise more men from somewhere, and that would take time. The pincer assault could not begin until both armies were in position. Since it would take time for Tiberius to raise a sufficient number of new troops, the offensive would have to be delayed until he had the number of men that he needed. While the Romans waited, Bato the Daesidiate used the time to further strengthen his positions.

Marcus Lepidus Ravages the Balkans

In the summer of 8 AD, after delaying military operations for months, Marcus Lepidus and his troops finally got under way. What exact route would Lepidus and his men have taken? It would seem natural for us to suppose that Lepidus' march lay along the route of the famed Roman roads. Many people have acclaimed these roads as engineering marvels, but contrary to what is often said or alluded to, these were not ancient versions of highways. Roman roads were not that wide. A typical Roman *via* or 'way' was only eight to ten feet wide, sufficiently wide for two waggons to travel in opposite directions without either one of them having to pull over so that the other could pass by.[10] Very few paved Roman roads were in Illyria during this early stage. There appears to have been one situated along Illyria's Adriatic coast called the Via Gemina, which connected the Italian city of Aquileia with the city of Salona. Another road, the Via Flavia, went down the Istrian peninsula to the city of Pula, which is located on the peninsula's tip.[11] One of the few Roman roads that lay in the interior of the region, the Via Pannonia, was constructed sometime within the first century BC and connected Aquileia to Sirmium.[12]

However, for the rest of Illyria, it seems that serious road construction took place after the Great Illyrian Revolt ended. We know of five Roman roads that were constructed within the province of Illyricum from 15 to 20 AD, well after the rebellion was crushed. Some roads, especially those connected to the city of Salona, are dated loosely to the early first century AD.[13] I find it difficult to believe that a massive road network spanning the whole of Illyria was constructed within the six years between the birth of Christ to the outbreak of hostilities in the western Balkans. Therefore I must conclude that the majority of iconic Roman paved roads that were constructed in Illyria were laid down, at the earliest, in the final years of Caesar Augustus' life. In fact, archaeology has shown that the vast majority of Roman roads constructed within this region were laid down during the third century.[14]

Yet these are just the famous paved cobblestone roads that we normally associate with travel in the ancient world. What about unpaved roads? Well, that is a very open-ended question, because there could have been many dirt roads criss-crossing the country connecting one settlement to another. Unlike the study of the cobblestone Roman roads, archaeology has a tough time trying to determine firstly if there was an unpaved road connecting one settlement to another, and secondly when such a road was developed. I say 'developed' instead of 'constructed' because dirt roads do indeed become developed over a prolonged period of time rather than being dug out in a single event. They start off as small footpaths winding their way through the land, then they develop into trails and then, after enough passage of people, waggons and livestock moving along them, they become roads. When did such pathways become roads? Who can say?

Looking at modern maps, it seems to me that Marcus Lepidus and his men may have marched eastwards along the course of the Sava River, moving from Segestica to the town of Sirmium. The Pannonians to the north had, for the most part, been defeated, with the small roving bands of rebel guerrillas being the exception. Two years earlier, the city of Sirmium had come under attack by rebel forces but Governor Aulus Caecina Severus managed to drive them off, though he suffered heavy losses later on at the Battle of the Dravus River. Having Marcus Lepidus march his men to Sirmium would reaffirm Roman control over the region, and it would definitely cut Illyria in half, splitting off Pannonia from Dalmatia and preventing any rebels from the south from infiltrating northwards to reawaken the Pannonians' rebellious spirit.

Paterculus states that along his march, Lepidus' force had to march through difficult terrain and repeatedly made contact with the enemy. Paterculus also states that the rebels 'barred his way', implying that they took up defensive positions in an attempt to stop or at least stall his advance. The historian concluded this part by saying that Lepidus managed to force his way through, inflicted heavy losses upon the rebels and utterly destroyed their lands.[15]

Paterculus does not state which tribes Marcus Lepidus and his troops encountered along their march. In order to determine this, we need to look at reconstructed maps and see which peoples were along Lepidus' supposed route from Segestica to Sirmium.

The Breucians, whose territory lay at or near the Bosna River, occupied a large area but they had already been defeated the previous year. Marcus Lepidus might have taken his troops on a tour through Breucian lands just to make sure that they stayed pacified. The next tribe that Lepidus would have encountered would have been the Cornacates, who lay between the Breucians and the Scordisci. They were a small tribe with only one prominent settlement, Cornacum (modern-day Sotin, Croatia, loated on the Danube River to the south-east of the modern town of Vukovar). Cornacum probably had a wall or at least a fence built around it, since the settlement's name stems from the Celtic word *caion*, meaning 'enclosure'.[16] Sometime during the first century AD, the Romans built a small fort here to house a battalion of auxiliaries. In 2009, excavations near here uncovered the remains of a Roman encampment, which was ringed by two V-shaped ditches.[17] Could this be the remains of a camp that was erected by Marcus Lepidus during his march into the region in the year 8 AD?

The Cornacates likely didn't give Marcus Lepidus and his legions much trouble since they were a minor tribe that only had one major settlement to their credit, but what was more daunting was the landscape. Their lands consisted mostly of boggy marshland, and Lepidus would have to take care that his men did not become entrapped. He must have been very conscious of what had happened to Severus and his soldiers the previous year at the Battle of the Volcaean Marshes, which likely took place not far from the location that Lepidus and his men were marching towards.

I imagine here a scene reminiscent of Germanicus' return to the Teutoburg Forest years after the infamous disaster that laid low three legions in the Germanic wilderness. In the year 15 AD, during Rome's revenge campaign against the Germanic rebels led by Arminius, Germanicus and his men returned to the old battlefield where Varus and many of his men lost their lives. In his account of this event Tacitus states that Germanicus and his troops discovered the bones of many men that had been chopped into pieces, lying scattered about everywhere exactly where the men had fallen, as well as fragments of weapons and the bones of war horses, and that the whole army was deeply filled with sorrow. They furthermore uncovered evidence of the Germans' barbarity when they saw decapitated heads that had been nailed onto trees, as well as altars where the victorious Germans had subjected their Roman captives to ritualistic human sacrifice.[18] Did Marcus Lepidus and his men visit the site of the old battlefield where Severus and his troops fought so bravely the year before? Did they discover any objects related to the battle, or perhaps uncover any human remains? The ancient sources do not make any mention of this, but as Lepidus and his men continued to march eastwards, I do not doubt that at some point they either arrived at the old battlefield or else passed very near to it. The memory of what had happened here must have been present in the minds of every soldier in that column, and it must have created a very ominous dark mood among the men.

After subjugating the Cornacates, which I imagine didn't take very long, the troops may have crossed over the Sava River and entered the land of the Andizetes. This tribe lived between the Sava and Drava Rivers, and they needed to be got out of the way so that Lepidus' troops could drive on further eastwards and still have their left flank protected.

After conquering the Andizetes, Lepidus likely continued to advance eastwards and his next target would have been the Amantini tribe. The

Amantini had previously occupied a large part of this area, including the city of Sirmium, but as the Scordisci Celts grew in power and expanded into the region, they gradually pushed the native Illyrians out, reducing the Amantini to a population existing between the Sava and Danube Rivers and forcing them into a subjected status. There is also evidence that a small pocket population broke off and migrated southwards into the region of Epirus, establishing the town of Amantia; either that, or Amantia was a Greek settlement that just happened to have an Illyrian-sounding name.

The clearest evidence for a Roman attack upon the Amantini comes from the fourth-century historian Festus, who writes with regard to the fighting in the Great Illyrian Revolt: 'After Batho [sic], King of the Pannonians, had been subdued, the Pannonians came under our sway. After the Amantians between the Save and Drave had been laid low, the area adjoining the Save and environs of Pannonia Secunda were obtained.'[19] This, to me, is confirmation that following the general surrender of the Pannonians, the Amantini tribe was one of the tribes that were targeted by General Marcus Lepidus.

Now that Lepidus was confident that his left and rear were secure, he turned his army south to attack his most formidable target: the Scordisci. They were a large and powerful tribe whose western territory lay at the junction of the Sava and Danube Rivers, not far from Sirmium. The Scordisci, known to the Greeks that they occasionally fought against as the 'Skordiskoi', were one of several Celtic tribes that had abandoned their traditional lands to the north-west and had migrated into south-eastern Europe. The Scordisci had migrated into the western Balkans sometime during the 200s BC. According to legend, following the Celtic invasion of Greece and their attack on the city of Delphi, the Celtic hordes left Greece, but afterwards they split up and different parties ventured off in search of new homes. One of these parties was led by a man named Bathanattos, and he and his party ventured into the land of the Illyrian Autariate tribe, which dwelled on the borders of Macedon. This Celtic band settled upon the slope of Mount Scordus, and thereupon took the name Scordisci, 'the people of Scordus'.[20] After establishing this initial outpost, the Scordisci gained more power and spread into the surrounding territory. They eventually became one of the major tribes in the region because they occupied a large portion of land and several of the neighbouring tribes were under their political domination, forced to acknowledge the Scordisci as their overlords and to pay regular tributes to them. Prominent settlements of the Scordisci included Singidunum (Belgrade, Serbia), Capedunum (possibly Banoštor, Serbia) and Viminacium (Kostolac, Serbia).[21] Part of the reason why they gained so much power was due to them controlling a vital natural resource found in the area: silver. In the years between their establishment in the western Balkans and their subjugation by the Romans, the Scordisci controlled the silver mines located near the Drina River.[22] In fact, their original home of Mount Scordus is now known as Shar-Dagh or 'Silver Mountain'.[23] When the Romans became involved in affairs in the western Balkans, and especially after the area was conquered by them, the Romans made sure to take possession of Scordisci lands in order to control the silver supply.

As for their relationship with the Romans, the Scordisci Celts had a mixed relationship with them, sometimes fighting alongside the legions and other times fighting against them. From the middle of the second century BC onwards, the Scordisci and the Romans fought each other. The Romans sent a total of twelve expeditions to attack them. One notable episode took place in the year 83 BC, when Lucius Scipio inflicted a major defeat upon them and compelled them to relocate across the Danube. However, five years later, they returned.[24] During Tiberius' conquest of Pannonia in 12–9 BC, the Scordisci acted as his allies, attacking from the east while Tiberius and his men attacked from the west.

Since the accounts of the Great Illyrian Revolt state that Lepidus had to frequently fight against those who he encountered, I can assume that this time the Scordisci were in a hostile mood rather than a friendly one. Several secondary authors claim that the Scordisci Celts were finally defeated once and for all in the year 8 AD, so I can conclude that the Scordisci did, in fact, resist Marcus Lepidus' advance with great tenacity and were finally crushed and forced to submit. Individual battles likely centred on the control of major settlements or strategic geographic locations. The ancient sources do not make any mention of Lepidus' army laying siege to or assaulting the cities of Singidunum or Viminacium or indeed any settlements in the area, but Lepidus' legions surely must have stormed some of them because Paterculus states that by the time Lepidus' force rendezvoused with Tiberius' force, Lepidus' legionnaires were laden with captured plunder. You don't get that from marching through farms and tiny villages, you get that from taking towns and cities. So Marcus Lepidus and his troops surely must have conducted at least one major assault against a rebel-held town or city. As to which one or ones he took, no one can say with any certainty.

This leads us to focus on Tiberius once again. If Tiberius was marching out of Italy, then he would be in Lepidus' rear, with Lepidus far to the east in Sirmium. Therefore, in order for Lepidus and Tiberius to link up, Lepidus' army would either have to about-face and march westwards back over the land that they had just devastated, or else possibly turn southwards and then wheel towards the west through more unconquered lands that he would have to fight through, essentially marching his army in a route shaped like a backwards C. I believe the second option. Paterculus states that Lepidus had to go through a lot of hard work to rendezvous with Tiberius' forces, that Lepidus' army was weighed down by plunder, and that he had to fight all the way through unconquered tribes and difficult terrain. If Lepidus merely retraced his steps and marched back where he came from, the journey homewards would be substantially easier; he would not have had to fight his way through the tribes a second time and he would not have had to struggle with the terrain as much since he now knew where the best routes would be. Therefore I believe that Lepidus, upon reaching Sirmium, turned his army southwards towards the traditional Pannonia–Dalmatia border and then marched westwards along this border region, conquering tribes that he met along the way.

Where was the rendezvous location? The sources don't say. All that Paterculus says is that after struggling through the landscape and enduring constant enemy attacks and after inflicting massive amounts of death and destruction along his path, Lepidus 'succeeded in reaching Caesar, rejoicing in victory and laden with booty'.[25] That's not much to go on. Was there a prearranged rendezvous point, or did the two forces move independently, gradually marching closer and closer towards each other, until they at last linked up at a random place? None of the sources say. If Tiberius was marching an army from Italy into Illyria, after he rounded the northern coast of the Adriatic, he would have been advancing from north-west to south-east. One hypothesis is that Tiberius arrived in Segestica and afterwards Marcus Lepidus and his men arrived on the scene. This is only one hypothesis, and there could be many other options that are equally valid such as Tiberius sailing across the Adriatic and landing in Salona and then fighting his way northwards. However, since the ancient accounts make no mention of any fighting on Tiberius' part during this stage, this hypothesis seems implausible. Remember, Tiberius was getting more and more cautious as the years rolled on and he did not want to engage in battle when it wasn't necessary. Furthermore, the war was draining and exhausting the empire's manpower. Repeatedly, the government had been required to relocate units from elsewhere in the empire, leaving those areas without protection. When this didn't work, they had called in the retired veterans, and when that didn't work they were forced to press-gang civilians and even slaves into military service. Quite simply, the empire was beginning to run out of available manpower. Tiberius could not afford to suffer more casualties in one battle or siege after another. It would have been better to circumvent these obstacles rather than charging directly at them, despite the lure of plunder and battlefield glory. So, with due caution and precision, Tiberius moved his men around in a wide C-shaped arc until they got to where they had to go.

If we reconstruct Lepidus' march of 8 AD, we can gauge that it was a horrendous ordeal. After leaving the security of Segestica at the beginning of summer, his men advanced south-east and then east along the course of the Sava River until he got to perhaps where the Sava and Bosna Rivers converge. From here, he would have marched his men overland north-eastwards towards the Danube, marching to what is now Vukovar. From this point, he would have proceeded along the Danube, making one detour in his march to take Sirmium and then continuing along his riverine march until he got to where the Sava joins the Danube. From here, he marched southwards through the land of the Scordisci Celts and then, along the foothills of the Dinaric Mountains, he made his return march westwards. He fought battles all along the way, smashing through armies and obstacles arrayed against him to block his path, crossing over the Drina River and making it to Brčko. Once again at the familiar flow of the Sava River, he would have followed it back to Segestica, where he would have presumably linked up with Tiberius' troops.

When word of these struggles reached the Senate, it was decided that Tiberius should be given some of the honours of a triumph (he would have been given a triumph if Tiberius had led the Roman force himself), even though it was Lepidus and not Tiberius who led the Roman force.[26] I imagine that Marcus Lepidus boiled at not being given the recognition that he felt he deserved, but if he did have such feelings it is likely that he kept them well hidden.

War in Bato's Backyard: Rome attacks the Daesidiates

Rome now turned its attention to the Perustae and Daesidiates. These two Dalmatian tribes were daunting opponents. According to Paterculus, their superb skills in warfare, their ferocious temper and, above all, their natural strongholds situated either atop mountains or in easily-defended narrow passes made them 'almost unconquerable'.[27] It wasn't until these two tribes were 'almost entirely exterminated',[28] as Paterculus puts it, that Rome was finally able to suppress them.

The fighting during this stage of the campaign must have been especially horrendous. After all, this was Bato's own tribe, and he was now fighting to defend his very own homeland. As such, he likely gave the Romans hell for every inch of ground that they gained. Tiberius remained cool-headed throughout these operations, as Paterculus records:

> Nothing in the course of this great war, nothing in the campaigns in Germany, came under my observation that was greater, or that aroused my admiration more, than these traits of its general; no chance of winning a victory ever seemed to him timely, which he would have to purchase by the sacrifice of his soldiers; the safest course was always regarded by him as the best; he consulted his conscience first and then his reputation, and, finally, the plans of the commander were never governed by the opinion of the army, but rather the army by the wisdom of its leader.[29]

Paterculus' words, though flowery at first glance, hide some unpleasant truths. In his own words, he admits that Tiberius was having a hard time bringing Bato to heel. Tiberius was never able to get an opportunity to defeat his Illyrian adversary or any of his subordinate commanders without losing a lot of his own men in the process. Knowing this, Tiberius was extremely hesitant to take on the Illyrian rebels in direct head-to-head clashes. The Roman commander tried to find or make opportunities to whittle down the rebel strength in a series of easy victories, but nothing worked. Paterculus also hints that Tiberius' troops were boiling for a fight. In fact, as you read the timelines of this entire war from beginning to end, it becomes increasingly clear that as the war went on, the legionnaires became all the keener to get it over and done with using whatever methods they could. As the war dragged on, the soldiers on both sides became more violent, more destructive and less concerned with morality. Tiberius was coming under a lot of pressure from his men to simply have at the rebels and destroy them all, but he knew that if he simply sent his soldiers forward against the well-entrenched enemy, they would be slaughtered.

It is here that I am reminded of the words of Major General James Wolfe, who fought against Montcalm in his campaign to take Quebec during the Seven Years' War. In a letter that Wolfe wrote to his mother, he relates the following:

> The enemy puts nothing to risk, and I can't in conscience put the whole army to risk. My antagonist has wisely shut himself up in inaccessible entrenchments, so that I can't get at him without spilling a torrent of blood, and that perhaps to little purpose. The Marquis de Montcalm is at the head of a great number of bad soldiers and I am at the head of a small number of good ones, that wish for nothing so much as to fight him; but the wary old fellow avoids an action, doubtful of the behaviour of his army. People must be of the [military] profession to understand the disadvantages and difficulties we labour under, arising from the uncommon natural strength of the country.[30]

Such feelings and words would have been easily applicable to the present situation in which Tiberius found himself when he and his men invaded Bato's home territory. Tiberius' subordinate commanders were likely eager to attack and bring the war to a conclusion due to the accolades and the titles that would be bestowed upon them once victory had been won, and the legionnaires as well would have wanted the war finished as soon as possible due to all of the horrors and hardships that they had to endure. Remember that these men had borne the brunt of the fighting and the conflict had been especially savage. The men were becoming increasingly worried about the war continuing indefinitely, and were consumed with the thoughts of all of the other battles and sieges that they might have to face in the future if the war dragged on any longer. So many had already been killed and wounded, and the longer the war went on, the greater the likelihood that they themselves would either end up on a stretcher or in a grave. Tiberius, too, must have been eager to get this operation finished. The months were passing and winter would be coming on soon. If he couldn't smash Bato's mountaintop fortresses before the weather turned harsh, then Tiberius would have to retire his army to their winter quarters with the work still unfinished and delay siege operations until the following spring.

The Romans weren't the only ones who were eager for a victory this year. The rebels were also likely anxious to smash the legions and have them limp away, or at least to keep them at a distance. The harvest was approaching and the Illyrians would need to get their crops in before the bite of winter. They remembered what the horrible winter of 6–7 AD had done. They did not want to see any more of their people starve to death. Therefore Bato needed to drive the Romans off as soon as possible so that his people could earnestly get to work bringing in the food from the fields.

As is the case so many times in wars like this, armies resort to general attrition when they cannot obtain specific primary objectives. We know from Cassius Dio that the Illyrians were suffering from a famine and starvation by the end of the year. However, not all of southern Europe shared this fate. In Italy the famine had ended, and Caesar Augustus celebrated the return of green growth by sponsoring games dedicated to his grandsons Germanicus and Claudius.[31] As for the condition of the rest of southern Europe, there's no information. However, I find it interesting that the historical sources say that while the famine had ended in Italy, it still persisted within Illyria. One hypothesis is that the Illyrian people were too busy fighting to tend to farming but this seems unlikely. Another hypothesis that might fill in the blanks is that Tiberius, being thwarted in his attacks against the fortified rebel positions, turned his men loose upon the countryside to destroy the rebel supply bases as well as to provoke the Illyrian rebels into abandoning their defensive positions and coming out into the open where they could be more easily destroyed. Once again, there is a parallel to the operation carried out by Tiberius against the Daesidiates with that of Wolfe's campaign to take Quebec. When assaulting the Canadian city failed, Wolfe resorted to devastating the surrounding landscape. On 2 September 1759, Wolfe wrote the following:

> At my first coming into the Country, I used all the Means in my Power, to engage the Canadians to lay down their Arms, by offers of such Protection & Security for themselves, their Property and Religion as was consistent with the known mildness of His Majesty's Government. I found that good treatment had not the desired Effect, so that of late I have changed my Measures & laid waste the Country; partly to engage the Marquis de Montcalm to try the Event of a Battle to prevent the Ravage, And partly in Return for many Insults offer'd to our People by the Canadians, As well as the frequent Inhumanitys exercised upon our own

Frontiers. It was necessary also to have some Prisoners as Hostages for their good Behaviour to our People in their Hands, whom I had reason to think they did not use very well. Major Dalling surprized [*sic*] the Guard of a village & brought in about 380 Prisoners, which I keep, not proposing any Exchange till the end of the Campaign. To the uncommon strength of the Country, the Enemy have added (for the Defence of the River) a great Number of Floating Batteries & Boats. By the vigilance of these, and the Indians round our different Posts, it has been impossible to execute anything by surprize. We have had almost daily skirmishes with these Savages, in which they are generally defeated. But not without Loss on our Side.[32]

Tiberius, too, might have made offers of peace to the Illyrian rebels, using promises and assurances of merciful treatment in order to induce the rebels to lay down their arms and submit. He had done the same thing in Germania years earlier on two occasions in order to get the hostile western Germanic tribes to submit to Rome. The historical records do not state whether or not Tiberius did indeed make overtures of peace to the Illyrians but if he did, then his entreaties failed because the Perustae and Daesidiate tribes resisted at every turn and Tiberius was forced to repeatedly confront them either in harrying the general population or in battle against the rebel forces. In the end, the Romans had done so much damage that both of these tribes were nearly wiped out entirely before the region could be deemed secure. Even so, Bato himself managed to escape.

Without large stores of food, these mountaintop strongholds would have had to rely upon regular shipments of food and supplies from outside. It would have been imperative to control the fertile wet valleys where much of the agriculture within the western Balkans took place. If Tiberius and his troops devastated the countryside, burning all of the area's farmland in order to deprive the Illyrians of their food supplies, then this would explain why the Illyrians were so desperate to eat whatever they could get their hands on, and it also explains why the campaign season of the following year was so abrupt.

On the Ropes

By the end of 8 AD, the Illyrian rebels began contemplating surrendering to the Romans because they were suffering greatly from famine and disease. In fact, they were becoming so desperate to find food, any food at all, that they were forced to eat plants that were toxic. Cassius Dio relates: 'They were afflicted first by famine and then by disease that followed it, since they were using for food roots and strange herbs.'[33] Imagine being so starved that you'll eat poison ivy.

However, even though they felt that the war was rapidly going against them and were looking for any way to bring the conflict to an end, they did not make these intentions known to the Romans, believing that the Romans would never spare their lives for rebelling against the empire. One of the Illyrian war chiefs named Scenobarbus, of whom we know nothing other than his name, wished to switch sides and fight alongside the Romans against his countrymen. He even sent a letter to Manius Ennius, who Tiberius had made the commander of the garrison at Segestica, but soon became afraid that his plans would be discovered and he would be killed before he could undertake his scheme. He likely remembered what happened to Bato the Breucian when he crossed his colleague Bato the Daesidiate. Scenobarbus didn't want to end up being publically beheaded as a collaborator and a traitor, so he changed his mind about joining the Romans.[34]

The Daesidiates, one of the major tribes that were involved in the Great Illyrian Revolt, had been conquered by the Romans just before winter set in. However, Bato was still alive and he had escaped every time that the Romans thought they had cornered him. With his flight also flew the prospect that this war could be brought to a conclusion that year. Tiberius, probably filled with dread at the thought of another year's fighting in the treacherous mountains of the western Balkans, left for Rome to give Caesar Augustus a report in person of what had been accomplished in Illyria thus far. He also ordered his troops to their winter quarters to rest and resupply and to ready themselves for the next round of bloody battles that they would have to fight once spring came.

Chapter Six

The End of the Road

The Last Year

It was now the year 9 AD, which would prove to be a formative year not only for the fighting in Illyria but for the Roman Empire in general. Quintus Sulpicius Camerinus and Gaius Sabinus were elected as the consuls for that year. Tiberius returned to Rome and was greeted by Caesar Augustus himself on the outskirts of the city. Marcus Messallinus, the governor of Illyricum, was relieved of command and Augustus appointed the former Senatorial *consul suffectus* Gaius Vibius Postumus to take his place. A man named Lucius Apronius was made one of Postumus' subordinates. Both men would conduct themselves very well during the last stages of the war and would earn the awards of a triumph.[1]

Publius Annius Florus writes in his *Epitome*:

> Augustus entrusted the task of completely subjugating them [the Illyrians] to Vibius, who forced this savage people to dig the earth and to melt from its veins the gold, which this otherwise most stupid of peoples seeks with such zeal and diligence that you would think they were extracting it for their own purposes.[2]

Danijel Dzino states that the Romans were fully aware that the western Balkans possessed a vast wealth of mineral resources. During the reign of Caesar Augustus, mining operations in the area increased but they did not increase to a substantial level until the second century AD.[3]

The Assault on Splonum

While Tiberius was in Rome participating in the celebrations commemorating the victories of the previous year, his nephew Germanicus was still fighting. Early in the year, he and his men had seized possession of numerous rebel-controlled settlements within Dalmatia. Now, he turned his attention towards capturing the fortified rebel stronghold of

Splonum, also called Splaunon. Cassius Dio describes the location as being naturally well-fortified and it was further strengthened by massive walls and had a large garrison of warriors to defend it. It is not clear where this fortified city was located; two possible contenders are Šipovo or possibly Plevlje, Bosnia.[4]

For a long time, Germanicus' army assaulted the fortress with siege weapons (presumably battering-rams and catapults) and repeated assaults by his men, but the fortress held firm and its defenders repulsed all of the Roman attacks. No other details are given with regard to these events.[5] What kinds of siege weapons did the Romans use during this time? Many of their weapons were copied from ancient Greek weapons, and others were modified based upon earlier Greek designs. The Romans had been making use of battering-rams for centuries. The earliest use of such a machine by the Romans may have been in 259 BC with the attack on Camarina, Sicily, using rams that had been loaned to the Roman army by the Greeks of Syracuse.[6] Rams would be used by the Romans in many future city assaults.

At first, the Romans did not possess artillery. Artillery itself, mechanically-operated projectile-shooters, was invented sometime in the late fifth century or early fourth century BC, and were machines that shot arrows with great velocity. These early throwing machines were not the stuff of the common imagination with rocks and hundred-pound boulders flying through the air. The historian Livy states that artillery was used by Romans for the first time in 386 BC when a Roman army assaulted the Volscian town of Antium. However, this appears to have been a one-off, since the Romans preferred either passively besieging a settlement by surrounding it and starving it into submission or else storming the settlement with infantry charges. It is because of this that the *testudo* or 'tortoise' formation appeared when it did.[7]

It would not be until the second half of the first century BC that artillery would become a core component of the Roman army. Each legion had a certain number of ballistae – large crossbow-like machines that could launch arrows, javelins or rocks with a mighty punch – and by the time of Caesar Augustus, each legion was supposed to be accompanied by sixty 'scorpion' ballistae, one for each century of infantry. As to how often each of the legions possessed the full number of artillery is unknown. Many times, the legions themselves were significantly understrength, and it would not be improbable to assume that the numbers of artillery were reduced as well. The scorpion was a small portable mechanical arrow-shooter, and operated much more like a high-powered sniper rifle than a cannon.[8]

However, arrows or javelins, no matter how forcefully they are propelled, are useless against thick stone walls. When the time came to batter enemy fortifications, large-calibre artillery that was able to fling heavy round stones was brought into play. The ancient Greeks called such a weapon the *lithobolos*, 'the stone-thrower'. Their range could be up to four hundred yards, depending upon the weight of the ammunition. The smallest projectiles could be about ten pounds, the same as an average-sized cannonball, while the largest stones could weigh as much as a hundred and fifty pounds and would have needed a large and cumbersome machine to launch them.[9] The historical records do not state if Germanicus had any large-calibre ballistae in his army, but he may have had them accompanying his men as attachments in addition to the smaller scorpion ballistae that were incorporated into the legions.

Germanicus' siege weapons had been employed against the walls of Splonum, but to little effect. Then Cassius Dio gives us something which I cannot believe to be true. A Germanic horseman named Pusio, who was fighting with Germanicus, picked up a stone and hurled it against the walls of Splonum, presumably in a fit of frustration. The wall crumbled, killing one of the wall's defenders in the process. The whole rebel garrison became so afraid when this happened that they abandoned their defence of the wall and retreated into the citadel. Later, the Illyrian defenders surrendered both themselves and the fortress to Germanicus.[10] The story of a single man simply picking up a rock and throwing it at the massive fortifications and causing them to crumble sounds very much like the story of David and Goliath, even though the similarities are almost surely coincidental. I highly doubt that chucking a stone at a giant fortified wall would cause it to fall, even after extensive pounding by battering-rams and artillery.

I believe that the siege *actually* went like this. A German horseman named Pusio, who was serving in Germanicus' army, discovered that there was a weak spot in the wall. After telling his commander of his observation, Germanicus ordered all of his artillery to concentrate on that single section of the fortifications. In due time, the walls crumbled and the Romans advanced into the breach. The Illyrians realized that once the Romans were inside they could not effectively defend the walls, and so they retreated into the fortress's central stronghold, the citadel. However, they were now pinned down inside this one location and had no hope of escape. They had two choices: resist to the last, taking as many Romans with them as they could, with the knowledge that the Romans would win the battle anyway, or they could surrender now and hopefully be spared. They chose to surrender.

Defeat at Raetinum

The Romans had taken Splonum after suffering many losses, but they had little time to celebrate or rest after such a hard-won victory. Germanicus marched his men to another rebel stronghold called Raetinum (possibly modern-day Golubic or Bihac, Bosnia[11]). This time, the battle would end in an horrific defeat for the Romans.

Based upon the evidence that Cassius Dio provides, Raetinum contained a central citadel with underground storerooms, and the whole town was surrounded by a wooden wall. The number of rebels defending this fortress is not provided, but the garrison must have been of substantial size. However, Cassius Dio clearly states that Germanicus' legions greatly outnumbered the rebel defenders.[12]

When the Romans arrived on the scene, the Illyrian rebels defending Raetinum saw that they were heavily outnumbered. They could not hope to withstand the legions' assaults for long. The Illyrians recognized that they would be easily defeated in a head-on fight, and the crude wooden fortifications were not enough to provide an edge. The rebels needed something to put the odds of victory in their favour. Then the defenders contrived a plan of how to do away with as many Romans as possible by luring them into a trap.

According to Cassius Dio, the Illyrian rebels deliberately made a weak spot in their defences, knowing that the sharp-eyed Romans would spot this and try to exploit it. The rebel garrison set fire to a section of the wooden wall that encircled Raetinum as well as the houses that were near the wall, but trying to keep the fire under control so that the entire wall didn't go up in flames. Their plan was to allow the Romans to enter and then lure them into the centre of the fortress just in time to have the entire encircling wall devoured in flames, thereby trapping the Romans inside with no hope of escape.[13]

One section of the wall was now burning, but the Romans didn't notice it. I'm not sure why, since they must have surely noticed the smoke. The defenders manning the walls abandoned their positions and retreated to the central stronghold. The Romans saw this and became bold, believing that the Illyrians were fleeing, and so chased after them, hoping to plunder the entire fortress. Their minds were so intent on killing the Illyrians, Cassius Dio states, that the Romans were completely ignorant of the fire that was steadily creeping around them until they were completely surrounded by a ring of fire. The Illyrians who had retreated to the citadel hurled missiles at the Roman soldiers down below. The Romans could not back up out of missile range because if they did they would be burned by the fire, but if they tried to avoid the fire, they would be shot full of arrows by the Illyrian warriors. Some of the Romans became so desperate to get out that they actually hurled the dead bodies of their comrades into the flames to form a bridge of corpses and thus a few managed to escape. However, Cassius Dio states that a majority of the Romans who entered the fortress perished either by the hand of the enemy or by the fire. The fire soon began raging out of control, and even the Illyrians deemed the citadel too unsafe to stay in and so retreated during the night to some underground chambers and stayed there while the fire raged above them. It is not recorded how many people perished in the fire.[14]

The Romans Regain the Upper Hand

After this hellish defeat, Germanicus needed another victory in order to revive his men's morale. He turned his attention to Seretium, which Tiberius had earlier attacked but was unable to take. Seizing possession of this rebel stronghold would help his men to regain their confidence. Cassius Dio reports that Seretium fell to Germanicus, though he gives no details about this event.[15] A man named Sir William Smith wrote in 1873 that Seretium 'which with Rhaetimus, was captured by Germanicus'.[16] This could mean that a person named Rhaetimus helped Germanicus to capture the town. No ancient source that I know of mentions anyone by this name, so this explanation is highly unlikely. Another possibility is that Rhaetimus refers to a place, not a person. In this case, Rhaetimus is almost certainly an incorrect spelling of Raetinum.

After Seretium was taken by Germanicus and his men, the Romans took control of other places in a series of easy fights. However, in spite of the fact that the Romans were steadily gaining ground, the Illyrians continued to resist, dragging out the war, determined to fight to the bitter end.[17]

Germanicus had been leading the Roman war effort during the campaign season of 9 AD. However, following Germanicus' terrifying defeat at Raetinum, Caesar Augustus once more sent Tiberius into Dalmatia to command the troops. Tiberius saw that the Roman soldiers had become increasingly impatient with the war dragging on for so long and wanted to bring the revolt to a quick end, even if it involved great danger to themselves. Knowing that the grumblings of soldiers often led to mutiny, Tiberius divided his force into three parts: one-third was led by General Marcus Plautius Silvanus, another third was led by General Marcus Aemilius Lepidus, and the last third was commanded jointly by Tiberius and Germanicus. Paterculus says that Germanicus commanded the vanguard, the front units, of Tiberius' army.[18] Tiberius ordered his subordinates to take their respective two parts of the army and go and conquer certain areas of the country (which particular areas each general was ordered to take are not stated in the historical accounts), but Tiberius would take his third with the specific purpose of marching against Bato the Daesidiate.[19]

Bato's Last Stand: The Battle of Andetrium

Aside from Germanicus' defeat at Raetinum, from which he quickly bounced back, the campaign season of 9 AD was going very well. After three years of obstinate resistance, the Illyrian rebels had been severely weakened by massive casualties, disease and a devastating famine. In 9 AD, the Romans had gained a lot of ground, in contrast to the hard fighting through which they had suffered during the previous year. By now, many of them could feel that the end was coming soon. After all this time, the Great Illyrian Revolt was drawing to a close and the knowledge of that lifted the Romans' spirits.

Silvanus and Lepidus easily defeated their respective opponents in battles, but Tiberius was having a very difficult time tracking his enemy down. Like Captain Ahab pursuing the white whale Moby Dick, Tiberius had become hell-bent on his mission to find and destroy the rebellion's ringleader, Bato the Daesidiate. Yet Bato was a crafty and elusive enemy, always managing to stay one step ahead of Tiberius' advance, so much so that Cassius Dio remarks that Tiberius and his men were forced to wander across the entire country in their pursuit of the rebel commander.[20]

At last, Bato and his followers stopped falling back and took up a defensive position within the mountain fortress of Andetrium (also spelled as Adetrium, Anderium or Anderitum; modern-day Muć[21] or Clissa[22]), located only a short distance from the province's capital of

Salona. Andetrium was an almost impregnable stronghold in classic Illyrian style: built atop a mountain, well-fortified and surrounded by deep ravines with fast-flowing rivers that would easily drown someone if they were unfortunate enough to fall in. The Illyrian defenders already had ample supplies necessary for a long siege, and more supplies were being carried to Andetrium by a vast number of porters who brought the provisions not with waggons or pack horses, but marched on foot carrying the supplies in their hands.[23]

Tiberius may have been glad that he at last had his opponent trapped, but he also knew he was in for a very long and difficult siege. The Illyrian defenders could not be starved out because they had plenty of food and water. Moreover, the Romans were being put into a worse position because roving parties of Illyrian warriors had swung around Tiberius' rear and had cut off his supply routes and his pathway of withdrawal. Cassius Dio remarks that thus the Romans who wished to besiege the Illyrians were themselves the ones who were besieged.[24] Within a stroke, the Roman force had been put on the defensive.

Tiberius realized that besieging Andetrium wasn't getting him anywhere, but he was at a complete loss as to what he should do. The Romans were hard pressed due to lack of supplies and they were not able to break into the fortress, but giving up would be disgraceful and shaming. No Roman commander wanted it to be known that he was bested by 'barbarians'. The Roman soldiers, who as said earlier were eager to bring the war to a quick end, became highly frustrated with the lack of progress and grew loud and disorderly. Cassius Dio states that the disaffected Roman soldiers raised such an outcry over such a prolonged period of time that the Illyrians defenders, believing that the Romans were about to launch a massive all-or-nothing attack, became so afraid that they retreated to the inner fortifications of the city.[25]

Tiberius assembled his men and reprimanded them for behaving in such an undisciplined manner, but this still left him in a quandary as to what to do. If he attacked Andetrium, his men would suffer heavy casualties, but if he withdrew, the rebel force would threaten his rear. So both sides appeared to be at an impasse. Tiberius chose to remain in his camp, wishing neither to attack such a strong position nor withdraw, and hoped that Bato would simply give up.[26]

It seemed that Tiberius would get his wish. Although Bato had doggedly dragged on the fighting for as long as he could, inflicting as many casualties as he could, and had managed to resist the Romans thus far, the Illyrian rebel commander knew that the revolt was dying. He repeatedly received messages from his subordinate officers urgently requesting aid to help them against the attacks by Silvanus' and Lepidus' troops, but Bato was unable to lend any assistance. There were always more Romans coming and Bato knew that their numbers were too great to keep the revolt going on any longer. By now, he knew that the war was lost but he didn't have the heart to ask his men to give themselves up to the Romans when they still wished to fight on. So the rebel leader secretly sent a messenger to the Roman commander asking what the Romans' terms would be if he was to surrender.[27]

When Tiberius received word that Bato himself wished to surrender but that the rest of his warriors wished to continue the war, he did something completely out of character. Rather than acting as the cautious old commander that he had become, he behaved instead like his younger self, the energetic fighter that he had once been, and immediately ordered his men to storm the fortress and to bring this long and costly war to an end once and for all. Believing that he could overwhelm the rebel position without heavy casualties, he ignored the constraints of the terrain and instead ordered his men to advance in a massive frontal assault. Tiberius himself stayed in the rear, keeping a portion of the army in reserve, which he would personally lead into the fray if necessity called for it. He even sat upon a platform so that he could watch the battle unfold like a spectator, believing that his men would fight all the harder knowing that their commander was watching them.[28]

Although it is not specifically stated in the accounts, the Roman legionnaires likely advanced upon the fortifications using the *testudo* or 'tortoise' formation. Our only clue to this is when Cassius Dio states that the Roman soldiers advanced on the Illyrians in a densely-packed square.[29] The Roman military used the tortoise formation for the first time during the Siege of Aquilonia in 293 BC.[30] The Greek historian Polybius, who lived during the second century BC, writes of an early use of the tortoise formation when the Romans assaulted Heraclea. In his account, he states that the Romans sent three maniples of infantry forward. The first of these held their shields aloft and overlapped them like roof shingles and formed a ramp so that the two maniples behind them could advance up to the enemy wall.[31]

Many people's conception of what the tortoise formation looked like is that of a square or rectangular box, with the legionnaires covering the sides and the top with their shields. However, it seems that in ancient times the tortoise formation actually looked more like a ramp than a box, a ramp that allowed other soldiers in the rear to advance, clamber up and reach the top of enemy-held walls.

In a single massive body, the Roman force advanced up the steep rocky slope towards the fortress of Andetrium. At first, their advance was a smooth and steady walk, but due to the unevenness of the terrain, some parts became separated from the main body. The single united force became fragmented, with smaller portions of men being either thrust further forward or lagging behind the bulk of the Roman force.[32]

This description sounds similar to the advance of the French infantry on the Plains of Abraham outside Quebec that took place on 13 September 1759. In this famous battle of the Seven Years' War, a British force of about 4,500 men, led by James Wolfe, threatened the city of Quebec by blocking the main road leading to the city. Defending Quebec was a French force led by Marquis de Montcalm. The British had managed to get into position very early in the day and took the French by surprise, who hastily assembled to meet them in battle. French artillery began firing upon the British line to drive them off, but despite taking casualties, Wolfe maintained his position. Montcalm realized that he would have to send in his infantry to force the British to leave. Although small in number, the British force had stretched itself out to encompass the width of the plain, a distance of nearly half a mile. That way, the French could not outmanoeuvre and swing around the British position; they would have no choice but to attack straight from the front. However, stretching the men out left the British line very thin and flimsy, at only two ranks deep and therefore vulnerable. A forceful attack could smash right through them. Montcalm was banking on this. Assembling his own force numbering about 4,500 troops, Montcalm ordered them to drive towards the British. However, things went badly even before the two sides engaged each other. While the professional French regulars advanced in step towards their foe, the Canadian militia broke ranks and charged towards the redcoats, who were 500 yards from the French lines. In addition to that, the coordination of the whole French force was lost as different units marched faster or slower than others, thereby breaking the single unified French line into several parts. As one witness recorded, the French left flank had lagged behind and was well in the rear, and the centre of the line had thrust itself too far forward. This disruption of the French force's advance escalated into chaos and confusion as pockets of

French troops fired upon the British ranks in a piecemeal fashion rather than the whole force attacking as a single unified body.[33]

The Illyrian defenders of Andetrium saw how the Roman advance was becoming more and more disorganized and so they decided to take a risk. Rather than continuing to maintain their positions atop Andetrium's walls and within, they arranged themselves *outside* of the fortifications and hurled down all manner of objects at the Romans as they advanced up the steep slope in an attempt to completely break up their cohesion. Some shot small sling stones, while others rolled down large boulders onto the Romans. Others rolled down wooden barrels that were filled with rocks, and others even resorted to unleashing supply waggons loaded with rocks to roll down and smash through the Roman lines like improvised battering-rams. The Romans were continuously bombarded in this manner, forcing them to scatter or else be crushed. Cassius Dio records: 'All these objects rushing down at once with great impetus kept striking here and there, as if discharged from a sling, separating the Romans from one another even more than before and crushing them.'[34]

Despite the vigour of the Illyrian defence and despite the heavy casualties that the Roman force was suffering, the men pressed onwards and upwards. As the Romans advanced closer to the rebel position, they came within range of enemy arrows and javelins. Cassius Dio states that many Roman troops were slain by enemy missiles.[35] Arrows and javelins seldom inflict damage upon a compact body of men with interlocking overlapping shields. So it seems that by now, if the Romans did indeed employ a tortoise formation, it was no longer in place. The forceful defensive measures undertaken by the Illyrians, especially sending down rock-filled waggons and barrels to smash through the Roman ranks, had disrupted the cohesion of the force to such an extent that they were probably no longer advancing in any semblance of unison at all. Most likely it was every man for himself. In such circumstances, the individual legionnaires were easy pickings for rebel marksmen. Casualties were becoming alarmingly high. The fighting was intense:

> One side endeavoured to ascend and conquer the heights, the other to repulse them and hurl them back…. Each side, both individually and collectively, was encouraging its own men, trying to hearten those who showed zeal and chiding those who gave way at any point. Those whose voices could be heard above the rest were also invoking the gods at the same time, both sides

praying for the safety of their warriors at the moment, and one side begging for its freedom, the other for peace, in the future.[36]

Tiberius watched in horror. His men were slowly advancing up the slope, but they were being slaughtered in the process. Several times, it looked as if the Romans would be forced to retreat, and to prevent this from happening, Tiberius had sent over detachments of his reserves to reinforce the main Roman assault force, but this was not enough. Tiberius decided to commit the last of his reserves. He sent some to aid their comrades, but he sent the rest in a flying column around the back and advanced upon the stronghold from the rear in a place where the slope was less steep and could thus be ascended with much less difficulty. The Illyrian garrison was small, and they only had enough men to fight on one front. Now, being attacked from both the front and the rear at the same time, they did not have enough men to keep both Roman forces at bay. The warriors wished to take shelter within their stronghold, but they were prevented from getting inside because they were continuously under attack, and so the entire Illyrian force was scattered all across the face of the mountain. The warriors cast off their armour to make them lighter so that they could flee, but the Romans were in hot pursuit, 'for they were very eager to end the war once and for all, and did not want the foe to unite again and cause them further trouble. They discovered most of them hiding in the forests and slew them as they would so many wild beasts.'[37]

It was now clear that the hard-fought Battle of Andetrium was going to end in failure for the Illyrian rebels. Bato, who was inside the city, knew that he would now have no choice but to surrender. He sent his son Sceuas to Tiberius as a peace hostage, carrying a message. The note said that Bato would surrender himself and all of his followers who were still inside the fort if he obtained a pardon; that is, he and his soldiers would surrender if the Romans promised not to kill him or any of his men. Tiberius sent a reply back to Bato, stating that if he and his rebels surrendered, Bato would not be executed. During the night, Bato went down to the Roman camp, and the following morning Bato was brought before Tiberius as the Roman commander sat in judgement of him. Bato asked nothing for himself, but he made a lengthy plea with Tiberius to spare his people, and even offered to submit to being executed in exchange for having all of those who still remained inside Andetrium spared. Cassius Dio reports that Bato actually stuck his head forwards, waiting for Tiberius to personally slice it off with his own sword. It must have been a very dramatic scene and it is a shame that we don't have any more details of it. Tiberius was apparently moved by Bato's entreaty and his willingness to die in order to save the lives of others. He consented to Bato's request. The remaining defenders who were still inside the fortifications surrendered. When Tiberius asked Bato why he and his people had decided to declare war on Rome and to resist for so many years, the rebel commander replied: 'You Romans are to blame for this; for you send as guardians of your flocks, not dogs or shepherds, but wolves.'[38]

The Last Rebel Stronghold: The Fall of Arduba

As soon as Tiberius began negotiating with Bato, Germanicus left, taking a portion of the army with him to go and hunt down and destroy the last surviving remnants of the rebellion.[39] At last, he and his men came to a place called Arduba, where the bulk of the surviving rebels had decided to make their futile last stand and had barricaded themselves within. Germanicus' troops outnumbered the fort's defenders, yet even so, he realized that he could not attack Arduba without suffering a large number of casualties. This late in the war, with the fighting all but over, he did not want to squander his men's lives unnecessarily.

It has been hypothesized that Arduba is the same as modern-day Vranduk, Bosnia, although there is not enough proof for this claim.[40] I am inclined to reject the idea that Arduba and Vranduk are the same place because the written records do not mention any place established on this spot before the medieval period and no artefacts have been recovered from this site that are dated to ancient times. So the site of the last battle of the Great Illyrian Revolt must lie elsewhere.

All was not well within Arduba's walls. Many of the rebels within were deserters from Bato's army who had regained their patriotic courage and had become determined to carry out the war to the bitter end, regardless of the fact that it was clear to everybody that it was already lost. The men of the town, knowing that the Roman troops that were encamped outside would force their way in sooner or later, and fearing that they would be slaughtered and the town destroyed, desired to make peace with Germanicus before he unleashed the fury of his legions upon them. They believed that if they surrendered now, before the battle began, they might be shown mercy. By contrast, the women of the town sided with the warriors, likely reminding their menfolk of what would happen to them and their families if the Romans prevailed. This argument between the rebel warriors and the people of Arduba turned violent, and they actually began brawling with each other within the town. During this 'battle', a fire broke out. The rebels were overwhelmed by the townsmen; many of them surrendered and a few escaped. The women of Arduba had a much greater love of their people's independence than their men, vowing that they would rather die than live under Roman rule. Thus, taking their children in their arms, they either deliberately hurled themselves into the fire to be burned alive or else they jumped off the cliffs that guarded the town and drowned themselves in the winding river below.[41] Images of the American attack on Saipan during the Second World War spring to mind when reading of these events.

The Roman soldiers, who were encamped only a short distance away, must have seen all that was going on. Germanicus was content to sit by and wait, watching the Illyrians attacking and killing each other, and beheld the whole of the mountaintop stronghold of Arduba roaring with flames like an Illyrian Mount Etna. When it was all over and when the fires had burned themselves out, Germanicus ordered his soldiers forward and seized possession of the ruined town. It is highly likely that Germanicus and his men did not do any actual fighting by this stage. As soon as Arduba was taken, other nearby places voluntarily submitted to Germanicus. After this was done, he and a group of his men rejoined Tiberius, leaving Vibius Postumus to complete the subjugation of the area.[42]

By the time that Arduba (or what was left of it) was taken, Tiberius had concluded his negotiations with the rebel leader. Germanicus likely returned to Tiberius' side just in time for the news to be relayed to him that Bato had surrendered. Germanicus would have then told his uncle that the last surviving remnants of Bato's rebel army had been defeated. Finally, it was over. The Great Illyrian Revolt was done.[43]

Chapter Seven

The Aftermath

Too Shameful to Remember, Too Painful to Forget

The Great Illyrian Revolt had begun, in all likelihood, in early March of the year 6 AD. Now, three and a half years later in September of 9 AD, it was over. The reason why we can be pretty confident in terms of dating when the rebellion ended is because it states in the ancient records that the Great Illyrian Revolt ended soon before Arminius led his own rebellion in Germania. Since it has been established through both history and forensic archaeology that the famed Battle of Teutoburg occurred in late September 9 AD, we can be certain that the Illyrian uprising ended sometime during that month, either in early or mid-September.

By any standards, the Great Illyrian Revolt was an immense and intense conflict. Surprisingly, the Romans don't appear to have taken much pride in this war. Ancient accounts about this uprising are few, and those that do write about it are mostly sparse. It is almost as if the Romans didn't want to talk about it. The ancient Romans usually gloried in their victories, writing down everything in the most minute detail about how they crushed their opponents. The fact that the Great Illyrian Revolt is not treated in such a manner makes me think that the Romans felt that this was not something to be remembered in the hallowed halls of their history. For three and a half years, the Romans and Illyrians slogged it out almost non-stop in an all-or-nothing war of attrition and annihilation. It is shocking to read the considerably long list of battles and sieges. Many times the Romans lost, and they lost *badly*. Body counts are not provided, but the death tolls in these engagements must have been unimaginable. There were blood-soaked defeats and even bloodier victories. There are certain scenes mentioned in some engagements that allude to the stuff of nightmares. The sheer scale of the war must have been at once awesome and terrifying. This was total war at its worst.

According to Suetonius, the Great Illyrian Revolt 'carried on for three years with fifteen legions and a corresponding force of auxiliaries, amid great difficulties of every kind and the utmost scarcity of supplies.'[1]

Fifteen legions? That's a full strength of 75,000 men! Added to that was a sizeable number of auxiliaries and support troops, as well as the men from Rome's Thracian allies, all of whose numbers are unknown. In total, the Roman force that fought during the war may have numbered as high as 100,000 men, at least in theory.

It is not recorded how many people were killed during the Great Illyrian Revolt, but it surely must be in the tens and perhaps even hundreds of thousands. I should state that casualty estimates are seldom recorded for ancient battles or wars, so it shouldn't be surprising that there isn't a butcher's bill for this conflict. With such a large number, it can be very difficult to put any names to numeric statistics and the further back in time, the less likely you will find anything. Amazingly, we know of one person by name that was killed in this conflict: Aulus Licinius Nerva Silianus. He was the son of the eminent Publius Silius, and he had a very high opinion of himself. Bluntly speaking, he was a haughty arrogant snob, and his nature made people shun him; Paterculus comments that he was not well-praised. Only his best friend (who is not named) stated that 'there were no qualities which he did not possess in the highest degree, whether as an excellent citizen or as an honest commander.'[2] He was an associate of Caesar Augustus, but 'his untimely death failed not only to reap the fruit of his close friendship with the emperor but also to realize that lofty conception of his powers which had been inspired by his father's eminence.'[3] The precise circumstances of Aulus Silianus' death are not recorded. He may have been killed in battle or he might have simply died from contagious camp diseases like dysentery or typhus, as did many soldiers in those days.

For the Illyrians, the Great Illyrian Revolt shattered their power in the region forever. This mass uprising was the last chance for the natives of the western Balkans to regain their ancient freedom. For the Romans, the Great Illyrian Revolt solved the problem of trying to control this volatile region. For more than two-hundred years, the Romans and Illyrians had fought each other. Now this would settle things permanently. The Great Illyrian Revolt was the last time that the Illyrians engaged in open hostility against the Romans. The native inhabitants would never challenge Rome's authority over them again.

With so much at stake in this war and with so many people involved in it, in the end what were the Romans able to show for it? Apparently, not much. Cassius Dio sums up his record of the war by stating depressingly that this revolt was a costly war for the Romans, both in men and money, and that it was a war in which much was lost and little was gained.[4] No wonder the Great Illyrian Revolt left a bad taste in Rome's mouth.

Bato's Fate

For three years, a man named Bato from the Daesidiate tribe had carried on one of the best-executed and bloodiest native resistance movements in Roman history. In terms of sheer fighting power and tenacity, this man ranks very high up on the scale. Unlike other native commanders like Vercingetorix and Arminius, Bato the Daesidiate won several battlefield victories during his rebellion, not just one or two, and he frequently gave the Romans a shocking and unexpected sucker-punch to the guts. Now he was in chains.

Bato had surrendered to the commander-in-chief of Rome's military in the area, Tiberius Claudius Nero, just before the end of the war. I can imagine what Bato thought his fate was going to be. Routinely, whenever the ringleaders of enemy forces were captured, they were executed but Bato was an exception. Rather than have him ceremonially killed, as Julius Caesar had done with Vercingetorix, Bato was exiled. Tiberius, who was never a very hard-line 'kill 'em all, boys!' sort of general, sent the Illyrian resistance fighter to the Italian port-city of Ravenna, located on the Adriatic Sea, along with a hefty supply of rich presents to keep him content. This highly uncharacteristic display of mercy (and some Romans might say 'softness', especially for a commander who appeared to be getting softer and less willing to fight with every passing year) by a Roman general to his defeated foe must have surprised and shocked many people, not the least of them being Bato himself, who probably expected to have his head cut off or be strangled to death. The Roman historian Suetonius explains that Tiberius did this out of gratitude because Bato had once allowed Tiberius to escape when he was trapped in a dangerous place. During that event, Bato had the opportunity to kill Tiberius but chose not to. Tiberius, though getting on in years and becoming less and less inclined to the martial life, realized that he owed this rebel leader his life and also probably recognized Bato as a worthy and challenging opponent. Noble adversaries were due a certain degree of honourable treatment. So Bato was released from his chains and would spend the rest of his life in Ravenna.[5]

During the early years of the first century AD, Ravenna seems to have been the unofficial 'retirement centre' of former Roman adversaries.

Several years after the war ended in Illyricum, Thusnelda, the wife of the Germanic rebel leader Arminius, was captured and her son Thumelicus was raised in Ravenna; perhaps she lived there as well.[6] A couple of years later, King Maroboduus of the Marcomanni tribe was granted permission to live in Ravenna after he had been ousted from power by Arminius.[7] One wonders if the three of them – Bato, Thusnelda and Maroboduus – saw each other, talked and even ate meals together, reminiscing about the good old times when they were independent and free, and when battle and honour were everything. We hear nothing of Bato the Daesidiate after his banishment to Ravenna. The date and circumstances of his death are not recorded.

Give Credit where Credit is Due

Both Augustus and Tiberius were permitted to add the title *imperator* to their various other titles. Tiberius was granted a triumph and received various other honours. Although his nephew Germanicus was not awarded a triumph for his efforts during the war, he was nevertheless given the various ornaments bestowed during a triumph and was given the rank of *praetor*. Moreover, Germanicus was given the privileges of casting his vote immediately after the ex-consuls and having himself hold the consulship earlier than otherwise would have been allowed. Two triumphal arches were erected within Pannonia in commemoration of the victory over the Illyrian rebels, further driving home the message to the cowed Pannonian Illyrians that Rome was indeed their master.[8]

In addition to this, some recommended that Tiberius should be given an honorific agnomen like his younger brother Drusus who, after such a valiant campaign in the wilderness of western Germania almost twenty years earlier, had been bestowed the honorific name *Germanicus*, a name that would be passed on to his children. Some recommended the agnomen *Pannonicus*, 'Victor of Pannonia', others *Invictus* 'the Undefeated' and others *Pius* 'the Devout'. Caesar Augustus, however, flatly rejected awarding his stepson an agnomen, stating that Tiberius would be satisfied enough with receiving his stepfather's surname when he died. In other words, Tiberius would be made the next emperor and he would take the name 'Caesar'.[9]

Some people didn't get the credit that they should have. Aelius Lamia, an old commander who had fought in the war, 'who always tempered his old-fashioned dignity by a spirit of kindliness, had performed splendid service in Germany and Illyricum, and was soon to do so in Africa, but failed to receive triumphal honours, not through any fault of his, but through lack of opportunity.'[10]

However, the time for merriment and celebration would be cut short. Scarcely had victory over the Illyrian rebels been won when terrible news arrived from Germania. The 17th, 18th and 19th Legions had been massacred in the Teutoburg Forest, resulting in the deaths of at least 10,000 men, among them Governor Publius Quinctilius Varus. Tiberius' triumph had already been scheduled, but he postponed it to deal with the German barbarians and their leader Arminius. A new war had begun.[11]

While Cassius Dio goes into detail regarding the deeds of Drusus Claudius Nero Germanicus during the Great Illyrian Revolt, Gaius Paterculus speaks little of the conduct and achievements of Germanicus other than stating that he had been dispatched to Dalmatia by Tiberius to act as a vanguard and had performed admirably in the service of the former consul Gaius Vibius Postumus. This man is described as 'the governor of Dalmatia', but the province wasn't split in half to create the provinces of Pannonia and Dalmatia until after the revolt was over, so this might be an historical error on Paterculus' part.[12]

Reconsolidation of Illyria

Now that the Great Illyrian Revolt was over, the Romans had to ensure that Illyria remained peaceful, obedient and submissive, now and for all time. For the past two-hundred years, the Romans had tried in piecemeal ways to bring stability to this region and they had always failed. They could not afford to have another war like this happen ever again.

Yet what could the Romans do? What method would work now when every other method that they used in the past hadn't? Unfortunately, the empire could not focus its attention on how to stabilize Illyria after the revolt was concluded because now it had to worry about the German rebels in the north. So while Tiberius and Germanicus readied their forces following the shock of the massacre of three legions in the Teutoburg Forest, the Illyrians were left alone. As far as we know, the only thing that was done was to divide the province of Illyricum in half, at least into two zones of military administration. The southern half was known as 'Illyricum Superius' and the northern half was called 'Illyricum Inferius'; for some reason, the Romans opted not to use the more well-known geographic names of Dalmatia and Pannonia. Each of these halves had a military commandant installed to oversee affairs within their respective area of operations.[13]

One would think that this would have been a golden opportunity for the Illyrians to rise up against the Romans yet again, to attack them while they were distracted elsewhere. Indeed, in hindsight, the Romans were very grateful that the Illyrian uprising ended just before Arminius' Germanic uprising began. Suetonius states that no one doubted that if the Great Illyrian Revolt had not been put down when it was, the Germanic barbarians surely would have joined forces with the Illyrian rebels and it would have been all the harder for the Romans to defeat the combined foe.[14]

However, it seems that the Illyrians were in no mood to go on fighting. They were thoroughly exhausted after three and a half years of virtually non-stop bloodshed and destruction. Many of their towns and cities were in blackened charred ruins, their farms and pastures had been ravaged and stripped bare, and an incalculable number of people had perished. Quite simply, they were worn out. Even if they wanted to reinitiate hostilities, what could they possibly do? The fighting force of the Illyrian people had been drastically reduced. Perhaps as much as a tenth of the region's population had been destroyed, maybe even more. What could a few survivors do against the ever-mighty Roman legions? No, it would be better not to waste the effort on such a foolish endeavour. So the Illyrians remained quiet.

Knowing this, or at least guessing it, Tiberius and other military commanders could afford to leave behind a small security force in Illyria to maintain order while the bulk of their men were speedily transferred to the north to attack the Germans in retribution for the disaster at Teutoburg. Three legions – the 8th Legion *Augusta*, the 9th Legion *Hispania* and the 11th Legion *Apollinaris* – were posted to Pannonia, and another two – the 7th Legion and the 11th Legion – were kept in Dalmatia. The gamble seems to have worked exactly the way that Tiberius and others guessed, because we hear no word of any disturbances in Illyria during this time.[15]

In 14 AD, Caesar Augustus sent Germanicus into Germania to deal with Arminius and his rebels, 'and was on the point of sending his son Tiberius to Illyricum to strengthen by peace the regions he had subjugated in war'.[16] The war against Arminius and his German rebels lasted a lot longer than the war against the Illyrian rebels and was no less hard-fought. In 14 AD, while Rome's war of revenge against the Germans entered its fourth year (and it wouldn't end until two years later in 16 AD), Rome's first emperor Caesar Augustus died. Tiberius Claudius Nero, who was about to depart for Illyricum to settle affairs there, was tasked with remaining within Rome and was crowned as the empire's new monarch. Upon his coronation as Rome's second emperor, he abandoned his birth name of Tiberius Claudius Nero and adopted the royal name Tiberius Julius Caesar.

Right away, he had to deal with problems. Decades earlier, Augustus had made all of the soldiers in the army swear a personal oath of allegiance to him. He did this to prevent factionalism and civil war, with different legions taking sides with different would-be national leaders. That simple tactic had kept the Roman army in a reasonable state of obedience and cooperation. Now Caesar Augustus was dead, and the army was no longer legally under anyone's control. Years of pent-up grumblings suddenly burst forth.

That year, three legions had been posted to Pannonia under the overall command of General Quintus Junius Blaesus, the military commandant of Illyricum Inferius. He was a man who was not particularly noteworthy, aside from being an ex-consul. Following Augustus' death, his men revolted at the harsh treatment they had had to endure for years. Paterculus comments that this mutiny could have easily morphed into a military coup d'état with the legions marching into Rome and declaring martial law. The mutiny spilled out from the army camps and into the civilian population, resulting in the town of Nauportus being ransacked along with several nearby villages. When word of all this reached the newly-crowned Emperor Tiberius, he sent his son Drusus Julius Caesar, nicknamed 'Castor', with some vague instructions to put a stop to all the disturbances. The emperor's son was an odd choice to act as a negotiator between the imperial government and rampaging soldiers, since Drusus Castor was not a very likeable person. He was prone to excessive drinking and he had a violent temper; not a good combination. Nevertheless, accompanied by a troop of nobles as well as 1,000 men from the Praetorian Guard, he asked what the soldiers' demands were so that he could present their case to the emperor and the Senate, provided that they stop their violence and act properly from then on. Later, Drusus and his staff quarrelled as to what ought to be done with the mutineers: pardon or punish? Being more inclined to bloodshed, Drusus stated that they would be punished. So he summoned the ringleaders to his tent, ostensibly for a conference, and had them all killed right then and there. This soon radically escalated into massacring every soldier who had taken part in the rebellion. A simultaneous mutiny in Germania was suppressed using means that were just as bloody.[17]

Once these military revolts were put down, the Romans could once more focus on beating up the Germans. For the remainder of that year, and for two more years after that, the Romans attacked and harassed the Germans, but Arminius himself was never killed or captured. However, while Rome was still licking its wounds from its war in Illyria and while the legions marched against the German barbarians, another area of the empire grew shaky with unrest and rebellion: Africa. The northern African territories had long served as a major exporter of grain and olive oil for the empire. Quite simply, Rome could not survive without bread made from grain that was imported from what are now Algeria, Tunisia and Libya. Then in the year 15 AD, while the war against Arminius and his German rebels was still under way, a Numidian warlord named Tacfarinas began causing trouble. This threat to Rome's food supply was a much greater danger to the security of the empire than Arminius and his northern barbarians. Emperor Tiberius was forced to divert more and more troops and support to Africa in order to keep the supply lines safe from attack. Finally, he realized that he could not fight both the African rebels and the Germanic rebels at the same time; he had to choose. At the end of 16 AD, Tiberius stated that the Romans had inflicted enough damage upon the Germans in retaliation for Rome's defeat at Teutoburg, and the troops could be pulled back to the Rhine. His nephew Germanicus, who was leading the legions in western Germania, strongly objected to this decision. He claimed that the Germans were on the brink of total defeat and that it would be incredibly stupid to give up and throw in the towel now, but Tiberius wouldn't listen and ordered all Roman soldiers to pull back to their bases along the Rhine and Danube Rivers. All Roman territory located on the eastern side of the Rhine River was to be abandoned. The following year in 17 AD, Tiberius returned to Rome to celebrate his triumph against the Illyrian rebels that he had put off for so long. Emperor Tiberius' son Drusus Castor was appointed as the new governor general of Illyricum Inferius, a post that he would hold for the next three years; he would be the last governor of a united Illyrian province.[18] It would take Rome six more years to finally bring Tacfarinas and his North African rebel army to heel.

Word of Tiberius' triumph eventually reached the Black Sea, where the poet Ovid had been exiled. To commemorate the event, he wrote a poem in which he celebrated the news of Tiberius' triumphal parade and he listed all of the various sights and attractions. According to Ovid's verses, crowds of people packed the route to gaze upon the victorious general. Although Rome had experienced several days of heavy rain in the days leading up to the parade, on the date of the triumph itself the weather was fine and sunny. Garbed in embroidered clothes, Tiberius advanced along a path scattered with rose petals while men carried facsimiles of the Illyrian mountains and defeated strongholds, but the most eye-catching spectacle was the many Illyrian prisoners chained to each other by their necks, forced to trudge on in ignominious defeat. At the end of his route, Tiberius made sacrifices in one of the temples to the ancient heroes and to the memory of Caesar Augustus.[19]

In either 19 or 20 AD, the two military zones of operation into which Illyricum had been divided following the Great Illyrian Revolt changed to being actual provinces. With this new development, the names changed again. Rather than keeping the awkward designations of Illyricum Superius and Illyricum Inferius, the Romans reverted to using the traditional names of Dalmatia and Pannonia, respectively.[20] Tiberius did this, in all likelihood, to create a more intense level of government control over the people, more effective military defence with more troops stationed in the area so that they could quickly respond in force to local problems without having to relocate units from hundreds of miles away, and to prevent the Illyrians from uniting again into a single block entity. The northern city of Segestica, the birthplace of the Great Illyrian Revolt, was renamed 'Siscia', possibly to further blur the memory of the rebellion and to deprive the native Illyrians of an identifiable place of national resistance, and it was designated as Pannonia's capital. The coastal city of Salona would serve as Dalmatia's capital. Both provinces were in turn divided into districts called *conventi* (sing. *conventus*, shortened from *conventus juridici*) composed of several settlements each, and were centred upon a major town. Dalmatia was divided into three *conventi*, named the *Conventus Scardonitanus*, the *Conventus Salonitanus* and the *Conventus Naronitanus*, while Pannonia only had one, the *Conventus Epidauritanus*. Each settlement was assigned a certain number of *decuriae* who would act on behalf of their settlement in matters of government, essentially a municipal representative body like a city assembly.[21]

One of the biggest problems during the opening stages of the Great Illyrian Revolt had been to get Roman troops quickly to the battlefield. As stated earlier, the first troops that were brought in to suppress the rebellion had to come all the way from central Bulgaria. Tiberius must have remembered the inherent problems in this. If rebellion should erupt in Illyricum in the future, he needed more soldiers on hand to be able to intercede quickly and not have to resort to hurriedly sending in men from more than a hundred miles away. Therefore the historian Suetonius states 'Tiberius safeguarded the country against banditry and local revolts by decreasing the distance between military posts.'[22] The addition of more military garrisons, with each one spaced a short distance apart from the others, meant that the Roman troops could serve as quick-reaction forces in case trouble brewed again.

However, forts need soldiers to man them and Illyria would be a place where the population could be recruited or press-ganged into military service. The Romans probably had a few reasons for doing this. Firstly, it was to refill the ranks that had suffered casualties during the various wars fought at this time. Secondly, it was a way for Rome to remove young men of fighting age from the region who might otherwise rekindle their rebellious spirit. Thirdly, it was a punishment. In terms of what the *delectus*, the conscription for military service, did to the population, we can't say. Increasingly, the Balkan population was singled out to be drafted, and taking these young men away for upwards of fifteen years where they would be cut off from their homes was one way to quell any ideas that they might have had, as well as to serve as a punitive measure towards the Illyrians. Auxiliary units with Illyrian names appear during the latter part of the Julio-Claudian dynasty. There were eight auxiliary cohorts staffed by Breucians, seven cohorts staffed by Dalmatians, one cohort of Liburnians and one mixed cohort of Pannonians and Dalmatians.[23]

However, forts rarely exist in isolation. Towns nearly always spring up around military posts because the people residing there supply goods and services to the soldiers. In addition to constructing new military posts, new settlements were also constructed in the region. These could have been homes for veterans, or they could have been settlements to create a higher Roman civilian presence in the area in order to overwhelm any more would-be native Illyrian rebels. Danijel Dzino states that in the years following the Great Illyrian Revolt, many of the urban coastal settlements on the Balkan side of the Adriatic had high numbers of Greek and Italian immigrants, and several of these settlements were in the process of being designated as either *municipiae* or *coloniae*, settlements for transplanted Roman citizens and subjects.[24] In the ancient town of Emona, two inscriptions commemorating the construction of the town's walls in the name of 'the Divine Augustus and Tiberius' were dated precisely to 20 March 15 AD.[25]

Forts and towns need a transportation system to connect them. In 14 AD, Publius Cornelius Dolabella, the former Senatorial consul for the year 10 AD, became the military commandant of Illyricum Superius (Dalmatia), and would hold that post until the year 20 AD. Dolabella took it upon himself to modernize the province's infrastructure, and so during his time in office he kept himself very busy. He instituted a programme of road-building within the coastal region of Dalmatia. Inscriptions known as the *Tabulae Dolabellae* have been found in Salona and can be dated to 16–20 AD. In the year 16 or 17 AD, two roads were constructed: the *Via Gabiniana*, which stretched from Salona to Andetrium, and the other one (whose name is not recorded) reached to the very border of the province. In 19–20 AD, three more roads were constructed in Dalmatia: one that reached from Salona to Fort Hedus (located within Daesidiate territory), another that connected Salona to the Bathinus River, and a third *imum montem Ditionum Ulcirum*, 'to the valley of Mount Ulcirus of the Ditiones' (modern-day Ilica, Bosnia). In addition to this, he also laid out permanent boundaries separating the territories of various townships within Illyricum and was responsible for the construction of many new forts and settlements such as the town of Emona. Finally, he commissioned a map to be made of his military zone, the *Forma Dolabelliana*. Military units patrolled the province and took note of the amount of real estate possessed by each community, and the sum of all this information was used to create the first truly accurate map of this region.[26]

Pannonia was turned into a heavily-militarized frontier province, guarding Rome's northern border from the Germans, Dacians and Sarmatians. By contrast, Dalmatia was an economic province, whose trading ports and abundance of mineral wealth were used to augment the imperial treasury. Following the Roman victory over the Illyrians, many of the old heavily-fortified hilltop settlments were abandoned and settlement on lower ground was favoured. These were places that could be easily accessible for trade and commerce. Economics, not defence, drove the creation and growth of these new settlements.[27]

In order to ensure that peace would prevail in this region from now on, certain changes had to be made. This included the Illyrian tribes themselves. According to Pliny, the names of many of the Illyrian tribes continued to be used, but new names also began to appear in the ancient records. The Romans took it upon themselves to not only redraw tribal borders, but even to erase and rewrite tribal identity. Many of the tribes that had existed in this region legally ceased to exist with a few strokes of a pen. In terms of the particulars, the Scordisci Celts were split in half, forming the 'Major Scordisci' and the 'Minor Scordisci'. The Breucian tribe was broken apart and several smaller 'tribes' were artificially created from it. Other tribes were combined together and were given a new name by their Roman masters to identify them. Most of these names were with reference to geographic place names to which the people had been forcibly relocated on Rome's order. Among the new tribes, if that word can be used, that were artificially created by the Romans were the following:

1. The *Colapiani*, who were named with reference to the Colapis River, now known as the Kupa River. They were formed by combining members of the Breuci along with the Osseriates and the Varciani.
2. The *Deraemestae*, who were also an amalgam of numerous tribes that were lumped together and given a single name.
3. The *Docleates*, who were named after their main settlement of Doclea. This tribe was also formed from numerous tribes that were combined together by the Romans.
4. The *Narensians* (also known as the Narensi, Narensii or Narensioi), 'the People of the Naro River', was composed of several tribes who lived along the Naro River. According to Pliny the Elder, their territory was divided into 102 *decuriae*.
5. The *Tricornenses*, 'the People of Tricornum', were named with reference to their main settlement (modern-day Ritopek, Serbia). This was a tribe that was artificially created by the Romans, comprising various Celtic and Thracian tribes who lived throughout Illyria. There were several Thracian tribes that lived within eastern Illyria, and there were Celtic tribes that were spread throughout Illyria from one end to the other. After the Great Illyrian Revolt ended, the Romans gathered these diverse people together and compelled all of them to live in one specific place for the purpose of observing and controlling them easily.

The Romans were essentially telling these people: 'This is who you are, this is where you live, this is where you call home, this is your culture, this is your history, and this is the name that you're going to call yourselves from now on.' There is something deeply disturbing about seeing this deliberate methodical step-by-step process of erasing old ethnic and tribal identities, making the tribes adopt new names, combining or splitting tribes to weaken them, relocating them away from their original lands and forcing them to live only within specific areas. As I was researching this particular aspect of ancient Roman policy within Illyria, I became struck by the realization that what the Romans were essentially doing here was making ancient versions of Indian reservations. All of this was done with the goal in mind of making the people's heritage disappear. By forcing them to relocate to other areas, they were depriving the people of their traditional ancestral homelands that they could identify with as being the homes of their people for generations. By taking away their names and giving them new ones, the Romans were attempting to erase their tribal self-consciousness, forcing the people to identify themselves based upon the reservation that they lived on rather than by their true ethnic origins. By giving them geographic-based names rather than names grounded in their heritage, the Romans were manipulating the people, or rather the future generations of these people, into believing that they had always lived in these places and didn't have any kind of history beforehand. By taking large numbers of different tribes and combining them together, the Romans were further attempting to erode the complex history of ancient Illyria and to erase the histories and dynamic relationships of the numerous peoples that once lived in this area. By breaking up powerful tribes like the Scordisci and the Breucians into smaller units, the Romans were crippling the strength of these hitherto dominant groups. It was a chillingly modern method of imperialism.

Epilogue

Tiberius Claudius Nero, now known as Emperor Tiberius Julius Caesar, would rule for another twenty years. As the old general's reign rolled on, Tiberius struggled with depression and indulged more and more in sexual perversion. The Roman upper classes grew to hate him due to his conduct as well as the conduct of his number two man, the commander of the Praetorian Guard, Lucius Aelius Sejanus, one of the most infamous names in Roman history. Tiberius lived as a recluse in his palatial estate on the island of Capri, preferring to let Sejanus do all his work for him. Sejanus became loathed and feared for his tyrannical treatment and the large number of executions that he ordered in Tiberius' name. In 23 AD, Tiberius' son Drusus Castor suddenly died. In 31 AD, Sejanus' wife committed suicide and in her note, she stated that Sejanus and Drusus' wife, with whom Sejanus was having an affair, had arranged for the murder of the emperor's son. Tiberius immediately ordered Sejanus to be arrested and executed. Emperor Tiberius died six years later in 37 AD, with only a few people mourning him.

Drusus Claudius Nero Germanicus, Emperor Tiberius' nephew who had fought beside him in Illyria and Germania, was sent to the east where he came into conflict with Gnaeus Calpurnius Piso, the governor of Syria. In 19 AD, Germanicus died under mysterious circumstances and rumours quickly spread that he had been assassinated. Gnaeus Calpurnius Piso was the main suspect in Germanicus' murder, but some have hypothesized that none other than Tiberius himself arranged his nephew's death. The emperor was never implicated but Piso was, and when it became clear that he was about to be convicted, Piso chose to commit suicide rather than face execution. Upon Tiberius' death, with no surviving sons to take the throne, the emperor's closest male relative and successor was Germanicus' son Gaius, more popularly known by his nickname 'Little Boots': *Caligula*.

Marcus Messallinus, who was the governor of Illyricum when the Great Illyrian Revolt erupted, became a lacky for Tiberius when he gained the throne. It was Messallinus who suggested to the emperor that the soldiers ought to swear an annual oath of loyalty to him. His name is vacant for much of the historical records, but he appears to have been eager to please the emperor at every opportunity, likely fearing being a victim of one of Sejanus' treason trials. Marcus Messallinus died in 21 AD.

Marcus Aemilius Lepidus, who had led Rome's forces in Illyricum during the campaign of 8 AD, was appointed governor of Spain. Shortly before Caesar Augustus died in 14 AD, the dying emperor briefly considered Marcus Lepidus to be a worthy contender for the throne, but Lepidus was an opponent of the idea of monarchy and therefore Augustus decided not to give him the crown and instead declared Tiberius to be his successor. Marcus Lepidus remained one of Tiberius' closest companions throughout his life. During the trial of Gnaeus Calpurnius Piso, Lepidus acted as Piso's attorney because he and Piso were distant relatives. In 21 AD, Emperor Tiberius offered to appoint Lepidus as governor of Africa in order to deal with the rebel warlord Tacfarinas, who was still threatening Rome's grain supply in the region. However, Lepidus rejected the offer, claiming ill health. Even so, he continued to involve himself with politics for the duration of his life. Marcus Aemilius Lepidus died in 33 AD, regarded by the historian Tacitus as a model senator who acted bravely in the face of tyranny.[28]

Aulus Caecina Severus, the governor of Moesia who had distinguished himself during the Great Illyrian Revolt, would fight in Germania against Arminius and his rebels and would gain further glory upon the battlefield in that theatre. Once the legions pulled out of western Germania, Severus seems to have devoted his time exclusively to politics. The date of his death is not recorded.

Quintus Junius Blaesus, who had been the commanding officer of the legions stationed in Pannonia during the soldiers' mutiny of 14 AD, became the governor of Africa in 21 AD, and it was he who defeated the North African rebel leader Tacfarinas. For this, he was awarded triumphal honours. However, both his career and his life would end soon. Blaesus was the uncle of Lucius Aelius Sejanus. In 31 AD, Sejanus was accused of treason and executed on Tiberius' orders. Blaesus was put on trial due to his family connection with Sejanus, but before he could be sentenced he committed suicide. Both of Blaesus' sons also committed suicide.

As for Illyria, it would continue to be part of the Roman Empire for the next 400 years and with little trouble among the people. The Great Illyrian Revolt of 6–9 AD was the largest, bloodiest and last of the Roman–Illyrian Wars. From then on, the western Balkans was firmly under imperial control. Gradually, native Illyrian culture faded away and was forgotten. During the third century AD, the empire was partitioned into four during the reign of Emperor Diocletian, who instituted the 'tetrarchy' system of government. In the fourth century AD, the empire was consolidated into western and eastern halves; Illyria was first apportioned to the Western Roman Empire, and then was transferred to the East. Despite attacks by Visigoths, Ostrogoths and Huns during the fourth and fifth centuries, the Praetorian Prefecture of Illyricum, as it was known, remained under the control of the Eastern Roman Empire and when the Western Empire fell in 476 AD, Illyricum remained under Roman control as a province in the Byzantine Empire.

Endnotes

Chapter 1: The Illyrians

1. Smithsonian Libraries Unbound. 'Twelfth Night Traditions: A Cake, a Bean, and a King', by Alexia MacClain (4 January 2013). https://blog. library.si.edu/blog/2013/01/04/twelfth-night-traditions-a-cake-a-bean-and-a-king/#.Wn4R1jRy6Uk Accessed on 9 February 2018.
2. William Shakespeare info. 'Twelfth Night by Shakespeare.' http://www. william-shakespeare.info/shakespeare-play-twelfth-night.htm
3. David Binder, *Fare Well, Illyria* (Budapest, Central European University Press, 2013), x.
4. Dragan Ledina and Dubravka Ledina (2002). 'Dinara – the Mountain of Extraordinary Beauty', *Croatian Medical Journal*, 43 (5): 517.
5. David Binder, *Fare Well, Illyria* (Budapest, Central European University Press, 2013), x-xii.
6. Dragan Ledina and Dubravka Ledina (2002). 'Dinara – the Mountain of Extraordinary Beauty', *Croatian Medical Journal*, 43 (5): 517; Alberto Fortis, *Travels into Dalmatia* (London, J. Robson, 1778), 248; John J. Wilkes, *Dalmatia* (London, Routledge & Kegan Paul, 1969), xxi-xxv.
7. Aleksandar Stipčević, *The Illyrians: History and Culture*. Translated by Stojana Čulić Burton (Park Ridge, Noyes Press, 1977), 21-23; John Wilkes, *The Illyrians* (Cambridge, Blackwell Publishers Inc., 1995), 94-97.
8. Strabo, *Geography*, book 7, chapter 5.
9. Pseudo-Scylax, *Periplus*. https://en.wikisource.org/wiki/Translation: Periplus_of_Pseudo-Scylax
10. John Wilkes, *The Illyrians* (Cambridge, Blackwell Publishers Inc., 1995), 69.
11. J.P. Mallory and Douglas Q. Adams, eds, *Encyclopedia of Indo-European Culture* (Chicago, Fitzroy Dearborn Publishers, 1997), 288.
12. Aleksandar Stipčević, *The Illyrians: History and Culture*. Translated by Stojana Čulić Burton (Park Ridge, Noyes Press, 1977), 24-25.
13. Homer, *The Iliad*, book 20, lines 210-245. http://www.perseus.tufts.edu/ hopper/text?doc=Perseus%3Atext%3A1999.01.0134%3Abook%3D20

14. Apollodorus, *Library*, book 3, chapter 12; Diodorus Siculus, *The Library of History*, book 4, chapter 75; book 5, chapter 48; Dionysius of Halicarnassus, *Roman Antiquities*, book 1, chapters 61-62; Virgil, *The Aeneid*, book 3, line 163.

15. Herodotus, *Histories*, book 7, chapters 73, 75.

16. Claude Brixhe, 'Phrygian', in Roger D. Woodard, ed., *The Ancient Languages of Asia Minor* (Cambridge, Cambridge University Press, 2008), 72.

17. Pseudo-Apollodorus, *Library*, book 3, chapter 5. http://www.perseus. tufts.edu/hopper/text?doc=Apollod.+3.5&fromdoc=Perseus%3 Atext%3A1999.01.0022

18. Appianus, *The Roman History*, book 9, appendix on the Illyrian Wars, chapter 2.

19. Aleksandar Stipčević, *The Illyrians: History and Culture*. Translated by Stojana Čulić Burton (Park Ridge, Noyes Press, 1977), 14-15, 24; John Wilkes, *The Illyrians* (Cambridge, Blackwell Publishers Inc., 1995), 3.

20. Aleksandar Stipčević, *The Illyrians: History and Culture*. Translated by Stojana Čulić Burton (Park Ridge, Noyes Press, 1977), 5.

21. J.P. Mallory and Douglas Q. Adams, eds, *Encyclopedia of Indo-European Culture* (Chicago, Fitzroy Dearborn Publishers, 1997), 288.

22. About Names. 'Albanian names'. http://www.aboutnames.ch/albanian. htm Accessed on 9 February 2018.

23. E. Bosch et al, 'Paternal and maternal lineages in the Balkans show a homogeneous landscape over linguistic barriers, except for the isolated Aromuns' (31 May 2006) http://onlinelibrary.wiley.com/ doi/10.1111/j.1469-1809.2005.00251.x/full

24. J.P. Mallory and Douglas Q. Adams, eds, *Encyclopedia of Indo-European Culture* (Chicago, Fitzroy Dearborn Publishers, 1997), 289.

25. Anthropology.net. 'A possible *Homo erectus* jaw from Sicevo Gorge, Serbia' (29 June 2008). http://anthropology.net/2008/06/29/a-possible-homo-erectus-jaw-from-sicevo-gorge-serbia Accessed on 29 November 2015; Reuters. 'Balkan caves, gorges were pre-Neanderthal haven', by Ljilja Cvekic (27 June 2008). http://www.reuters.com/article/2008/06/27/ us-balkans-prehistoric-idUSL2768278020080627 Accessed on 29 November 2015.

26. John Wilkes, *The Illyrians* (Cambridge, Blackwell Publishers Inc., 1995), 28.

27. Sarunas Milisauskas, ed., *European Prehistory: A Survey* (New York, Springer, 2002), 56; Science Daily. '40,000-year-old Skull Shows Both Modern Human And Neanderthal Traits' (16 January 2007). https:// www.sciencedaily.com/releases/2007/01/070115215252.htm Accessed on 29 January 2018.

28. John Wilkes, *The Illyrians* (Cambridge, Blackwell Publishers Inc., 1995), 29-30; R. Bollongino, et al (2013). '2000 Years of Parallel Societies in Stone Age Central Europe', *Science*, 342 (6157): 479-481. http://science. sciencemag.org/content/342/6157/479

29. PanaComp. 'Lepenski vir Archaeological site Lepen Whirlpool.' http:// www.panacomp.net/lepenski-vir-archaeological-site-lepen-whirlpool Accessed on 19 February 2018; Radic, Zoran M. (2000). 'Some puzzles about the Danubian and European Cultural History and Connections of Civilization Development with Climate, Water and Hydrology.' http:// medhycos.mpl.ird.fr/doc/zoran.htm

30. Radovanović, Ivana (2000). 'Houses and burials at Lepenski Vir', *European Journal of Archaeology*, Vol. 3(3): 333-334.

31. Radovanović, Ivana (2000). 'Houses and burials at Lepenski Vir', *European Journal of Archaeology*, Vol. 3(3): 336-337.

32. John Boardman et al, eds, *The Cambridge Ancient History, volume III, part 1 – The Prehistory of the Balkans; and the Middle East and Aegaean World, tenth to eighth centuries B.C.* (Cambridge, Cambridge University Press, 2003), 85; Marija Gimbutas, *The Living Goddesses* (Berkeley, University of California Press, 2001), 31; Radovanović, Ivana (2000). 'Houses and burials at Lepenski Vir', *European Journal of Archaeology*, Vol. 3(3): 335; PanaComp. 'Lepenski vir Archaeological site Lepen Whirlpool.' http:// www.panacomp.net/lepenski-vir-archaeological-site-lepen-whirlpool Accessed on 19 February 2018.

33. Aleksandar Stipčević, *The Illyrians: History and Culture*. Translated by Stojana Čulić Burton (Park Ridge, Noyes Press, 1977), 134-135; John Wilkes, *The Illyrians* (Cambridge, Blackwell Publishers Inc., 1995), 29-30.

34. John Wilkes, *The Illyrians* (Cambridge, Blackwell Publishers Inc., 1995), 29-31.

35. John Wilkes, *The Illyrians* (Cambridge, Blackwell Publishers Inc., 1995), 31; John Boardman et al, eds, *The Cambridge Ancient History, volume III, part 1 – The Prehistory of the Balkans; and the Middle East and Aegaean World, tenth to eighth centuries B.C.* (Cambridge, Cambridge University Press, 2003), 86-87.

36. Marija Gimbutas, *The Goddesses and Gods of Old Europe, 6500–3500 BC: Myths and Cult Images*. New and updated edition (Berkeley, University of California Press, 1982), 24-25; Sarajevo School of Science and Technology. 'Butmir Culture – General Facts' (2006). http://dmc.ssst.edu.ba/ButmirNeolithicCulture/ english/gfacts.html; Bosnia and Herzegovina Commission to Preserve National Monuments. 'Prehistoric settlement of Butmir, the archaeological

site', by Dubravko Lovrenoviae (31 August 2004). http://www.kons.gov.ba/main.php?id_struct=50&lang=4&action=view&id=2500

37. Old European Culture. 'Baba – earthen bread oven' (21 December 2015). http://oldeuropeanculture.blogspot.com/2015/12/baba-earthen-bread-oven.html; Sarajevo School of Science and Technology. 'Butmir Culture – General Facts' (2006). http://dmc.ssst.edu.ba/ButmirNeolithicCulture/english/gfacts.html; Sarajevo School of Science and Technology. 'Butmir Culture – Okolište' (2006). http://dmc.ssst.edu.ba/ButmirNeolithicCulture/english/okoliste.html

38. Sarajevo School of Science and Technology. 'Butmir Culture – General Facts' (2006). http://dmc.ssst.edu.ba/ButmirNeolithicCulture/english/gfacts.html

39. Arne Windler (2013). 'From the Aegean Sea to the Parisian Basin. How Spondylus can change our view on trade and exchange.' *Metalla*, Nr. 20.2: 95-106. https://www.academia.edu/5464477/From_the_Aegean_Sea_to_the_Parisian_Basin._How_Spondylus_can_rearrange_our_view_on_trade_and_exchange

40. Ancient Origins. 'Is the Danube Valley Civilization script the oldest writing in the world?' by John Black (15 February 2014). http://www.ancient-origins.net/ancient-places-europe/danube-valley-civilisation-script-oldest-writing-world-001343; 'Origins of Writing: Danube Scripts led to Pharaonic Egyptian Hieroglyphs: Confirmation by Pottery Comparison' (6 February 2005). http://ancientworldblog.blogspot.com/2005/02/origins-of-writing-danube-scripts-led.html

41. *Thaindian News*. 'Ancient axe find suggests Copper Age began earlier than believed' (8 October 2008). http://www.thaindian.com/newsportal/india-news/ancient-axe-find-suggests-copper-age-began-earlier-than-believed_100105122.html

42. UCL Institute of Archaeology. 'Serbian site may have hosted first copper-makers' (23 September 2010). http://www.ucl.ac.uk/archaeology/calendar/articles/20100924

43. John Wilkes, *The Illyrians* (Cambridge, Blackwell Publishers Inc., 1995), 31-32.

44. John Wilkes, *The Illyrians* (Cambridge, Blackwell Publishers Inc., 1995), 32.

45. John Wilkes, *The Illyrians* (Cambridge, Blackwell Publishers Inc., 1995), 34-35.

46. John Wilkes, *The Illyrians* (Cambridge, Blackwell Publishers Inc., 1995), 223.

47. John Wilkes, *The Illyrians* (Cambridge, Blackwell Publishers Inc., 1995), 35-37, 224-225; A.F. Harding, *European Societies in the Bronze Age* (Cambridge, Cambridge University Press, 2000), 191.

48. Aleksandar Stipčević, *The Illyrians: History and Culture*. Translated by Stojana Čulić Burton (Park Ridge, Noyes Press, 1977), 35-36.

49. John Wilkes, *The Illyrians* (Cambridge, Blackwell Publishers Inc., 1995), 224.

50. John Wilkes, *The Illyrians* (Cambridge, Blackwell Publishers Inc., 1995), 39, 104.

51. John Wilkes, *The Illyrians* (Cambridge, Blackwell Publishers Inc., 1995), 38-39, 223.

52. John Wilkes, *The Illyrians* (Cambridge, Blackwell Publishers Inc., 1995), 41.

53. A.F. Harding, *European Societies in the Bronze Age* (Cambridge, Cambridge University Press, 2000), 77, 100-102.

54. John Wilkes, *The Illyrians* (Cambridge, Blackwell Publishers Inc., 1995), 41, 44, 104-105.

55. Peter Bogucki and Pam J. Crabtree, eds, *Ancient Europe 8000 B.C.–A.D. 1000: Encyclopedia of the Barbarian World*, volume II (New York, Charles Scribner's Sons, 2004), 299.

56. John Wilkes, *The Illyrians* (Cambridge, Blackwell Publishers Inc., 1995), 223-224.

57. John Wilkes, *The Illyrians* (Cambridge, Blackwell Publishers Inc., 1995), 225.

58. Aleksandar Stipčević, *The Illyrians: History and Culture*. Translated by Stojana Čulić Burton (Park Ridge, Noyes Press, 1977), 110-111.

59. Aleksandar Stipčević, *The Illyrians: History and Culture*. Translated by Stojana Čulić Burton (Park Ridge, Noyes Press, 1977), 111.

60. Aleksandar Stipčević, *The Illyrians: History and Culture*. Translated by Stojana Čulić Burton (Park Ridge, Noyes Press, 1977), 107, 108-109.

61. Aleksandar Stipčević, *The Illyrians: History and Culture*. Translated by Stojana Čulić Burton (Park Ridge, Noyes Press, 1977), 107-108.

62. Aleksandar Stipčević, *The Illyrians: History and Culture*. Translated by Stojana Čulić Burton (Park Ridge, Noyes Press, 1977), 108.

63. Aleksandar Stipčević, *The Illyrians: History and Culture*. Translated by Stojana Čulić Burton (Park Ridge, Noyes Press, 1977), 108.

64. Aleksandar Stipčević, *The Illyrians: History and Culture*. Translated by Stojana Čulić Burton (Park Ridge, Noyes Press, 1977), 3-4; John Wilkes, *The Illyrians* (Cambridge, Blackwell Publishers Inc., 1995), 97.

65. Aleksandar Stipčević, *The Illyrians: History and Culture*. Translated by Stojana Čulić Burton (Park Ridge, Noyes Press, 1977), 83.

66. J.J. Wilkes, *Dalmatia* (London, Routledge & Kegan Paul, 1969), 3.

67. Aleksandar Stipčević, *The Illyrians: History and Culture*. Translated by Stojana Čulić Burton (Park Ridge, Noyes Press, 1977), 108.

68. Strabo, *Geography*, book 7, chapter 5.

69. John Wilkes, *The Illyrians* (Cambridge, Blackwell Publishers Inc., 1995), 186.
70. Aleksandar Stipčević, *The Illyrians: History and Culture*. Translated by Stojana Čulić Burton (Park Ridge, Noyes Press, 1977), 36, 107-108.
71. John Wilkes, *The Illyrians* (Cambridge, Blackwell Publishers Inc., 1995), 186-187.
72. John Wilkes, *The Illyrians* (Cambridge, Blackwell Publishers Inc., 1995), 95.
73. John Wilkes, *The Illyrians* (Cambridge, Blackwell Publishers Inc., 1995), 187.
74. Strabo, *Geography*, book 7, chapter 5.
75. Strabo, *Geography*, book 7, chapter 5; Cassius Dio, *The Roman History*, book 49, chapter 35.
76. Strabo, *Geography*, book 7, chapter 5.
77. Appianus, *The Roman History*, book 9, appendix on the Illyrian Wars, chapter 18.
78. Strabo, *Geography*, book 7, chapter 5.
79. Appianus, *The Roman History*, book 9, appendix on the Illyrian Wars, chapter 18.
80. Sextus Julius Frontinus, *Stratagems*, book 2, chapter 5.
81. Cassius Dio, *The Roman History*, book 49, chapter 36.
82. Cassius Dio describes the Daesidiate tribe as being Dalmatian, not Pannonian.
83. Strabo, *Geography*, book 7, chapter 5.
84. Appianus, *The Roman History*, book 9, appendix on the Illyrian Wars, chapters 14, 18, 22.
85. Publius Annius Florus, *Epitome*, book 2, chapter 14.
86. Cassius Dio, *The Roman History*, book 49, chapter 36.
87. Cassius Dio, *The Roman History*, book 49, chapter 36.
88. Strabo, *Geography*, book 7, chapter 5.
89. According to Peter Kovacs, Segestica and Siscia were two separate towns, even though they were located close to each other. Segestica was the more noteworthy, located on the Pogorelec Peninsula, while Siscia was located on the left bank of the Sava River. This comes from Pliny's description of the area, in which Segestica is stated to be on the right bank of the Kupa River and with Siscia situated upon the left bank. Strabo also states that Segestica and Siscia were two separate settlements, but both Strabo and Pliny lived and wrote their works during the reign of Tiberius. Peter Kovacs, *A History of Pannonia during the Principate* (Bonn, Dr Rudolf Habelt GMBH, 2014), 23; Rajka Makjanić, *Siscia Pannonia Superior*. BAR International Series 621 (Oxford, Hadrian Books, Ltd, 1995), 1.

90. Danijel Dzino, *Illyricum in Roman Politics, 229 BC–AD 68* (Cambridge, Cambridge University Press, 2010), 154.

91. Strabo, *Geography*, book 7, chapter 5.

92. Gaius Velleius Paterculus, *The Roman History*, book 2, chapter 110.

93. Herodianus of Antioch, *The History of the Roman Empire*, book 2, chapter 9.

94. Strabo, *Geography*, book 7, chapter 5.

95. Publius Cornelius Scipio Nasica Corculum, who destroyed Dalmium in 155 BC. http://penelope.uchicago.edu/Thayer/E/Roman/Texts/Strabo/7E*.html#note308

96. Strabo, *Geography*, book 7, chapter 5.

97. Aleksandar Stipčević, *The Illyrians: History and Culture*. Translated by Stojana Čulić Burton (Park Ridge, Noyes Press, 1977), 35; Peter Michael Swan, *The Augustan Succession* (New York, Oxford University Press, 2004), 198.

98. Pliny the Elder, *Natural History*, book 3, chapter 28.

99. John Wilkes, *The Illyrians* (Cambridge, Blackwell Publishers Inc., 1995), 44.

100. John Wilkes, *The Illyrians* (Cambridge, Blackwell Publishers Inc., 1995), 44.

101. John Wilkes, *The Illyrians* (Cambridge, Blackwell Publishers Inc., 1995), 41, 44.

102. John Wilkes, *The Illyrians* (Cambridge, Blackwell Publishers Inc., 1995), 51, 54.

103. John Wilkes, *The Illyrians* (Cambridge, Blackwell Publishers Inc., 1995), 43.

104. Aleksandar Stipčević, *The Illyrians: History and Culture*. Translated by Stojana Čulić Burton (Park Ridge, Noyes Press, 1977), 176-177.

105. Aleksandar Stipčević, *The Illyrians: History and Culture*. Translated by Stojana Čulić Burton (Park Ridge, Noyes Press, 1977), 177-178.

106. *Sabretooth* (2000).

107. Quintus Ennius, *Annales*, fragment 249.

108. Aulus Gellius, *Noctes Atticae*, book 10, chapter 25; Sir William Smith et al, eds, *A Dictionary of Greek and Roman Antiquities*, Volume 1, Third Edition, Revised and Enlarged (London, John Murray, 1901), 937.

109. Sir William Smith et al, eds, *A Dictionary of Greek and Roman Antiquities*, Volume 1, Third Edition, Revised and Enlarged (London, John Murray, 1901), 937.

110. Aleksandar Stipčević, *The Illyrians: History and Culture*. Translated by Stojana Čulić Burton (Park Ridge, Noyes Press, 1977), 127-128.

111. Aleksandar Stipčević, *The Illyrians: History and Culture*. Translated by Stojana Čulić Burton (Park Ridge, Noyes Press, 1977), 138.

112. Paulus Aegineta, *De Re Medica*, book 6, chapter 88. In *The Seven Books of Paulus Aegineta*, Volume II, translated by Francis Adams (London, C. and J. Adlard, 1846), 420.

113. Aleksandar Stipčević, *The Illyrians: History and Culture*. Translated by Stojana Čulić Burton (Park Ridge, Noyes Press, 1977), 138, John Wilkes, *The Illyrians* (Cambridge, Blackwell Publishers Inc., 1995), 222.

114. Aleksandar Stipčević, *The Illyrians: History and Culture*. Translated by Stojana Čulić Burton (Park Ridge, Noyes Press, 1977), 85.

115. Henri Hubert, *The Greatness and Decline of the Celts* (New York, Routledge, 1996), 58.

116. Publius Annius Florus, *Epitome*, book 1, chapter 39.

117. Aleksandar Stipčević, *The Illyrians: History and Culture*. Translated by Stojana Čulić Burton (Park Ridge, Noyes Press, 1977), 85, 263.

118. Aleksandar Stipčević, *The Illyrians: History and Culture*. Translated by Stojana Čulić Burton (Park Ridge, Noyes Press, 1977), 179.

119. Aleksandar Stipčević, *The Illyrians: History and Culture*. Translated by Stojana Čulić Burton (Park Ridge, Noyes Press, 1977), 178.

120. John Wilkes, *The Illyrians* (Cambridge, Blackwell Publishers Inc., 1995), 44, 240.

121. Aleksandar Stipčević, *The Illyrians: History and Culture*. Translated by Stojana Čulić Burton (Park Ridge, Noyes Press, 1977), 67-68.

122. Tacitus, 'Germania' in *Chronicles of the Barbarians* (New York, History Book Club, 1998), 80-81.

123. Aleksandar Stipčević, *The Illyrians: History and Culture*. Translated by Stojana Čulić Burton (Park Ridge, Noyes Press, 1977), 186.

124. Pliny the Elder, *Natural History*, book 7, chapter 2.

125. Arrian, *Anabasis*, book 1, chapter 5.

126. Aleksandar Stipčević, *The Illyrians: History and Culture*. Translated by Stojana Čulić Burton (Park Ridge, Noyes Press, 1977), 230-232; John Wilkes, *The Illyrians* (Cambridge, Blackwell Publishers Inc., 1995), 241.

127. Aleksandar Stipčević, *The Illyrians: History and Culture*. Translated by Stojana Čulić Burton (Park Ridge, Noyes Press, 1977), 74, 231.

128. John Wilkes, *The Illyrians* (Cambridge, Blackwell Publishers Inc., 1995), 44.

129. Aleksandar Stipčević, *The Illyrians: History and Culture*. Translated by Stojana Čulić Burton (Park Ridge, Noyes Press, 1977), 98.

130. Sanjin Đumišić. 'Ancient Megalithic Site of Daorson in Bosnia & Herzegovina' (28 January 2017). https://sanjindumisic.com/ancient-megalithic-site-of-daorson-in-bosnia-herzegovina/; UNESCO. 'The natural and architectural ensemble of Stolac' (12 November 2007). http://whc.unesco.org/en/tentativelists/5282

131. Aleksandar Stipčević, *The Illyrians: History and Culture*. Translated by Stojana Čulić Burton (Park Ridge, Noyes Press, 1977), 100-101.

132. Aleksandar Stipčević, *The Illyrians: History and Culture*. Translated by Stojana Čulić Burton (Park Ridge, Noyes Press, 1977), 100-103.
133. Aleksandar Stipčević, *The Illyrians: History and Culture*. Translated by Stojana Čulić Burton (Park Ridge, Noyes Press, 1977), 103-104; John Wilkes, *The Illyrians* (Cambridge, Blackwell Publishers Inc., 1995), 227.
134. Aleksandar Stipčević, *The Illyrians: History and Culture*. Translated by Stojana Čulić Burton (Park Ridge, Noyes Press, 1977), 167.
135. Aleksandar Stipčević, *The Illyrians: History and Culture*. Translated by Stojana Čulić Burton (Park Ridge, Noyes Press, 1977), 86-89; John Wilkes, *The Illyrians* (Cambridge, Blackwell Publishers Inc., 1995), 227-228.
136. Aleksandar Stipčević, *The Illyrians: History and Culture*. Translated by Stojana Čulić Burton (Park Ridge, Noyes Press, 1977), 90-94; John Wilkes, *The Illyrians* (Cambridge, Blackwell Publishers Inc., 1995), 229-230.
137. Aleksandar Stipčević, *The Illyrians: History and Culture*. Translated by Stojana Čulić Burton (Park Ridge, Noyes Press, 1977), 89; John Wilkes, *The Illyrians* (Cambridge, Blackwell Publishers Inc., 1995), 229.
138. Aleksandar Stipčević, *The Illyrians: History and Culture*. Translated by Stojana Čulić Burton (Park Ridge, Noyes Press, 1977), 89-90.
139. John Wilkes, *The Illyrians* (Cambridge, Blackwell Publishers Inc., 1995), 229.
140. Aleksandar Stipčević, *The Illyrians: History and Culture*. Translated by Stojana Čulić Burton (Park Ridge, Noyes Press, 1977), 123; John Wilkes, *The Illyrians* (Cambridge, Blackwell Publishers Inc., 1995), 231-233.
141. Aleksandar Stipčević, *The Illyrians: History and Culture*. Translated by Stojana Čulić Burton (Park Ridge, Noyes Press, 1977), 111, 114, 121.
142. Aleksandar Stipčević, *The Illyrians: History and Culture*. Translated by Stojana Čulić Burton (Park Ridge, Noyes Press, 1977), 121.
143. Aleksandar Stipčević, *The Illyrians: History and Culture*. Translated by Stojana Čulić Burton (Park Ridge, Noyes Press, 1977), 123; John Wilkes, *The Illyrians* (Cambridge, Blackwell Publishers Inc., 1995), 233-235.
144. Aleksandar Stipčević, *The Illyrians: History and Culture*. Translated by Stojana Čulić Burton (Park Ridge, Noyes Press, 1977), 80; John Wilkes, *The Illyrians* (Cambridge, Blackwell Publishers Inc., 1995), 220; Herodotus, 'Scythians and Thracians' in *Chronicles of the Barbarians* (New York, History Book Club, 1998), 24.
145. Aleksandar Stipčević, *The Illyrians: History and Culture*. Translated by Stojana Čulić Burton (Park Ridge, Noyes Press, 1977), 137-139.
146. Aleksandar Stipčević, *The Illyrians: History and Culture*. Translated by Stojana Čulić Burton (Park Ridge, Noyes Press, 1977), 84, 134; John

Wilkes, *The Illyrians* (Cambridge, Blackwell Publishers Inc., 1995), 220-221; Strabo, *Geography*, book 7, chapter 5.

147. Aleksandar Stipčević, *The Illyrians: History and Culture*. Translated by Stojana Čulić Burton (Park Ridge, Noyes Press, 1977), 83-85, 134, 137; John Wilkes, *The Illyrians* (Cambridge, Blackwell Publishers Inc., 1995), 220-222.

148. Aleksandar Stipčević, *The Illyrians: History and Culture*. Translated by Stojana Čulić Burton (Park Ridge, Noyes Press, 1977), 128-129, 135-136; John Wilkes, *The Illyrians* (Cambridge, Blackwell Publishers Inc., 1995), 221, 230-231.

149. Athanaeus, *Deipnisophistae*, book 10, chapter 440.

150. Polybius, *Histories*, fragments of book 29, chapter 13. http://penelope.uchicago.edu/Thayer/E/Roman/Texts/Polybius/29*.html

151. Athanaeus, *Deipnisophistae*, book 10, chapter 443.

152. Aleksandar Stipčević, *The Illyrians: History and Culture*. Translated by Stojana Čulić Burton (Park Ridge, Noyes Press, 1977), 128-129.

153. Aleksandar Stipčević, *The Illyrians: History and Culture*. Translated by Stojana Čulić Burton (Park Ridge, Noyes Press, 1977), 128-129; John Wilkes, *The Illyrians* (Cambridge, Blackwell Publishers Inc., 1995), 231.

154. Aleksandar Stipčević, *The Illyrians: History and Culture*. Translated by Stojana Čulić Burton (Park Ridge, Noyes Press, 1977), 127-128, 131-132, 135; John Wilkes, *The Illyrians* (Cambridge, Blackwell Publishers Inc., 1995), 231.

155. Web Citation. 'Pod, a prehistoric hillfort settlement, the archaeological site.' Published in the ďž″Official Gazette of BiHďž″ no. 75/08, Bosnia and Herzegovina Commission to Preserve National Monuments. http://www.webcitation.org/5t3n3Effr Accessed on 27 November 2015; John Wilkes, *The Illyrians* (Cambridge, Blackwell Publishers Inc., 1995), 194, 204.

Chapter 2: Rome and the Balkans

1. Strabo, *Geography*, book 6, chapter 2.

2. Aleksandar Stipčević, *The Illyrians: History and Culture*. Translated by Stojana Čulić Burton (Park Ridge, Noyes Press, 1977), 37-40; Anthony Everitt, *Augustus: The Life of Rome's First Emperor* (New York, Random House Trade Paperbacks, 2006), 51.

3. Aleksandar Stipčević, *The Illyrians: History and Culture*. Translated by Stojana Čulić Burton (Park Ridge, Noyes Press, 1977), 4.

4. Thucydides, *The History of the Peloponnesian War*, book 4, chapter 126.

5. Diodorus Siculus, *The Library of History*, book 16, chapter 2.

6. Thucydides, *The History of the Peloponnesian War*, book 4, chapters 124-128; Diodorus Siculus, *The Library of History*, book 14, chapter 92; Aleksandar Stipčević, *The Illyrians: History and Culture*. Translated by Stojana Čulić Burton (Park Ridge, Noyes Press, 1977), 43; John Wilkes, *The Illyrians* (Cambridge, Blackwell Publishers Inc., 1995), 117-122.

7. Strabo, *Geography*, book 6, chapter 3.

8. Aleksandar Stipčević, *The Illyrians: History and Culture*. Translated by Stojana Čulić Burton (Park Ridge, Noyes Press, 1977), 27.

9. Strabo, *Geography*, book 6, chapter 3; T.H. Carpenter et al, *The Italic People of Ancient Apulia* (Cambridge, Cambridge University Press, 2014), 37-39.

10. L'Anticopedie. 'Daunia.' http://www.anticopedie.fr/mondes/mondes-gb/daunie-doc.html Accessed on 19 February 2018.

11. Strabo, *Geography*, book 6, chapter 3; Michael Grant, *A Guide to the Ancient World: A Dictionary of Classical Place Names* (New York, Barnes & Noble Books, 1997), 106-107, 122-123, 146.

12. Strabo, *Geography*, book 6, chapter 3.

13. Strabo, *Geography*, book 6, chapter 3.

14. Strabo, *Geography*, book 6, chapter 3.

15. Aleksandar Stipčević, *The Illyrians: History and Culture*. Translated by Stojana Čulić Burton (Park Ridge, Noyes Press, 1977), 36.

16. Aleksandar Stipčević, *The Illyrians: History and Culture*. Translated by Stojana Čulić Burton (Park Ridge, Noyes Press, 1977), 36.

17. Pliny the Elder, *Natural History*, 3.110, 112; Aleksandar Stipčević, *The Illyrians: History and Culture*. Translated by Stojana Čulić Burton (Park Ridge, Noyes Press, 1977), 27.

18. Aleksandar Stipčević, *The Illyrians: History and Culture*. Translated by Stojana Čulić Burton (Park Ridge, Noyes Press, 1977), 28.

19. Polybius, *The Rise of the Roman Empire*, book 2, chapter 2 (London, Penguin Classics, 1979), 112.

20. Cassius Dio, *The Roman History*, book 12, chapter 19; Publius Annius Florus, *Epitome*, book 1, chapter 21; Polybius, *The Rise of the Roman Empire*, book 2, chapter 2 (London, Penguin Classics, 1979), 112-118; Polybius, *The Rise of the Roman Empire*, map of northern Greece (London, Penguin Classics, 1979), 551; Appianus, *The Roman History*, book 9, appendix on the Illyrian Wars, chapter 7.

21. Cassius Dio, *The Roman History*, book 12, chapter 19; Publius Annius Florus, *Epitome*, book 1, chapter 21; Polybius, *The Rise of the Roman Empire*, book 2, chapter 2 (London, Penguin Classics, 1979), 118-119;

Appianus, *The Roman History*, book 9, appendix on the Illyrian Wars, chapter 7.

22. Cassius Dio, *The Roman History*, book 12, chapter 19; Publius Annius Florus, *Epitome*, book 1, chapter 21; Polybius, *The Rise of the Roman Empire*, book 2, chapter 2 (London, Penguin Classics, 1979), 119-123; Appianus, *The Roman History*, book 9, appendix on the Illyrian Wars, chapters 7-8.

23. UNRV. 'First Illyrian War' http://www.unrv.com/empire/first-illyrian-war.php

24. Appianus, *The Roman History*, book 9, appendix on the Illyrian Wars, chapters 7-8.

25. Polybius, *The Rise of the Roman Empire*, book 2, chapter 2 (London, Penguin Classics, 1979), 192-193; Appianus, *The Roman History*, book 9, appendix on the Illyrian Wars, chapter 8.

26. Polybius, *The Rise of the Roman Empire*, book 2, chapter 2 (London, Penguin Classics, 1979), 192-193; Appianus, *The Roman History*, book 9, appendix on the Illyrian Wars, chapter 8.

27. Polybius, *The Rise of the Roman Empire*, book 2, chapter 2 (London, Penguin Classics, 1979), 195.

28. Appianus, *The Roman History*, book 9, appendix on the Illyrian Wars, chapter 8; Polybius, *The Rise of the Roman Empire*, book 2, chapter 2 (London, Penguin Classics, 1979), 195.

29. Polybius, *The Rise of the Roman Empire*, book 2, chapter 2 (London, Penguin Classics, 1979), 195-197; Appianus, *The Roman History*, book 9, appendix on the Illyrian Wars, chapter 8.

30. Aleksandar Stipčević, *The Illyrians: History and Culture*. Translated by Stojana Čulić Burton (Park Ridge, Noyes Press, 1977), 53.

31. Aleksandar Stipčević, *The Illyrians: History and Culture*. Translated by Stojana Čulić Burton (Park Ridge, Noyes Press, 1977), 53-54.

32. Aleksandar Stipčević, *The Illyrians: History and Culture*. Translated by Stojana Čulić Burton (Park Ridge, Noyes Press, 1977), 54.

33. Aleksandar Stipčević, *The Illyrians: History and Culture*. Translated by Stojana Čulić Burton (Park Ridge, Noyes Press, 1977), 54.

34. Appianus, *The Roman History*, book 9, appendix on the Illyrian Wars, chapter 9; Polybius, *Histories*, fragments of book 29, chapter 13. http://penelope.uchicago.edu/Thayer/E/Roman/Texts/Polybius/29*.html; UNRV. 'Third Macedonian War' http://www.unrv.com/empire/third-macedonian-war.php; J.J. Wilkes, *Dalmatia* (London, Routledge & Kegan Paul, 1969), 22-24.

35. Cassius Dio, *The Roman History*, book 20, chapter 24; Appianus, *The Roman History*, book 9, appendix on the Illyrian Wars, chapter 9; Aleksandar Stipčević, *The Illyrians: History and Culture*. Translated by Stojana Čulić Burton (Park Ridge, Noyes Press, 1977), 54.

36. Cassius Dio, *The Roman History*, book 20, chapter 24; Appianus, *The Roman History*, book 9, appendix on the Illyrian Wars, chapter 9; Aleksandar Stipčević, *The Illyrians: History and Culture*. Translated by Stojana Čulić Burton (Park Ridge, Noyes Press, 1977), 54-55.

37. Aleksandar Stipčević, *The Illyrians: History and Culture*. Translated by Stojana Čulić Burton (Park Ridge, Noyes Press, 1977), 54-55.

38. Danijel Dzino, *Illyricum in Roman Politics, 229 BC–AD 68* (Cambridge, Cambridge University Press, 2010), 57-58, 80.

39. Aleksandar Stipčević, *The Illyrians: History and Culture*. Translated by Stojana Čulić Burton (Park Ridge, Noyes Press, 1977), 55-56.

40. Appianus, *The Roman History*, book 9, appendix on the Illyrian Wars, chapter 11; Cassius Dio, *The Roman History*, book 20, chapter 25; Strabo, *Geography*, book 7, chapter 5; Aleksandar Stipčević, *The Illyrians: History and Culture*. Translated by Stojana Čulić Burton (Park Ridge, Noyes Press, 1977), 56.

41. Aleksandar Stipčević, *The Illyrians: History and Culture*. Translated by Stojana Čulić Burton (Park Ridge, Noyes Press, 1977), 58-59.

42. Appianus, *The Roman History*, book 9, appendix on the Illyrian Wars, chapter 11.

43. Appianus, *The Roman History*, book 9, appendix on the Illyrian Wars, chapter 11.

44. Appianus, *The Roman History*, book 9, appendix on the Illyrian Wars, chapter 11; Cassius Dio, *The Roman History*, book 20, chapter 25; Aleksandar Stipčević, *The Illyrians: History and Culture*. Translated by Stojana Čulić Burton (Park Ridge, Noyes Press, 1977), 56.

45. Strabo, *Geography*, book 7, chapter 5.

46. J.S. Richardson, *Hispaniae: Spain and the Development of Roman Imperialism, 218–82 BC* (Cambridge, Cambridge University Press, 1986), 136.

47. Appianus, *The Roman History*, book 9, appendix on the Illyrian Wars, chapter 10; Aleksandar Stipčević, *The Illyrians: History and Culture*. Translated by Stojana Čulić Burton (Park Ridge, Noyes Press, 1977), 56-57.

48. Aleksandar Stipčević, *The Illyrians: History and Culture*. Translated by Stojana Čulić Burton (Park Ridge, Noyes Press, 1977), 59.

49. Appianus, *The Roman History*, book 9, appendix on the Illyrian Wars, chapter 10; Aleksandar Stipčević, *The Illyrians: History and Culture.* Translated by Stojana Čulić Burton (Park Ridge, Noyes Press, 1977), 59.
50. Aleksandar Stipčević, *The Illyrians: History and Culture.* Translated by Stojana Čulić Burton (Park Ridge, Noyes Press, 1977), 59.
51. UNRV History. 'First Triumvirate.' http://www.unrv.com/fall-republic/first-triumvirate.php
52. 'Solin.' http://w3.mrki.info/split/solin.html; Arthur L. Frothingham, *Roman Cities in Italy and Dalmatia* (New York, Sturgis & Walton Company, 1910), 267.
53. Arthur L. Frothingham, *Roman Cities in Italy and Dalmatia* (New York, Sturgis & Walton Company, 1910), 267.
54. 'Solin.' http://w3.mrki.info/split/solin.html
55. Arthur L. Frothingham, *Roman Cities in Italy and Dalmatia* (New York, Sturgis & Walton Company, 1910), 267-268.
56. 'Solin.' http://w3.mrki.info/split/solin.html; Arthur L. Frothingham, *Roman Cities in Italy and Dalmatia* (New York, Sturgis & Walton Company, 1910), 271.
57. 'Solin.' http://w3.mrki.info/split/solin.html
58. Aleksandar Stipčević, *The Illyrians: History and Culture.* Translated by Stojana Čulić Burton (Park Ridge, Noyes Press, 1977), 65.
59. Aleksandar Stipčević, *The Illyrians: History and Culture.* Translated by Stojana Čulić Burton (Park Ridge, Noyes Press, 1977), 66-67.
60. Aleksandar Stipčević, *The Illyrians: History and Culture.* Translated by Stojana Čulić Burton (Park Ridge, Noyes Press, 1977), 66-67.
61. Aleksandar Stipčević, *The Illyrians: History and Culture.* Translated by Stojana Čulić Burton (Park Ridge, Noyes Press, 1977), 66-68.
62. Strabo, *Geography*, book 5, chapter 1.
63. Appianus, *The Roman History*, book 9, appendix on the Illyrian Wars, chapters 12, 25.
64. Appianus, *The Roman History*, book 9, appendix on the Illyrian Wars, chapter 12.
65. Appianus, *The Roman History*, book 9, appendix on the Illyrian Wars, chapters 12, 25; Aleksandar Stipčević, *The Illyrians: History and Culture.* Translated by Stojana Čulić Burton (Park Ridge, Noyes Press, 1977), 59-60.
66. Appianus, *The Roman History*, book 9, appendix on the Illyrian Wars, chapter 13; Aleksandar Stipčević, *The Illyrians: History and Culture.* Translated by Stojana Čulić Burton (Park Ridge, Noyes Press, 1977), 60.

67. Appianus, *The Roman History*, book 9, appendix on the Illyrian Wars, chapter 13; Aleksandar Stipčević, *The Illyrians: History and Culture*. Translated by Stojana Čulić Burton (Park Ridge, Noyes Press, 1977), 60.

68. Appianus, *The Roman History*, book 9, appendix on the Illyrian Wars, chapter 13; Aleksandar Stipčević, *The Illyrians: History and Culture*. Translated by Stojana Čulić Burton (Park Ridge, Noyes Press, 1977), 60.

69. Theodor Mommsen, *A History of Rome under the Emperors* (London, Routledge, 1996), 65-71.

70. Anthony Everitt, *Augustus: The Life of Rome's First Emperor* (New York, Random House Trade Paperbacks, 2006), 113-114; Theodor Mommsen, *A History of Rome under the Emperors* (London, Routledge, 1996), 72-73.

71. Anthony Everitt, *Augustus: The Life of Rome's First Emperor* (New York, Random House Trade Paperbacks, 2006), 146; Aleksandar Stipčević, *The Illyrians: History and Culture*. Translated by Stojana Čulić Burton (Park Ridge, Noyes Press, 1977), 60.

72. Sextus Julius Frontinus, *Stratagems*, book 2, chapter 15.

73. Aleksandar Stipčević, *The Illyrians: History and Culture*. Translated by Stojana Čulić Burton (Park Ridge, Noyes Press, 1977), 60.

74. Theodor Mommsen, *A History of Rome under the Emperors* (London, Routledge, 1996), 74-75; Anthony Everitt, *Augustus: The Life of Rome's First Emperor* (New York, Random House Trade Paperbacks, 2006), 154-155.

75. Appianus, *The Roman History*, book 9, appendix on the Illyrian Wars, chapters 16-17.

76. Cassius Dio, *The Roman History*, book 49, chapter 34.

77. Appianus, *The Roman History*, book 9, appendix on the Illyrian Wars, chapters 19-20; Cassius Dio, *The Roman History*, book 49, chapter 35.

78. Cassius Dio, *The Roman History*, book 49, chapter 34.

79. Cassius Dio, *The Roman History*, book 49, chapters 34-35.

80. Appianus, *The Roman History*, book 9, appendix on the Illyrian Wars, chapters 17-21; Cassius Dio, *The Roman History*, book 49, chapters 34-35; Publius Annius Florus, *Epitome*, book 2, chapter 13.

81. Cassius Dio, *The Roman History*, book 49, chapter 36.

82. Cassius Dio, *The Roman History*, book 49, chapter 36-37; Appianus, *The Roman History*, book 9, appendix on the Illyrian Wars, chapters 22-24; Aleksandar Stipčević, *The Illyrians: History and Culture*. Translated by Stojana Čulić Burton (Park Ridge, Noyes Press, 1977), 61.

83. Cassius Dio, *The Roman History*, book 49, chapter 38; Appianus, *The Roman History*, book 9, appendix on the Illyrian Wars, chapter 25; Anthony

Everitt, *Augustus: The Life of Rome's First Emperor* (New York, Random House Trade Paperbacks, 2006), xix, 157, 159; Aleksandar Stipčević, *The Illyrians: History and Culture*. Translated by Stojana Čulić Burton (Park Ridge, Noyes Press, 1977), 61.

84. Cassius Dio, *The Roman History*, book 49, chapter 38; Appianus, *The Roman History*, book 9, appendix on the Illyrian Wars, chapters 26-28; Aleksandar Stipčević, *The Illyrians: History and Culture*. Translated by Stojana Čulić Burton (Park Ridge, Noyes Press, 1977), 61-62; Anthony Everitt, *Augustus: The Life of Rome's First Emperor* (New York, Random House Trade Paperbacks, 2006), 159; *Warrior Challenge*, episode 1: 'Romans' (PBS, 2003).

85. Aleksandar Stipčević, *The Illyrians: History and Culture*. Translated by Stojana Čulić Burton (Park Ridge, Noyes Press, 1977), 62; Anthony Everitt, *Augustus: The Life of Rome's First Emperor* (New York, Random House Trade Paperbacks, 2006), 165.

86. Theodor Mommsen, *A History of Rome under the Emperors* (London, Routledge, 1996), 80, 510.

87. Theodor Mommsen, *A History of Rome under the Emperors* (London, Routledge, 1996), 80, 510.

88. Theodor Mommsen, *A History of Rome under the Emperors* (London, Routledge, 1996), 80, 510.

89. Theodor Mommsen, *A History of Rome under the Emperors* (London, Routledge, 1996), 80, 510.

90. Danijel Dzino (2005), *Illyrian Policy of Rome in the Late Republic and Early Principate* (University of Adelaide), 120-121, 124. https://digital.library.adelaide.edu.au/dspace/bitstream/2440/37806/10/02whole.pdf

91. Theodor Mommsen, *A History of Rome under the Emperors* (London, Routledge, 1996), 81.

92. Suetonius, *The Twelve Caesars*, book 3, chapter 1.

93. Suetonius, *The Twelve Caesars*, book 3, chapter 9; Cassius Dio, *The Roman History*, book 54, chapter 20; Danijel Dzino (2005), *Illyrian Policy of Rome in the Late Republic and Early Principate* (University of Adelaide), 128-130. https://digital.library.adelaide.edu.au/dspace/bitstream/2440/37806/10/02whole.pdf

94. Cassius Dio, *The Roman History*, book 54, chapters 20 and 24.

95. Cassius Dio, *The Roman History*, book 54, chapters 28 and 31; Danijel Dzino (2005), *Illyrian Policy of Rome in the Late Republic and Early Principate* (University of Adelaide), 132. https://digital.library.adelaide.edu.au/dspace/bitstream/2440/37806/10/02whole.pdf

96. Cassius Dio, *The Roman History*, book 54, chapter 28.

97. Cassius Dio, *The Roman History*, book 54, chapters 28 and 31; Publius Annius Florus, *Epitome*, book 2, chapter 14; Danijel Dzino (2005), *Illyrian Policy of Rome in the Late Republic and Early Principate* (University of Adelaide), 132. https://digital.library.adelaide.edu.au/dspace/bitstream/2440/37806/10/02whole.pdf

98. Cassius Dio, *The Roman History*, book 54, chapter 31; Gaius Velleius Paterculus, *The Roman History*, book 2, chapter 96.

99. András Mócsy, *Pannonia and Upper Moesia* (New York, Routledge, 1974), 34.

100. Barbara Levick, *Tiberius the Politician* (London, Thames and Hudson, 1976), 31; Suetonius, *The Twelve Caesars*, book 3, chapter 14.

101. Gaius Velleius Paterculus, *The Roman History*, book 2, chapter 96.

102. Gaius Velleius Paterculus, *The Roman History*, book 2, chapter 96.

103. Cassius Dio, *The Roman History*, book 54, chapter 31.

104. Cassius Dio, *The Roman History*, book 54, chapter 34.

105. Cassius Dio, *The Roman History*, book 54, chapter 34.

106. Cassius Dio, *The Roman History*, book 54, chapter 36.

107. Sextus Julius Frontinus, *Stratagems*, book 2, chapter 1.

108. Publius Annius Florus, *Epitome*, book 2, chapter 14. 'Vinnius' is supposed to be Marcus Vinicius.

109. Caesar Augustus, *Res Gestae*, 30.

110. Theodor Mommsen, *A History of Rome under the Emperors* (London, Routledge, 1996), 110.

Chapter 3: Outbreak

1. Cassius Dio, *The Roman History*, book 55, chapter 22.

2. Live Science. 'Hurricane Katrina: Facts, Damage & Aftermath' by Kim Ann Zimmermann (27 August 2015). https://www.livescience.com/22522-hurricane-katrina-facts.html Accessed on 19 February 2018.

3. *Jaws in the Mediterranean*, The Discovery Channel, 1995.

4. Cassius Dio, *The Roman History*, book 55, chapter 23.

5. David Brownstone and Irene Franck, eds, *Timelines of War: A Chronology of Warfare from 100,000 BC to the Present* (Boston, Little, Brown and Company, 1994), 68.

6. Cassius Dio, *The Roman History*, book 55, chapter 26.

7. Cassius Dio, *The Roman History*, book 55, chapter 27.

8. Cassius Dio, *The Roman History*, book 55, chapter 28.

9. Cassius Dio, *The Roman History*, book 55, chapter 28; Michael Grant, *A Guide to the Ancient World: A Dictionary of Classical Place Names* (New York, Barnes & Noble Books, 1997), 563-564.

10. Cassius Dio, *The Roman History*, book 55, chapter 28.

11. Cassius Dio, *The Roman History*, book 55, chapter 28; Michael Grant, *A Guide to the Ancient World: A Dictionary of Classical Place Names* (New York, Barnes & Noble Books, 1997), 310.

12. Cassius Dio, *The Roman History*, book 55, chapter 28.

13. Gaius Velleius Paterculus, *The Roman History*, book 2, chapter 108.

14. Publius Annius Florus, *Epitome*, book 1, chapter 38; Plutarch, *Parallel Lives*, 'The Life of Marius', 11-27; Livy, *Periochae*, books 67-68, 142; Theodor Mommsen, *History of Rome – The Revolution*, pages 67-68; Gaius Julius Caesar, *Commentaries*, book 1, chapters 31-54; book 4, chapters 6-19; book 5, chapter 29; Adrian Murdoch, *Rome's Greatest Defeat* (Sutton Publishing Limited, 2006), 25-33, 41-42, 129; *The Germanic Tribes*, episode 1: 'Barbarians against Rome'; *The Germanic Tribes*, episode 3: 'Pax Romana'; Cassius Dio, *The Roman History*, book 53, chapter 26; book 54, chapters 20-22, 32-36; book 55, chapters 1-2, 6, 9-10, 28; book 56, chapter 18; Gaius Velleius Paterculus, *The Roman History*, book 2, chapters 97, 104-106; Ovid, *The Heroïdes, or Epistles of the Heroines; The Amours; Art of Love; Remedy of Love; and, Minor Works of Ovid* (G. Bell, 1893), 503; Suetonius, *The Twelve Caesars*, book 3, chapter 7; book 5, chapter 1; book 6, chapter 4; Tacitus, *The Annals*, book 4, chapter 44 (Indianapolis, Hackett Publishing Company, Inc., 2004), 144.

15. Strabo, *Geography*, book 7, chapter 1, verse 3.

16. Gaius Velleius Paterculus, *The Roman History*, book 2, chapter 108.

17. 'Barbarian Europe: Germanic or Gaulish?' by Edward Dawson (2 July 2011). http://www.historyfiles.co.uk/FeaturesEurope/BarbarianTribes01.htm; Strabo, *Geography*, book 7, chapter 1, verse 3.

18. Strabo, *Geography*, book 7, chapter 1, verse 3; Gaius Velleius Paterculus, *The Roman History*, book 2, chapters 108-110.

19. Gaius Velleius Paterculus, *The Roman History*, book 2, chapters 108-110.

20. Robin Seager, *Tiberius*, second edition (Oxford, Blackwell Publishing, Ltd, 2005), 30.

21. Cassius Dio, *The Roman History*, book 53, chapter 26; Gaius Velleius Paterculus, *The Roman History*, book 2, chapters 104-106.

22. Gaius Velleius Paterculus, *The Roman History*, book 2, chapters 109-110.

23. Gaius Velleius Paterculus, *The Roman History*, book 2, chapter 109.

24. Henri Hubert, *The Greatness and Decline of the Celts* (New York, Routledge, 1996), 58.

25. Mária Bizubová et al, *The Slovak-Austrian-Hungarian Danubeland*, second edition (Wauconda, Bolchazy-Carducci Publishers, 2001), 13.

26. The *Telegraph*, 'Remains of Roman army base found in Austria' (19 June 2014). http://www.telegraph.co.uk/news/earth/environment/archaeology/10912474/Remains-of-Roman-army-base-found-in-Austria.html; Ludwig Boltzmann Institute, 'The first Romans in Carnuntum.' http://archpro.lbg.ac.at/press-release/first-romans-carnuntum
27. Gaius Velleius Paterculus, *The Roman History*, book 2, chapter 109.
28. Theodor Mommsen, *A History of Rome under the Emperors* (London, Routledge, 1996), 96.
29. Theodor Mommsen, *A History of Rome under the Emperors* (London, Routledge, 1996), 96-97.
30. Gaius Velleius Paterculus, *The Roman History*, book 2, chapter 110.
31. Gaius Velleius Paterculus, *The Roman History*, book 2, chapter 111.
32. Robin Seager, *Tiberius*, second edition (Oxford, Blackwell Publishing Ltd, 2005), 42; Tacitus, *The Annals*, book 3, chapter 34 (Indianapolis, Hackett Publishing Company Inc., 2004), 101; George Gilbert Ramsay, ed., *Selections from Tibullus and Propertus* (Oxford, Clarendon Press, 1900), 164.
33. Cassius Dio, *The Roman History*, book 55, chapter 29.
34. Peter Michael Swan, *The Augustan Succession* (New York, Oxford University Press, 2004), 197.
35. Gaius Velleius Paterculus, *The Roman History*, book 2, chapter 111.
36. Cassius Dio, *The Roman History*, book 55, chapter 29.
37. 'Roman Social Class and Public Display' by Barbara F. McManus (January 2009). http://www.vroma.org/~bmcmanus/socialclass.html; 'Civitas' by William Smith (1875) http://penelope.uchicago.edu/Thayer/E/Roman/Texts/secondary/SMIGRA*/Civitas.html
38. Cassius Dio, *The Roman History*, book 55, chapter 29.
39. Cassius Dio, *The Roman History*, book 55, chapter 29.
40. Gaius Velleius Paterculus, *The Roman History*, book 2, chapter 110.
41. Peter Michael Swan, *The Augustan Succession* (New York, Oxford University Press, 2004), 198.
42. Cassius Dio, *The Roman History*, book 55, chapter 29.
43. Cassius Dio, *The Roman History*, book 55, chapter 29.
44. Academia.edu. 'Archaeological Traces of the Pannonian Revolt: Evidence and Conjectures' by Ivan Radman-Livaja and Marko Dizdar (April 2008). http://www.academia.edu/512324/Archaeological_traces_of_the_Pannonian_revolt_evidence_and_conjectures
45. De Imperatoribus Romanis. Festus, *Breviarium*, 7. Translated by Thomas M. Banchich and Jennifer A. Meka. Canisius College Translated Texts,

Number 2 (Buffalo, Canisius College, 2001). http://www.roman-emperors.org/festus.htm

46. Cassius Dio, *The Roman History*, book 55, chapter 29.

47. Derek Williams, *Romans and Barbarians: Four Views from the Empire's Edge, 1st Century AD* (New York, St Martin's Press, 1998), 34-37, 46-47, 52-56.

48. Tacitus, *The Annals*, book 3, chapter 33 (Indianapolis, Hackett Publishing Company Inc., 2004), 100-101.

49. Peter Michael Swan, *The Augustan Succession* (New York, Oxford University Press, 2004), 199.

50. Cassius Dio, *The Roman History*, book 55, chapter 29; Michael Grant, *A Guide to the Ancient World: A Dictionary of Classical Place Names* (New York, Barnes & Nobel Inc., 1997), 593.

51. Croatian History. 'Osijek – Essek – Mursa' by Zvonko Springer (1999). http://www.croatianhistory.net/etf/osijek.html Accessed on 7 February 2018.

52. Cassius Dio, *The Roman History*, book 55, chapter 29.

53. Cassius Dio, *The Roman History*, book 55, chapter 29; Gaius Velleius Paterculus, *The Roman History*, book 2, chapter 112.

54. Herodotus, 'Scythians and Thracians' in *Chronicles of the Barbarians* (New York, History Book Club, 1998), 23; Michael Grant, *A Guide to the Ancient World: A Dictionary of Classical Place Names* (New York, Barnes & Nobel Inc., 1997), 652-654; Strabo, *Geography*, book 7, chapter 5.

55. Michael Grant, *A Guide to the Ancient World: A Dictionary of Classical Place Names* (New York, Barnes & Nobel Inc., 1997), 112-113, 652-654; Cassius Dio, *The Roman History*, book 55, chapter 30.

56. Wildwinds. 'Ancient Coinage of Thrace, Kings, Rhoemetalkes I.' http://www.wildwinds.com/coins/greece/thrace/kings/rhoemetalkes_I/i.html Accessed on 10 February 2018.

57. Cassius Dio, *The Roman History*, book 55, chapter 29-30.

58. *National Geographic*, 'Ancient Slingshot Was as Deadly as a .44 Magnum', by Heather Pringle (24 May 2017) http://news.nationalgeographic.com/2017/05/ancient-slingshot-lethal-44-magnum-scotland

59. Cassius Dio, *The Roman History*, book 55, chapter 29.

60. Cassius Dio, *The Roman History*, book 55, chapter 29.

61. Cassius Dio, *The Roman History*, book 55, chapter 29.

62. Gaius Velleius Paterculus, *The Roman History*, book 2, chapter 110.

63. Danijel Dzino (2005), *Illyrian Policy of Rome in the Late Republic and Early Principate* (University of Adelaide), 147. https://digital.library.adelaide.edu.au/dspace/bitstream/2440/37806/10/02whole.pdf

64. Gaius Velleius Paterculus, *The Roman History*, book 2, chapter 110.

65. Gaius Velleius Paterculus, *The Roman History*, book 2, chapter 110.
66. Suetonius, *The Twelve Caesars*, book 3, chapter 16.
67. Gaius Velleius Paterculus, *The Roman History*, book 2, chapter 110.
68. Gaius Velleius Paterculus, *The Roman History*, book 2, chapter 111.
69. Gaius Velleius Paterculus, *The Roman History*, book 2, chapter 111.
70. Gaius Velleius Paterculus, *The Roman History*, book 2, chapter 110.
71. Cassius Dio, *The Roman History*, book 55, chapter 30; Gaius Velleius Paterculus, *The Roman History*, book 2, chapter 111.
72. Cassius Dio, *The Roman History*, book 55, chapter 30.
73. Cassius Dio, *The Roman History*, book 55, chapter 30; Gaius Velleius Paterculus, *The Roman History*, book 2, chapter 111.
74. Gaius Velleius Paterculus, *The Roman History*, book 2, chapter 111.
75. Cassius Dio, *The Roman History*, book 55, chapter 30.
76. Gaius Velleius Paterculus, *The Roman History*, book 2, chapter 112.
77. Gaius Velleius Paterculus, *The Roman History*, book 2, chapter 112.
78. Gaius Velleius Paterculus, *The Roman History*, book 2, chapter 112.
79. Stephen Dando-Collins, *Legions of Rome: The Definitive History of Every Imperial Roman Legion* (New York, St Martin's Press, 2010), 144.
80. Cassius Dio, *The Roman History*, book 55, chapter 30.
81. Academia.edu. 'Archaeological Traces of the Pannonian Revolt: Evidence and Conjectures' by Ivan Radman-Livaja and Marko Dizdar (April 2008). http://www.academia.edu/512324/Archaeological_traces_of_the_Pannonian_revolt_evidence_and_conjectures; Peter Michael Swan, *The Augustan Succession* (New York, Oxford University Press, 2004), 201.
82. Cassius Dio, *The Roman History*, book 55, chapter 30.
83. Strabo, *Geography*, book 9, chapter 2.
84. Polyaenus, *Stratagems*, book 7, chapter 43.
85. Polyaenus, *Stratagems*, book 2, chapter 2.
86. Derek Williams, *Romans and Barbarians: Four Views from the Empire's Edge, 1st Century AD* (New York, St Martin's Press, 1998), 46-47.
87. Christopher Webber, *The Thracians 700 BC–AD 46* (Oxford, Osprey Publishing, 2001), 35.
88. Christopher Webber, *The Thracians 700 BC–AD 46* (Oxford, Osprey Publishing, 2001), 35-36.
89. Cassius Dio, *The Roman History*, book 55, chapter 30.
90. Gaius Velleius Paterculus, *The Roman History*, book 2, chapter 112.
91. Gaius Velleius Paterculus, *The Roman History*, book 2, chapter 112.
92. Gaius Velleius Paterculus, *The Roman History*, book 2, chapter 112.

93. Gaius Velleius Paterculus, *The Roman History*, book 2, chapter 112.

94. Gaius Velleius Paterculus, *The Roman History*, book 2, chapter 112.

95. *Weapons that Made Britain*, episode 5: 'Armour.'

96. Gaius Velleius Paterculus, *The Roman History*, book 2, chapter 112.

97. Gaius Velleius Paterculus, *The Roman History*, book 2, chapter 110.

98. Gaius Velleius Paterculus, *The Roman History*, book 2, chapter 111.

99. Gaius Velleius Paterculus, *The Roman History*, book 2, chapter 113.

100. Gaius Velleius Paterculus, *The Roman History*, book 2, chapter 118; The date of Arminius' birth is based upon Tacitus' description of Arminius' lifespan: '37 years of life and 12 in power' (Tacitus, *The Annals*, book 2, chapter 88). If Arminius came to power in 9 AD, the year of the Battle of Teutoburg, and reigned as the leader of the Germanic rebels for twelve years, he would have died in 21 AD. Having lived for thirty-seven years, this means he was born in the year 16 BC. Tacitus, *The Annals*, book 11, chapter 16 (Indianapolis, Hackett Publishing Company Inc., 2004), 203; 2, chapter 9 (Indianapolis, Hackett Publishing Company Inc., 2004), 45.

101. Gaius Velleius Paterculus, *The Roman History*, book 2, chapter 118.

102. Gaius Velleius Paterculus, *The Roman History*, book 2, chapter 113.

103. Cassius Dio, *The Roman History*, book 55, chapter 30.

104. Gaius Velleius Paterculus, *The Roman History*, book 2, chapter 111.

105. Cassius Dio, *The Roman History*, book 55, chapter 30.

106. Gaius Velleius Paterculus, *The Roman History*, book 2, chapter 104.

107. Suetonius, *The Twelve Caesars*, book 3, chapter 18.

108. Cassius Dio, *The Roman History*, book 55, chapter 31.

109. Lindsay Powell, *Germanicus*, second edition (Barnsley, Pen & Sword Books, 2016), 4, 7-8, 19-20.

110. Cassius Dio, *The Roman History*, book 55, chapter 31-32.

111. Cassius Dio, *The Roman History*, book 55, chapter 31.

112. Cassius Dio, *The Roman History*, book 55, chapter 31.

113. Gaius Velleius Paterculus, *The Roman History*, book 2, chapter 113.

114. Cassius Dio, *The Roman History*, book 55, chapter 30.

115. Derek Williams, *Romans and Barbarians: Four Views from the Empire's Edge, 1st Century AD* (New York, St Martin's Press, 1998), 29.

116. Derek Williams, *Romans and Barbarians: Four Views from the Empire's Edge, 1st Century AD* (New York, St Martin's Press, 1998), 31, 45, 50.

117. Derek Williams, *Romans and Barbarians: Four Views from the Empire's Edge, 1st Century AD* (New York, St Martin's Press, 1998), 51-52.

118. Derek Williams, *Romans and Barbarians: Four Views from the Empire's Edge, 1st Century AD* (New York, St Martin's Press, 1998), 52-59.

119. Cassius Dio, *The Roman History*, book 55, chapter 30.
120. Gaius Velleius Paterculus, *The Roman History*, book 2, chapter 114.
121. Gaius Velleius Paterculus, *The Roman History*, book 2, chapter 112, footnote 241. http://penelope.uchicago.edu/Thayer/E/Roman/Texts/Velleius_Paterculus/2D*.html#note241; Danijel Dzino, *Illyricum in Roman Politics, 229 BC–AD 68* (Cambridge, Cambridge University Press, 2010), 150.
122. Gaius Velleius Paterculus, *The Roman History*, book 2, chapter 112.
123. Cassius Dio, *The Roman History*, book 55, chapter 30.
124. Gaius Velleius Paterculus, *The Roman History*, book 2, chapter 112.

Chapter 4: The Tide Turns

 1. Cassius Dio, *The Roman History*, book 55, chapter 31.
 2. Lindsay Powell, *Germanicus*, second edition (Barnsley, Pen & Sword Books, 2016), 42-43.
 3. Academia.edu. 'Archaeological Traces of the Pannonian Revolt: Evidence and Conjectures' by Ivan Radman-Livaja and Marko Dizdar (April 2008). http://www.academia.edu/512324/Archaeological_traces_of_the_Pannonian_revolt_evidence_and_conjectures
 4. Cassius Dio, *The Roman History*, book 55, chapter 32.
 5. Peter Michael Swan, *The Augustan Succession* (New York, Oxford University Press, 2004), 212.
 6. Academia.edu. 'Archaeological Traces of the Pannonian Revolt: Evidence and Conjectures' by Ivan Radman-Livaja and Marko Dizdar (April 2008). http://www.academia.edu/512324/Archaeological_traces_of_the_Pannonian_revolt_evidence_and_conjectures
 7. Academia.edu. 'Archaeological Traces of the Pannonian Revolt: Evidence and Conjectures' by Ivan Radman-Livaja and Marko Dizdar (April 2008). http://www.academia.edu/512324/Archaeological_traces_of_the_Pannonian_revolt_evidence_and_conjectures
 8. Thomas Hodgkin, *Italy and her Invaders, 476–535*, Volume 3, second edition (Oxford, Clarendon Press, 1896), 184-185.
 9. Sextus Aurelius Victor, *Epitome de Cesaribus*, chapter 41, verse 5. My translation.
10. Zosimus, *New History*, book 2, chapter 18; Thomas Hodgkin, *Italy and her Invaders, 476–535*, Volume 3, second edition (Oxford, Clarendon Press, 1896), 186.
11. Péter Kovács (2006), 'The Sebasteion of Aphrodisias and Pannonia.' *Hungarian Polis Studies*, 13: 176.

12. *Diccionario Universal De Historia Y De Geographica*, volume 1 (Andrade, Mexico 1853), 424.
13. Tacitus, *The Annals*, book 1, chapters 63-70 (Indianapolis, Hackett Publishing Company Inc., 2004), 33-37.
14. Nic Fields, *The Roman Army of the Principate 27 BC–AD 117* (Oxford, Osprey Publishing, 2009), 50-52.
15. Cassius Dio, *The Roman History*, book 55, chapter 32.
16. Cassius Dio, *The Roman History*, book 55, chapter 32.
17. Cassius Dio, *The Roman History*, book 55, chapter 32.
18. Cassius Dio, *The Roman History*, book 55, chapter 32.
19. Cassius Dio, *The Roman History*, book 55, chapter 32.
20. Pliny the Elder, *Natural History*, book 3, chapter 26 (22).
21. Lindsay Powell, *Germanicus*, second edition (Barnsley, Pen & Sword Books, 2016), 45.
22. Cassius Dio, *The Roman History*, book 55, chapter 34.
23. Cassius Dio, *The Roman History*, book 55, chapter 34.
24. Cassius Dio, *The Roman History*, book 55, chapter 34.
25. Cassius Dio, *The Roman History*, book 55, chapter 34.
26. Cassius Dio, *The Roman History*, book 55, chapter 34.
27. Cassius Dio, *The Roman History*, book 55, chapter 34.
28. Cassius Dio, *The Roman History*, book 55, chapter 34.
29. Cassius Dio, *The Roman History*, book 55, chapter 34; Gaius Velleius Paterculus, *The Roman History*, book 2, chapter 114.
30. Thomas Smith, *Arminius: A history of the German people and of their legal and constitutional customs, from the days of Julius Caesar to the time of Charlemagne* (London, James Blackwood, 1861) 86.
31. Gaius Velleius Paterculus, *The Roman History*, book 2, chapter 114. The date of the surrender, 3 August 7 AD, is written in the *Fasti Antiates* (3 August: CIL X 6638 col. II, v. 3. = I² p. 248).
32. Cassius Dio, *The Roman History*, book 55, chapter 34.
33. Sextus Julius Frontinus, *Strategems*, book 1, chapter 3.
34. *Soldiers: A History of Men in Battle*, episode 12: 'Irregular.'
35. *Soldiers: A History of Men in Battle*, episode 12: 'Irregular.'
36. Gaius Velleius Paterculus, *The Roman History*, book 2, chapters 114-115.

Chapter 5: A Long Hard Slog

1. Cassius Dio, *The Roman History*, book 55, chapter 34.
2. Gaius Velleius Paterculus, *The Roman History*, book 2, chapter 115.
3. Gaius Velleius Paterculus, *The Roman History*, book 2, chapter 115.

4. Anthony A. Barrett, *Caligula: The Corruption of Power* (London, Taylor & Francis e-Library, 2001), 82.
5. Gaius Velleius Paterculus, *The Roman History*, book 2, chapter 114.
6. Tacitus, *The Annals*, book 4, chapter 20 (Indianapolis, Hackett Publishing Company Inc., 2004), 132.
7. Gaius Velleius Paterculus, *The Roman History*, book 2, chapter 115.
8. Cassius Dio, *The Roman History*, book 56, chapter 1.
9. Austria Forum. Map of Limes in Austria, Slovakia, Hungary, Croatia and Serbia. https://austria-forum.org/af/AEIOU/Eiserner_Vorhang_Slowakei_Ungarn
10. A. Deluka, V. Dragcevic and T. Rukavina (2003). 'Roman Roads in Croatia.' Proceedings of the First International Congress on Construction History: 734.   http://www.sedhc.es/biblioteca/actas/CIHC1_073_Deluka%20A.pdf
11. A. Deluka, V. Dragcevic and T. Rukavina (2003). 'Roman Roads in Croatia.' Proceedings of the First International Congress on Construction History: 737.   http://www.sedhc.es/biblioteca/actas/CIHC1_073_Deluka%20A.pdf
12. A. Deluka, V. Dragcevic and T. Rukavina (2003). 'Roman Roads in Croatia.' Proceedings of the First International Congress on Construction History: 739.   http://www.sedhc.es/biblioteca/actas/CIHC1_073_Deluka%20A.pdf
13. A. Deluka, V. Dragcevic and T. Rukavina (2003). 'Roman Roads in Croatia.' Proceedings of the First International Congress on Construction History: 738. http://www.sedhc.es/biblioteca/actas/CIHC1_073_Deluka%20A.pdf
14. A. Deluka, V. Dragcevic and T. Rukavina (2003). 'Roman Roads in Croatia.' Proceedings of the First International Congress on Construction History: 739. http://www.sedhc.es/biblioteca/actas/CIHC1_073_Deluka%20A.pdf
15. Gaius Velleius Paterculus, *The Roman History*, book 2, chapter 115.
16. Henri Hubert, *The Greatness and Decline of the Celts* (New York, Routledge, 1996), 58.
17. Danube *Limes* in Croatia. 'Sotin'. http://limescroatia.eu/sotin-3 Accessed on 19 February 2018.
18. Tacitus, *The Annals*, book 1, chapters 55-61 (Indianapolis, Hackett Publishing Company Inc., 2004), 29-32; Suetonius, *The Twelve Caesars*, book 4, chapter 3.
19. De Imperatoribus Romanis. Festus, *Breviarium*, 7. Translated by Thomas M. Banchich and Jennifer A. Meka. Canisius College Translated Texts,

Number 2 (Buffalo, Canisius College, 2001). http://www.roman-emperors.org/festus.htm

20. Henri Hubert, *The Greatness and Decline of the Celts* (New York, Routledge, 1996), 42; Harry Mountain, *The Celtic Encyclopedia*, volume 1 (Universal Publishers, 1998), 215.

21. Henri Hubert, *The Greatness and Decline of the Celts* (New York, Routledge, 1996), 58-59.

22. Henri Hubert, *The Greatness and Decline of the Celts* (New York, Routledge, 1996), 62, 102.

23. Harry Mountain, *The Celtic Encyclopedia*, volume 1 (Universal Publishers, 1998), 215.

24. Henri Hubert, *The Greatness and Decline of the Celts* (New York, Routledge, 1996), 88.

25. Gaius Velleius Paterculus, *The Roman History*, book 2, chapter 115.

26. Gaius Velleius Paterculus, *The Roman History*, book 2, chapter 115.

27. Gaius Velleius Paterculus, *The Roman History*, book 2, chapter 115.

28. Gaius Velleius Paterculus, *The Roman History*, book 2, chapter 115.

29. Gaius Velleius Paterculus, *The Roman History*, book 2, chapter 115.

30. Beckles Wilson, *The Life and Letters of James Wolfe* (London, William Heinemann, 1909), 469.

31. Cassius Dio, *The Roman History*, book 55, chapter 33.

32. Edward Salmon, *General Wolfe* (London, Sir Isaac Pitman & Sons Ltd, 1909), 239.

33. Cassius Dio, *The Roman History*, book 55, chapter 33.

34. Cassius Dio, *The Roman History*, book 55, chapter 33.

Chapter 6: The End of the Road

1. Cassius Dio, *The Roman History*, book 56, chapter 1; Gaius Velleius Paterculus, *The Roman History*, book 2, chapter 116.

2. Publius Annius Florus, *Epitome*, book 2, chapter 25.

3. Danijel Dzino, *Illyricum in Roman Politics, 229 BC–AD 68* (Cambridge, Cambridge University Press, 2010), 173.

4. Cassius Dio, *The Roman History*, book 56, chapter 11; Brill Online Reference Works. 'Splonum.' http://referenceworks.brillonline.com/entries/brill-s-new-pauly/splonum-e1119590?s.num=2&s.au=%22Cabanes%2C+Pierre+(Clermont-Ferrand)%22&s.f.s2_parent_title=Brill%E2%80%99s+New+Pauly Accessed on 19 February 2018.

5. Cassius Dio, *The Roman History*, book 56, chapter 11.

6. Konstantin Nossov, *Ancient and Medieval Siege Weapons* (Guilford, The Lyons Press, 2005), 44.
7. Konstantin Nossov, *Ancient and Medieval Siege Weapons* (Guilford, The Lyons Press, 2005), 44.
8. *Warrior Challenge*, episode 1: 'Romans' (PBS, 2003).
9. Konstantin Nossov, *Ancient and Medieval Siege Weapons* (Guilford, The Lyons Press, 2005), 136-141.
10. Cassius Dio, *The Roman History*, book 56, chapter 11.
11. Ivan Lovrenović, *Bosnia: A Cultural History* (London, Saqi, 2001), 24; Aleksandar Stipčević, *The Illyrians: History and Culture*. Translated by Stojana Čulić Burton (Park Ridge, Noyes Press, 1977), 63.
12. Cassius Dio, *The Roman History*, book 56, chapter 11.
13. Cassius Dio, *The Roman History*, book 56, chapter 11.
14. Cassius Dio, *The Roman History*, book 56, chapter 11.
15. Cassius Dio, *The Roman History*, book 56, chapter 12.
16. Sir William Smith, *A Dictionary of Greek and Roman Geography*, volume II (London, John Murray, 1873), 967.
17. Cassius Dio, *The Roman History*, book 56, chapter 12.
18. Gaius Velleius Paterculus, *The Roman History*, book 2, chapter 116.
19. Cassius Dio, *The Roman History*, book 56, chapter 12.
20. Cassius Dio, *The Roman History*, book 56, chapter 12.
21. Aleksandar Stipčević, *The Illyrians: History and Culture*. Translated by Stojana Čulić Burton (Park Ridge, Noyes Press, 1977), 64.
22. Sir John Gardner Wilkinson, *Dalmatia and Montenegro*, volume II (London, John Murray, 1848), 442.
23. Cassius Dio, *The Roman History*, book 56, chapter 12.
24. Cassius Dio, *The Roman History*, book 56, chapter 12.
25. Cassius Dio, *The Roman History*, book 56, chapter 13.
26. Cassius Dio, *The Roman History*, book 56, chapter 13.
27. Cassius Dio, *The Roman History*, book 56, chapter 13.
28. Cassius Dio, *The Roman History*, book 56, chapter 13.
29. Cassius Dio, *The Roman History*, book 56, chapter 13.
30. Konstantin Nossov, *Ancient and Medieval Siege Weapons* (Guilford, The Lyons Press, 2005), 44.
31. Polybius, *Histories*, book 28, chapter 11.
32. Cassius Dio, *The Roman History*, book 56, chapter 13.
33. Fred Anderson, *Crucible of War* (New York, Alfred A. Knopf, 2000), 355-361.
34. Cassius Dio, *The Roman History*, book 56, chapter 14.

35. Cassius Dio, *The Roman History*, book 56, chapter 14.
36. Cassius Dio, *The Roman History*, book 56, chapter 14.
37. Cassius Dio, *The Roman History*, book 56, chapter 14.
38. Cassius Dio, *The Roman History*, book 56, chapter 16.
39. Cassius Dio, *The Roman History*, book 56, chapter 15.
40. Ivan Lovrenović, *Bosnia: A Cultural History* (London, Saqi, 2001), 24; Aleksandar Stipčević, *The Illyrians: History and Culture*. Translated by Stojana Čulić Burton (Park Ridge, Noyes Press, 1977), 64; *National Geographic*, Western Balkans Geotourism Map Guide. 'The Royal City of Vranduk, Bosnia and Herzegovina.' http://www.balkansgeotourism. travel/content/the-royal-city-of-vranduk-bosnia-and-herzegovina/ see26C9365E209209A9A
41. Cassius Dio, *The Roman History*, book 56, chapter 15.
42. Cassius Dio, *The Roman History*, book 56, chapter 15.
43. Cassius Dio, *The Roman History*, book 56, chapter 16.

Chapter 7: The Aftermath

1. Suetonius, *The Twelve Caesars*, book 3, chapter 16.
2. Gaius Velleius Paterculus, *The Roman History*, book 2, chapter 116.
3. Gaius Velleius Paterculus, *The Roman History*, book 2, chapter 116.
4. Cassius Dio, *The Roman History*, book 56, chapter 16.
5. Suetonius, *The Twelve Caesars*, book 3, chapter 20.
6. Tacitus, *The Annals*, book 1, chapters 58 (Indianapolis, Hackett Publishing Company Inc., 2004), 31.
7. Tacitus, *The Annals*, book 2, chapters 44-46, 62-63 (Indianapolis, Hackett Publishing Company Inc., 2004), 62-63, 71-72.
8. Cassius Dio, *The Roman History*, book 56, chapter 17.
9. Suetonius, *The Twelve Caesars*, book 3, chapter 17.
10. Gaius Velleius Paterculus, *The Roman History*, book 2, chapter 116.
11. Suetonius, *The Twelve Caesars*, book 3, chapter 17.
12. Gaius Velleius Paterculus, *The Roman History*, book 2, chapter 116.
13. Danijel Dzino (2005), *Illyrian Policy of Rome in the Late Republic and Early Principate* (University of Adelaide), 161. https://digital.library.adelaide. edu.au/dspace/bitstream/2440/37806/10/02whole.pdf
14. Suetonius, *The Twelve Caesars*, book 3, chapter 17.
15. Danijel Dzino (2005), *Illyrian Policy of Rome in the Late Republic and Early Principate* (University of Adelaide), 156, 166. https://digital.library. adelaide.edu.au/dspace/bitstream/2440/37806/10/02whole.pdf
16. Gaius Velleius Paterculus, *The Roman History*, book 2, chapter 123.

17. Tacitus, *The Annals*, book 1, chapters 16-30 (Indianapolis, Hackett Publishing Company Inc., 2004), 11-18; Gaius Velleius Paterculus, *The Roman History*, book 2, chapter 125.

18. John Hazel, *Who's Who in the Roman World* (London, Routledge, 2002), 100; Tacitus, *The Annals*, book 1, chapters 51-72 (Indianapolis, Hackett Publishing Company Inc., 2004), 27-37; book 2, chapters 1-26 (Indianapolis, Hackett Publishing Company Inc., 2004), 42-52.

19. Ovid, *Ex Ponto*, book 2, poem 1: 'To Germanicus: The Triumph.' Translated by A.S. Kline. http://www.poetryintranslation.com/PITBR/Latin/OvidExPontoBkTwo.htm#_Toc34217665

20. Danijel Dzino (2005), *Illyrian Policy of Rome in the Late Republic and Early Principate* (University of Adelaide), 161. https://digital.library.adelaide.edu.au/dspace/bitstream/2440/37806/10/02whole.pdf

21. John Wilkes, *The Illyrians* (Cambridge, Blackwell Publishers Inc., 1995), 215-216; Danijel Dzino, *Illyricum in Roman Politics, 229 BC–AD 68* (Cambridge, Cambridge University Press, 2010), 163-165.

22. Suetonius, *The Twelve Caesars*, book 3, chapter 37.

23. Danijel Dzino, *Illyricum in Roman Politics, 229 BC–AD 68* (Cambridge, Cambridge University Press, 2010), 172-173.

24. Danijel Dzino, *Illyricum in Roman Politics, 229 BC–AD 68* (Cambridge, Cambridge University Press, 2010), 163.

25. Peter Kovacs, *A History of Pannonia during the Principate* (Bonn, Dr Rudolf Habelt GMBH, 2014), 36.

26. Peter Kovacs, *A History of Pannonia during the Principate* (Bonn, Dr Rudolf Habelt GMBH, 2014), 44-45; Danijel Dzino, *Illyricum in Roman Politics, 229 BC–AD 68* (Cambridge, Cambridge University Press, 2010), 162-163; Danijel Dzino (2005), *Illyrian Policy of Rome in the Late Republic and Early Principate* (University of Adelaide), 164. https://digital.library.adelaide.edu.au/dspace/bitstream/2440/37806/10/02whole.pdf; Trismegistos Geo. 'Ulcirus Mons (Ilica). Bosnia and Herzegovina (Pannonia).' http://www.trismegistos.org/geo/detail.php?tm=44997. Accessed on 19 February 2018.

27. John Wilkes, *The Illyrians* (Cambridge, Blackwell Publishers Inc., 1995), 227.

Epilogue

1. Tacitus, *The Annals*, book 3, chapter 35 (Indianapolis, Hackett Publishing Company Inc., 2004), 102.

Bibliography

Primary Sources:

Aegineta, Paulus, *De Re Medica*, book 6, chapter 88. *In The Seven Books of Paulus Aegineta*, Volume II, translated by Francis Adams (London, C. and J. Adlard, 1846)

Apollodorus, *Library*, book 3, chapter 12. Translation by Sir James George Frazer, F.B.A. (Cambridge, Harvard University Press, 1921) http://www.perseus.tufts.edu/hopper/text?doc=Perseus: text:1999.01.0022:text=Library:book=3:chapter=12

Appian of Alexandria, *The Roman History*, book 9, appendix on the Illyrian Wars. Translated by Horace White. Livius. http://www.livius. org/sources/content/appian/appian-the-illyrian-wars

Arrian, *Anabasis*, book 1, chapter 5. Translated by E.J. Chinnock (London, Hodder and Stoughton, 1884) https://en.wikisource.org/ wiki/The_Anabasis_of_Alexander/Book_I/Chapter_V#18

Athanaeus, *Deipnisophistae*. Translated by Charles Burton Gulick. Loeb Classical Library (Harvard University Press, 1927). Lacus Curtius. http://penelope.uchicago.edu/thayer/e/roman/texts/athenaeus/ home.html

Augustus, Caesar, *Res Gestae*, 30. Translated by Frederick W. Shipley. Loeb Classical Library, 1924. Lacus Curtius. http://penelope. uchicago.edu/Thayer/E/Roman/Texts/Augustus/Res_Gestae/5*. html

Caesar, Gaius Julius, *Commentaries on the Gallic and Civil Wars* http:// etext.virginia.edu/toc/modeng/public/CaeComm.html

Dio, Cassius, The Roman History. Translated by Earnest Cary. Loeb Classical Library (Harvard University Press, 1914–1927) Lacus Curtius. http://penelope.uchicago.edu/Thayer/E/Roman/Texts/ cassius_dio/home.html

Dionysius of Halicarnassus, *Roman Antiquities*. Translated by Earnest Cary. Loeb Classical Library, 1937–1950. Lacus Curtius. http://

penelope.uchicago.edu/Thayer/e/roman/texts/dionysius_of_
halicarnassus/home.html

Ennius, Quintus, *Annales*, fragment 249. Translated by E.H. Warmington
(1935). Attalus. http://www.attalus.org/poetry/ennius2.html#book7

Festus, *Breviarium*, 7. Translated by Thomas M. Banchich and Jennifer
A. Meka. Canisius College Translated Texts, Number 2 (Buffalo,
Canisius College, 2001) De Imperatoribus Romanis. http://www.
roman-emperors.org/festus.htm

Florus, Publius Annius, *Epitome*. Translated by E.S. Forster. Loeb
Classical Library, 1929. Lacus Curtius. http://penelope.uchicago.
edu/Thayer/E/Roman/Texts/Florus/Epitome/home.html

Frontinus, Sextus Julius, *Strategems*. Translated by Charles E. Bennett.
Loeb Classical Library, 1925. Lacus Curtius. http://penelope.
uchicago.edu/Thayer/E/Roman/Texts/Frontinus/Strategemata/
home.html

Gellius, Aulus, *Noctes Atticae*, book 10, chapter 25. Translated by J.C.
Rolfe. Loeb Classical Library, 1927. Lacus Curtius. http://penelope.
uchicago.edu/Thayer/E/Roman/Texts/Gellius/10*.html

Gronovius, Joannes Fredericus, ed., *The Delphin Classics*, Volume 33;
Aulus Gellius, *Noctes Atticae*, volume 1 (London, A.J. Valpy, 1824)

Herodian of Antioch, *The History of the Roman Empire*, book 2,
chapter 9. Translated by Edward C. Echols (Berkeley and
Los Angeles, 1961). http://www.tertullian.org/fathers/herodian_02_
book2.htm#C9

Herodotus, *Histories*, book 7, chapter 73. Translated by A.D. Godley
(Cambridge, Harvard University Press, 1920) http://www.perseus.
tufts.edu/hopper/text?doc=Perseus%3Atext%3A1999.01.0126%
3Abook%3D7%3Achapter%3D73%3Asection%3D1

Herodotus, *Histories*, book 7, chapter 75. Translated by A.D. Godley
(Cambridge, Harvard University Press, 1920) http://www.perseus.
tufts.edu/hopper/text?doc=Perseus%3Atext%3A1999.01.0126%3
Abook%3D7%3Achapter%3D75%3Asection%3D2

Herodotus, 'Scythians and Thracians' in *Chronicles of the Barbarians:
Firsthand Accounts of Pillage and Conquest from the Ancient World to the
Fall of Constantinople* (New York, History Book Club, 1998), 17-24.

Homer, *The Iliad*, book 20, lines 210-245. http://www.perseus.tufts.
edu/hopper/text?doc=Perseus%3Atext%3A1999.01.0134%3
Abook%3D20

Livy, *Periochae*. Livius. http://www.livius.org/li-ln/livy/periochae/periochae00.html

Ovid, *Ex Ponto*, book 2, poem 1: 'To Germanicus: The Triumph'. Translated by A.S. Kline, 2003. http://www.poetryintranslation.com/PITBR/Latin/OvidExPontoBkTwo.htm#_Toc34217665

Ovid, *The Heroïdes, or Epistles of the Heroines; The Amours; Art of Love; Remedy of Love; and, Minor Works of Ovid* (G. Bell, 1893)

Paterculus, Gaius Velleius, *The Roman History*. Translated by Frederick W. Shipley. Loeb Classical Library, 1924. Lacus Curtius. http://penelope.uchicago.edu/thayer/e/roman/texts/velleius_paterculus/home.html

Pliny the Elder, *Natural History*. Translated by John Bostock (London, Taylor and Francis, 1855) http://www.perseus.tufts.edu/hopper/text?doc=Plin.%20Nat

Plutarch, *Parallel Lives*, 'The Life of Marius'. Translated by Bernadotte Perrin. Loeb Clasical Library, 1923. Lacus Curtius. http://penelope.uchicago.edu/Thayer/E/Roman/Texts/Plutarch/Lives/Marius*.html

Polyaenus, *Stratagems*. Translated by R. Shepherd (1793). Attalus. http://www.attalus.org/translate/polyaenus.html

Polybius, *The Rise of the Roman Empire*. Translated by Ian Scott-Kilvert (London, Penguin Classics, 1979)

Polybius, *Histories*, book 28, chapter 11. Translated by H.J. Edwards. Loeb Classical Library, 1922. Lacus Curtius. http://penelope.uchicago.edu/Thayer/E/Roman/Texts/Polybius/28*.html

Polybius, *Histories*, fragments of book 29, chapter 13. Translated by H.J. Edwards. Loeb Classical Library, 1922. Lacus Curtius. http://penelope.uchicago.edu/Thayer/E/Roman/Texts/Polybius/29*.html

Pseudo-Apollodorus, *The Library of Greek Mythology*. http://www.perseus.tufts.edu/hopper/text?doc=Apollod.+3.5&fromdoc=Perseus%3Atext%3A1999.01.0022

Pseudo-Scylax, *Periplus*. Translated by Wikisource. https://en.wikisource.org/wiki/Translation:Periplus_of_Pseudo-Scylax

Pseudo-Scymnus, *Periodos to Nicomedes*, fragment 405. http://topostext.org/work.php?work_id=130

Siculus, Diodorus, *The Library of History*. Translated by Charles Henry Oldfather. Loeb Classical Library edition, 1939. Lacus Curtius. http://penelope.uchicago.edu/Thayer/e/roman/texts/diodorus_siculus/home.html

Strabo, *Geography*. Translated by Horace Leonard Jones. Loeb Classical Library (Harvard University Press, 1917–1932) Lacus Curtius. http://penelope.uchicago.edu/Thayer/E/Roman/Texts/Strabo/home.html

Suetonius, *The Twelve Caesars*. Translated by J.C. Rolfe. Loeb Classical Library, 1913–1914. Lacus Curtius. http://penelope.uchicago.edu/Thayer/E/Roman/Texts/Suetonius/12Caesars/home.html

Tacitus, 'Germania' in *Chronicles of the Barbarians: Firsthand Accounts of Pillage and Conquest from the Ancient World to the Fall of Constantinople* (New York, History Book Club, 1998), 77-98.

Tacitus, *The Annals*. Translated with Introduction and Notes by A.J. Woodman (Indianapolis, Hackett Publishing Company Inc., 2004)

Thucydides, *The History of the Peloponnesian War*. 1910. http://www.perseus.tufts.edu/hopper/text?doc=Perseus%3Atext%3A1999.01.0200

Victor, Sextus Aurelius, *Epitome de Cesaribus. From the edition of Franz Pichlmayr (Teubner 1911). Corpus Scriptorum Latinorum. http://www.forumromanum.org/literature/victor_ep.html*

Victor, Sextus Aurelius, *Epitome de Cesaribus*. Translated by Thomas M. Banchich, *Canisius College Translated Texts*, Number 1, second edition (Canisius College, Buffalo, New York, 2009) https://www.roman-emperors.org/epitome.htm

Virgil, *The Aeneid*, book 3. Translated by John Dryden. http://classics.mit.edu/Virgil/aeneid.3.iii.html

Zosimus, *New History*, book 2, chapter 18 (London, Green and Chaplin (1814)) Tertullian. http://www.tertullian.org/fathers/zosimus02_book2.htm

Secondary Sources:

Books:

Anderson, Fred, *Crucible of War: The Seven Years' War and the Fate of Empire in British North America* (New York, Alfred A. Knopf, 2000)

Barrett, Anthony A., *Caligula: The Corruption of Power* (London, Taylor & Francis e-Library, 2001)

Binder, David, *Fare Well, Illyria* (Budapest, Central European University Press, 2013)

Bizubová, Mária; Kollár, Daniel; Lacika, Ján; Zubrický, Gabriel, *The Slovak-Austrian-Hungarian Danubeland*, 2nd Edition. Translated by Hana Contrerasová (Wauconda, Bolchazy-Carducci Publishers, 2001)

Boardman, John; Edwards, I.E.S.; Hammond, N.G.L.; Sollberger, E., eds, *The Cambridge Ancient History, volume III, part 1: The Prehistory of the Balkans; and the Middle East and Aegaean World, tenth to eighth centuries B.C. (Cambridge, Cambridge University Press, 2003)*

Bogucki, Peter; Crabtree, Pam J., eds, *Ancient Europe 8000 B.C.–A.D. 1000: Encyclopedia of the Barbarian World*, volume II (New York, Charles Scribner's Sons, 2004)

Brownstone, David; Franck, Irene, eds, *Timelines of War: A Chronology of Warfare from 100,000 BC to the Present* (Boston, Little, Brown and Company, 1994)

Carpenter, T.H; Lynch, K.M; Robinson, E.G.D., eds, *The Italic People of Ancient Apulia: New Evidence from Pottery for Workshops, Markets, and Customs* (Cambridge, Cambridge University Press, 2014)

Dando-Collins, Stephen, *Legions of Rome: The Definitive History of Every Imperial Roman Legion* (New York, St Martin's Press, 2010)

Dzino, Danijel, *Illyricum in Roman Politics, 229 BC–AD 68* (Cambridge, Cambridge University Press, 2010)

Everitt, Anthony, *Augustus: The Life of Rome's First Emperor* (New York, Random House Trade Paperbacks, 2006)

Fields, Nic, *The Roman Army of the Principate 27 BC–AD 117* (Oxford, Osprey Publishing, 2009)

Fine, Jr, John V.A., *When Ethnicity Did Not Matter in the Balkans: A Study of Identity in Pre-Nationalist Croatia, Dalmatia and Slavonia in the Medieval and Early-Modern Periods* (Ann Arbor, University of Michigan Press, 2006)

Fortis, Alberto, *Travels into Dalmatia* (London, J. Robson, 1778)

Frothingham, Arthur L., *Roman Cities in Italy and Dalmatia* (New York, Sturgis & Walton Company, 1910)

Gimbutas, Marija, *The Goddesses and Gods of Old Europe, 6500–3500 BC: Myths and Cult Images*. New and updated edition. (Berkeley, University of California Press, 1982)

Gimbutas, Marija, *The Living Goddesses* (Berkeley, University of California Press, 2001)

Grant, Michael, *A Guide to the Ancient World: A Dictionary of Classical Place Names* (New York, Barnes & Noble Books, 1997)

Harding, A.F., *European Societies in the Bronze Age* (Cambridge, Cambridge University Press, 2000)

Hazel, John, *Who's Who in the Roman World* (London, Routledge, 2002)

Hodgkin, Thomas, *Italy and her Invaders, 476–535*, volume 3, second edition (Oxford, Clarendon Press, 1896)

Hubert, Henri, *The Greatness and Decline of the Celts* (New York, Routledge, 1996)

Kovacs, Peter, *A History of Pannonia during the Principate* (Bonn, Dr Rudolf Habelt GMBH, 2014)

Levick, Barbara, *Tiberius the Politician* (London, Thames and Hudson, 1976)

Lovrenović, Ivan, *Bosnia: A Cultural History* (London, Saqi, 2001)

Makjanić, Rajka, *Siscia Pannonia Superior*, BAR International Series 621 (Oxford, Hadrian Books Ltd, 1995)

Mallory, J.P. and Adams, Douglas Q., eds., *Encyclopedia of Indo-European Culture* (Chicago, Fitzroy Dearborn Publishers, 1997)

Milisauskas, Sarunas, ed., *European Prehistory: A Survey* (New York, Springer, 2002)

Mócsy, András, *Pannonia and Upper Moesia: A History of the Middle Danube Provinces of the Roman Empire* (New York, Routledge, 1974)

Mommsen, Theodor, *A History of Rome under the Emperors* (London, Routledge, 1996)

Mommsen, Theodor, *History of Rome: The Revolution*, p. 67. http://italian.classic-literature.co.uk/history-of-rome/04-the-revolution/ebook-page-67.asp Accessed on 8 January 2013.

Mommsen, Theodor, *History of Rome: The Revolution*, p. 68. http://italian.classic-literature.co.uk/history-of-rome/04-the-revolution/ebook-page-68.asp Accessed on 8 January 2013.

Mountain, Harry, *The Celtic Encyclopedia*, volume 1 (Universal Publishers, 1998)

Murdoch, Adrian, *Rome's Greatest Defeat: Massacre in the Teutoburg Forest* (Sutton Publishing Ltd, 2006)

Nossov, Konstantin, *Ancient and Medieval Siege Weapons* (Guilford, The Lyons Press, 2005)

Powell, Lindsay, *Germanicus: The Magnificent Life and Mysterious Death of Rome's Most Popular General*, second edition (Barnsley, Pen & Sword Books, 2016)

Ramsay, George Gilbert, ed., *Selections from Tibullus and Propertus*, third edition, revised (Oxford, Clarendon Press, 1900)

Richardson, J.S., *Hispaniae: Spain and the Development of Roman Imperialism, 218–82 BC* (Cambridge, Cambridge University Press, 1986)

Salmon, Edward, *General Wolfe* (London, Sir Isaac Pitman & Sons Ltd, 1909)

Seager, Robin, *Tiberius*, second edition (Oxford, Blackwell Publishing Ltd, 2005)

Shoberl, Frederic, *Illyria and Dalmatia; containing a description of the manners, customs, habits, dress and other peculiarities characteristic of their inhabitants, and those of the adjacent countries; illustrated with thirty-two coloured engravings*, volume I (London, R. Ackermann, 1821)

Smith, Thomas, *Arminius: A history of the German people and of their legal and constitutional customs, from the days of Julius Caesar to the time of Charlemagne* (London, James Blackwood, 1861)

Smith, Sir William, *A Dictionary of Greek and Roman Geography*, volume II (London, John Murray, 1873)

Smith, Sir William; Wayte, William; Marindin, George E., eds, *A Dictionary of Greek and Roman Antiquities*, Volume 1, Third Edition, Revised and Enlarged (London, John Murray, 1901)

Southern, Pat, *Augustus* (New York, Routledge, 1998)

Stipčević, Aleksandar, *The Art of the Illyrians*. Translated by Leslie van Rensselaer White (Milan, Edizioni Del Milione, 1963)

Stipčević, Aleksandar, *The Illyrians: History and Culture*. Translated by Stojana Čulić Burton (Park Ridge, Noyes Press, 1977)

Swan, Peter Michael, *The Augustan Succession: An Historical Commentary on Cassius Dio's Roman History Books 55-56 (9 B.C.–A.D. 14)* (New York, Oxford University Press, 2004)

Watling, Maurice, *This is Illyria: Black Earth and Rainbow Waters* (Ilfracombe, Arthur H. Stockwell Ltd, 1958)

Webber, Christopher, *The Thracians 700 BC–AD 46* (Oxford, Osprey Publishing, 2001)

Wilkes, John, *The Illyrians* (Cambridge, Blackwell Publishers Inc., 1995)

Wilkes, John J., *Dalmatia* (London, Routledge & Kegan Paul, 1969)

Wilkinson, Sir John Gardner, *Dalmatia and Montenegro*, volume II (London, John Murray, 1848)

Williams, Derek, *Romans and Barbarians: Four Views from the Empire's Edge, 1st Century AD* (New York, St Martin's Press, 1998)

Wilson, Beckles, *The Life and Letters of James Wolfe* (London, William Heinemann, 1909)

Woodard, Roger D., ed., *The Ancient Languages of Asia Minor* (Cambridge, Cambridge University Press, 2008)

Articles:

Bollongino, Ruth; Nehlich, Olaf; Richards, Michael P.; Orschiedt, Jörg; Thomas, Mark G.; Sell, Christian; Fajkosova, Zuzana; Powell, Adam; Burger, Joachim (2013), '2000 Years of Parallel Societies in Stone Age Central Europe.' *Science*, 342 (6157): 479-481. http://science.sciencemag.org/content/342/6157/479 Accessed on 29 January 2018.

Bosch, E. et al (May 31, 2006) 'Paternal and maternal lineages in the Balkans show a homogeneous landscape over linguistic barriers, except for the isolated Aromuns.' *Annals of Human Genetics*, 70 (4) (July 2006): 459-487. http://onlinelibrary.wiley.com/doi/10.1111/j.1469-1809.2005.00251.x/full. Accessed on 19 February 2018.

Deluka, A., Dragcevic, V. and Rukavina, T. (2003), 'Roman Roads in Croatia.' Proceedings of the First International Congress on Construction History: 733-742. http://www.sedhc.es/biblioteca/actas/CIHC1_073_Deluka%20A.pdf

Dzino, Danijel (August 2005), 'Illyrian policy of Rome in the late republic and early principate.' PhD Thesis. School of Humanities, University of Adelaide. https://digital.library.adelaide.edu.au/dspace/bitstream/2440/37806/10/02whole.pdf

Kovacs, Peter (2006), 'The Sebasteion of Aphrodisias and Pannonia.' *Hungarian Polis Studies*, 13: 171-179. http://www.academia.edu/5577237/The_Sebasteion_of_Aphrodisias_and_Pannonia. Accessed on 11 July 2017.

Ledina, Dragan; Ledina, Dubravka (2002), 'Dinara – the Mountain of Extraordinary Beauty.' *Croatian Medical Journal*, 43 (5): 517-518. http://neuron.mefst.hr/docs/CMJ/issues/2002/43/5/12402388.pdf Accessed on 9 October 2016.

Radic, Zoran M. (2000), 'Some puzzles about the Danubian and European Cultural History and Connections of Civilization Development with Climate, Water and Hydrology.' http://medhycos.mpl.ird.fr/doc/zoran.htm

Radman-Livaja, Ivan; Dizdar, Marko (April 2008), 'Archaeological Traces of the Pannonian Revolt: Evidence and Conjectures.' Beiträge zum internationalen Kolloquiumdes LWL-Römermuseums. http://www.

academia.edu/512324/Archaeological_traces_of_the_Pannonian_
revolt_evidence_and_conjectures

Radovanović, Ivana (2000), 'Houses and burials at Lepenski Vir.' *European
Journal of Archaeology*, Vol. 3 (3): 330-349. http://www.academia.
edu/547069/Houses_and_burials_at_Lepenski_Vir Accessed on 23
January 2016.

Wallace, Jennifer (1998), 'A (Hi)Story of Illyria.' *Greece & Rome*, volume
45, no. 2 (Cambridge University Press, October 1998): 213-225.

Windler, Arne (2013), 'From the Aegean Sea to the Parisian Basin. How
Spondylus can change our view on trade and exchange.' *Metalla*,
Nr. 20.2: 95-106. https://www.academia.edu/5464477/From_
the_Aegean_Sea_to_the_Parisian_Basin._How_Spondylus_can_
rearrange_our_view_on_trade_and_exchange

Websites:

About Names. 'Albanian names.' http://www.aboutnames.ch/albanian.
htm Accessed on 9 February 2018.

Ancient Origins. 'Is the Danube Valley Civilization script the oldest
writing in the world?' by John Black (15 February 2014). http://
www.ancient-origins.net/ancient-places-europe/danube-valley-
civilisation-script-oldest-writing-world-001343 Accessed on 26
December 2016.

Ancient World Blog. 'Origins of Writing: Danube Scripts led to Pharaonic
Egyptian Hieroglyphs: Confirmation by Pottery Comparison (6
February 2005). http://ancientworldblog.blogspot.com/2005/02/
origins-of-writing-danube-scripts-led.html

Anthropology.net. 'A possible *Homo erectus* jaw from Sicevo Gorge, Serbia'
(29 June 2008). http://anthropology.net/2008/06/29/a-possible-
homo-erectus-jaw-from-sicevo-gorge-serbia Accessed on 29
November 2015.

Archive.org. *Diccionario Universal De Historia Y De Geographica*,
volume 1 (Andrade, Mexico, 1853). https://archive.org/details/
diccionariouniv00alamgoog Accessed on 19 February 2018.

Austria Forum. Map of Limes in Austria, Slovakia, Hungary,
Croatia and Serbia. https://austria-forum.org/af/AEIOU/
Eiserner_Vorhang_Slowakei_Ungarn

Bosnia and Herzegovina Commission to Preserve National Monuments.
'Prehistoric settlement of Butmir, the archaeological site' by Dubravko
Lovrenoviae (31 August 2004). http://www.kons.gov.ba/main.

php?id_struct=50&lang=4&action=view&id=2500 Accessed on 1 January 2018.

Brill Online Reference Works. 'Splonum.' http://referenceworks. brillonline.com/entries/brill-s-new-pauly/splonum-e1119590?s. num=2&s.au=%22Cabanes%2C+Pierre+(Clermont-Ferrand)%22&s.f.s2_parent_title=Brill%E2%80%99s+New+Pauly Accessed on 19 February 2018.

Croatian History. 'Osijek – Essek – Mursa' by Zvonko Springer (1999). http://www.croatianhistory.net/etf/osijek.html Accessed on 7 February 2018.

Danube *Limes* in Croatia. 'Sotin.' http://limescroatia.eu/sotin-3 Accessed on 19 February 2018.

History Files. 'Barbarian Europe: Germanic or Gaulish?' by Edward Dawson (2 July 2011). http://www.historyfiles.co.uk/ FeaturesEurope/BarbarianTribes01.htm

Lacus Curtius. 'Civitas' by William Smith (1875). http://penelope. uchicago.edu/Thayer/E/Roman/Texts/secondary/SMIGRA*/ Civitas.html

L'Anticopedie. 'Daunia.' http://www.anticopedie.fr/mondes/ mondes-gb/daunie-doc.html Accessed on 19 February 2018.

Live Science. 'Hurricane Katrina: Facts, Damage & Aftermath' by Kim Ann Zimmermann (27 August 2015). https://www.livescience. com/22522-hurricane-katrina-facts.html Accessed on 19 February 2018.

Ludwig Boltzmann Institute. 'The first Romans in Carnuntum.' http:// archpro.lbg.ac.at/press-release/first-romans-carnuntum Accessed on 26 December 2015.

Mrki.info. 'Solin.' http://w3.mrki.info/split/solin.html Accessed on 19 February 2018.

National Geographic. 'Ancient Slingshot Was as Deadly as a .44 Magnum' by Heather Pringle (24 May 2017) http://news.nationalgeographic. com/2017/05/ancient-slingshot-lethal-44-magnum-scotland

National Geographic, Western Balkans Geotourism Map Guide. 'The Royal City of Vranduk, Bosnia and Herzegovina.' http://www. balkansgeotourism.travel/content/the-royal-city-of-vranduk-bosnia-and-herzegovina/see26C9365E209209A9A

Old European Culture. 'Baba – earthen bread oven' (21 December 2015). http://oldeuropeanculture.blogspot.com/2015/12/baba-earthen-bread-oven.html

PanaComp. 'Lepenski vir Archaeological site Lepen Whirlpool.' http://www.panacomp.net/lepenski-vir-archaeological-site-lepen-whirlpool Accessed on 19 February 2018.

Reuters. 'Balkan caves, gorges were pre-Neanderthal haven' by Ljilja Cvekic (27 June 2008). http://www.reuters.com/article/2008/06/27/us-balkans-prehistoric-idUSL2768278020080627 Accessed on 29 November 2015.

Roman Emperors. 'Military Occupation of the Middle and Lower Danube Valley in the Late Republic and Early Empire to the End of the Flavian Period (A.D. 96)' by Thomas H. Watkins (3 December 2005). http://www.roman-emperors.org/wardoc.htm

Sanjin Đumišić. 'Ancient Megalithic Site of Daorson in Bosnia & Herzegovina' (28 January 2017). https://sanjindumisic.com/ancient-megalithic-site-of-daorson-in-bosnia-herzegovina Accessed on 27 January 2018.

Sarajevo School of Science and Technology. 'Butmir Culture – General Facts' (2006). http://dmc.ssst.edu.ba/ButmirNeolithicCulture/english/gfacts.html

Sarajevo School of Science and Technology. 'Butmir Culture – Okolište' (2006). http://dmc.ssst.edu.ba/ButmirNeolithicCulture/english/okoliste.html

Science Daily. '40,000-year-old Skull Shows Both Modern Human And Neanderthal Traits' (16 January 2007). https://www.sciencedaily.com/releases/2007/01/070115215252.htm Accessed on 29 January 2018.

Smithsonian Libraries Unbound. 'Twelfth Night Traditions: A Cake, a Bean, and a King' by Alexia MacClain (4 January 2013). https://blog.library.si.edu/blog/2013/01/04/twelfth-night-traditions-a-cake-a-bean-and-a-king/#.Wn4R1jRy6Uk Accessed on 9 February 2018.

'Some puzzles about the Danubian and European Cultural History and Connections of Civilization Development with Climate, Water and Hydrology' by Zoran M. Radic, PhD (December 2000). http://medhycos.mpl.ird.fr/doc/zoran.htm Accessed on 23 January 2016.

Thaindian News. 'Ancient axe find suggests Copper Age began earlier than believed' (8 October 2008). http://www.thaindian.com/newsportal/india-news/ancient-axe-find-suggests-copper-age-began-earlier-than-believed_100105122.html

The *Telegraph*. 'Remains of Roman army base found in Austria' (19 June 2014). http://www.telegraph.co.uk/news/earth/environment/archaeology/10912474/Remains-of-Roman-army-base-found-in-Austria.html Accessed on 26 December 2015.

Trismegistos Geo. 'Ulcirus Mons (Ilica). Bosnia and Herzegovina (Pannonia).' http://www.trismegistos.org/geo/detail.php?tm=44997 Accessed on 19 February 2018.

UCL Institute of Archaeology. 'Serbian site may have hosted first copper-makers' (23 September 2010). http://www.ucl.ac.uk/archaeology/calendar/articles/20100924

UNESCO. 'The natural and architectural ensemble of Stolac' (12 November 2007). http://whc.unesco.org/en/tentativelists/5282 Accessed on 27 January 2018.

UNRV. 'First Illyrian War.' http://www.unrv.com/empire/first-illyrian-war.php

UNRV. 'Third Macedonian War.' http://www.unrv.com/empire/third-macedonian-war.php

UNRV History. 'First Triumvirate.' http://www.unrv.com/fall-republic/first-triumvirate.php

VROMA. 'Roman Social Class and Public Display' by Barbara F. McManus (January 2009). http://www.vroma.org/~bmcmanus/socialclass.html

Web citation. 'Pod, a prehistoric hillfort settlement, the archaeological site.' Published in the dż"Official Gazette of BiHdż" no. 75/08, Bosnia and Herzegovina Commission to Preserve National Monuments. http://www.webcitation.org/5t3n3Effr Accessed on 27 November 2015.

Wildwinds. 'Ancient Coinage of Thrace, Kings, Rhoemetalkes I.' http://www.wildwinds.com/coins/greece/thrace/kings/rhoemetalkes_I/i.html Accessed on 10 February 2018.

William Shakespeare info. 'Twelfth Night by Shakespeare.' http://www.william-shakespeare.info/shakespeare-play-twelfth-night.htm

Videos/DVDs:

Jaws in the Mediterranean. The Discovery Channel, 1995. Narrated by Malcolm McDowell.

Sabretooth. BBC and the Discovery Channel, 2000. Narrated by Jonathan Pryce.

Soldiers: A History of Men in Battle, episode 12: 'Irregular'. BBC, 1985. Hosted by Frederick Forsyth.

The Germanic Tribes, episode 1: 'Barbarians against Rome'. Kultur International Films Ltd, 2007.

The Germanic Tribes, episode 3: 'Pax Romana'. Kultur International Films Ltd, 2007.

Warrior Challenge, episode 1: 'Romans'. PBS, 2003. Narrated by Henry Strozier.

Weapons that Made Britain, episode 5: 'Armour'. BBC, 2004. Hosted by Mike Loades.

Index